LOOK
FOR THE
ENEMY

'Bette Dam is a unique voice among Western journalists, providing a hard look at the U.S. justification for war in Afghanistan. *Looking for the Enemy* is a fascinating biographical account of Mullah Omar's life and an important contribution to our understanding of the war. This should be required reading for journalists and policy makers covering Afghanistan.'
                    – Jessica Donati, author of *Eagle Down: The Last Special
                                    Forces Fighting the Forever War*

'Bette Dam was one of the bravest, best-connected and most committed investigative journalists working in Afghanistan during the five years I spent in the country. She was one of the very few Western journalists to gain real access to the Taliban movement, through years of painstaking work building relationships with senior ex-Talibs, and with people around the group's fringes still connected to its center.'
                            – Emma Graham-Harrison, *The Guardian*

'Bette Dam's *Looking for the Enemy* is an in-depth, insightful, and engaging addition to the world's knowledge of the Taliban's enigmatic founding leader.'
                – Jeff W. Hayes, former Director at the National Security Council staff,
                                    involved in talks with the Taliban since 2010

'Dam's work looks consistent, across the various sources.'
                    – Afghan independent researcher Borhan Osman, as quoted in
                                                    The Wall Street Journal

'Bette is like Carry in *Homeland*. A fascinating book.'
                                                    – *The Correspondent*

'The account exposes an embarrassing failure of U.S. intelligence.'
                                                    – *The Guardian*

LOOKING FOR THE ENEMY

Mullah Omar and
the Unknown
Taliban

BETTE DAM

HarperCollins *Publishers* India

First published in Dutch as *Op Zoek Naar De Vijand* by
De Bezige Bij 2019

First published in English in India by
HarperCollins *Publishers* 2021
A-75, Sector 57, Noida, Uttar Pradesh 201301, India
www.harpercollins.co.in

2 4 6 8 10 9 7 5 3 1

P-ISBN: 978-93-5489-279-0
E-ISBN: 978-93-5489-286-8

Cover design: Saurav Das
Front cover photo: Getty Images
Back cover photo: Joel van Houdt

Typeset in 12/16 Arno Pro
Manipal Technologies Limited, Manipal

Printed and bound at
Thomson Press (India) Ltd

 HarperCollinsIn

'Explaining is not excusing; understanding is not forgiving.'
– Christopher Browning
(*The Logic of Violence in Civil War*, Stathis N. Kalyvas)

'I've always felt that it is impossible to engage properly with a place or a person without engaging with all of the stories of that place and that person. The consequence of the single story is this: It robs people of dignity. It makes our recognition of our equal humanity difficult. It emphasizes how we are different rather than how we are similar.'
– Chimamanda Ngozi Adichie, 'The Danger of a Single Story'

Contents

The author would like to thank the following organizations
for their financial help:

Fonds Bijzondere Journalistieke Projecten

Fonds Pascal de Croos voor Bijzondere Journalistieke Projecten

NOREF

Norwegian Center for Conflict Resolution

Foreword

WHEN this book first came out in Dutch in February 2019, the Islamic Republic of Afghanistan, with President Ashraf Ghani at the helm, was still in place. The U.S., keen to extricate itself from the Afghan war, had started formal negotiations with the Taliban's political office in Doha. A year later, in February 2020, the two parties signed an agreement which allowed the U.S. to withdraw its troops by 2021 and which was meant to kick-start an intra-Afghan peace process.

It went differently. The peace process never took off and, throughout the summer of 2021, while U.S. presence dwindled, Afghan military forces gradually ceded the whole country to the Taliban, district by district and province by province – sometimes after fierce battles but mostly through deals and surrenders. The government in Kabul, in the meantime, continued to behave as if this were only a temporary setback. Then on August 15, 2021, while the U.S. troops had not yet finalized their withdrawal, the Taliban entered Kabul and took over the government after the sudden departure of President Ghani.

The speed of the collapse of the Republic took everyone, including the Taliban, by surprise and they are now scrambling to transform their military movement into something resembling a government. It is unclear how this will go. In contrast to their previous reign, the Taliban currently have no clear center of gravity. Although they nominally have a leader – Sheikh al-Hadith Hebatullah Akhundzadah, Mullah Omar's latest successor – the man has not been seen in public for years and is probably either sidelined or dead, as Mullah Omar had been before him.

With the Taliban back in power, the world is scrambling to figure out what their reign might look like. There have been striking parallels with how the movement tried to consolidate its previous regime in the 1990s – most prominently the lack of clarity on issues like girls' education and women's employment, the threat of violent reprisals, and a tendency towards harsh punishments. There are also clear divergences – for instance, the heavy use of social media, videos and photography, and the push towards establishing uniformed security forces. But, although journalists and analysts have had all these years of international involvement to acquaint themselves more deeply and meaningfully with Afghanistan and its politics, much of the current reporting seems stuck in the 1990s – as if we have collectively learned nothing.

This book is fuelled by a thinly veiled exasperation. Over how much the military, the policy establishment and the media have missed during the last twenty years. How the different frames – the War on Terror, the state-building project, the counterinsurgency – meant that what happened in Afghanistan was often only viewed and interpreted in relation to the international presence and, because of that, often misunderstood.

This book is also fuelled by curiosity. It tries to do something different: to understand Mullah Omar and his movement on their own terms and within their own context. And, in doing so, it tells a very Afghan story, from a vantage point that is rarely seen in the West.

Bette and I were regularly in touch during her years-long research, particularly towards the end when she was in Afghanistan pursuing a new lead, only weeks before the original Dutch edition of this book was scheduled to come out. New and promising contacts sounded like they could shed light on where and how Mullah Omar had spent the last years of his life. We discussed the details as a fascinating story emerged. We weighed the sources, going back and forth to see whether they were solid enough. When the book came out, this was the part that attracted most attention and pushback, as it ran counter to the main narrative and the related worldview and self-image that had been put forward by the Afghan government, the U.S. military and most of the Western media.

This book, though deeply researched, obviously does not claim to be the final word on what happened in Afghanistan, the Taliban as a movement, or even the life Mullah Omar. But it is one of the very few books on Afghanistan in which the author has taken the time to listen deeply and follow a thread until clarity emerged beyond what seemed known already. With the Taliban now embarking on a new era, this is an invaluable resource on their roots, their past dealings with the rest of the world, and how the people in their orbit view the events of the last few decades.

Martine van Bijlert
Co-founder of the Afghanistan Analysts Network,
Former political adviser to the EU Special Representative for Afghanistan
October 2021

Prologue

In My Name
(2010)

THE air is still humid with the morning dew as I saunter casually into Aziz's orchard, with no inkling of what I'm about to find out. Aziz, a hunchbacked man, walks beside me among the almond trees with their pale pink blossoms. His face is like that of a typical grandfather, his creased, translucent skin framed by greyish-white hair, his beady eyes still full of life. He is wearing a satiny grey turban and a long, loose-fitting white robe. With a welcoming gesture as if he's drawing aside a stage curtain, he shows me his riches: dozens of pink trees in neat rows.

Aziz is at least seventy-five and I enjoy listening to his memories. He tells me that he was already living in this region when King Zahir Shah drew up the first borders in 1964 in an effort to curb the power of the hundreds of Pashtun tribes. All at once this area was turned into provinces. Where Aziz lived became the middle province, which is why it was given the ancient Persian name Uruzgan, meaning 'in the middle of the day', the time when the sun is highest in the sky.

We talk about how he managed to climb up the tribal hierarchy. He started out in the tribe as a nobody, an orphan who was hated by his stepfather. He would roam the mountains of Uruzgan for days on end with only a few sheep for company. Eventually, his clan began to appreciate him for his serene demeanor. They gave him the title Pir, which is given to spiritual guides in Sufism. This is the mystical, transcendental form of Islam that most Afghans practice. To be honest, Aziz says with a smile, he is not a real Pir. His fellow tribesmen merely bestowed this honorary title on him because they thought he was such a good man.

While I'm standing among the pale pink trees, losing myself in these stories about Sufism, Aziz natters on about his supporters in Tarin Kowt, the capital of Uruzgan. 'But I have plenty of enemies around here too, you know. One of them lives over there,' laughs the man who, after 2001, became part of the inner circle of the country's new leader, Hamid Karzai. The tribal community in which Aziz lives can be incredibly hospitable and yet at the same time harsh, a society of unwritten rules and customs where it is also a question of the survival of the fittest. 'During the Taliban era, that neighbor made my life so impossible that I had to go into temporary exile,' he tells me. Like so many others, Aziz fell out with one of his brothers' sons; in this tribal society, such a rival cousin or nephew is known as a *turbur*.

All of a sudden, Aziz remarks, 'You know, we're not that far from where Mullah Omar used to live.' His voice is calm, my response astonished. '*The* Mullah Omar?' I was not expecting this. Filled with curiosity, I follow his finger, which is pointing west.

I had been living in Afghanistan for some time and had even written a book about the country, but the thought of Omar still filled me with dread: he was the great enemy whom they had never managed to catch, the mysterious Taliban leader who was wanted by just about the entire world. Ever since 2001, tens of thousands of U.S. soldiers had been

hunting this Mullah Omar for his alleged role in the attacks on the Twin
Towers on 9/11. The Americans thought he was sheltering the wealthy
Arab terrorist Osama bin Laden. And because Omar was offering him
protection, he was assumed to have known all along exactly what Bin
Laden was up to. Omar had been accused of all but piloting the planes
that were flown into the World Trade Center. Now that Mullah Omar
had disappeared, it was believed he must be plotting with Al Qaeda to set
up more terrorist training camps, from where new attacks on Europe and
the U.S. would be orchestrated.

But there was another important reason why Omar was wanted,
namely, the extreme cruelty perpetrated by his fundamentalist regime
in the late 1990s. It seemed as if he loathed the female sex: under his
regime, girls were deprived of their right to an education and women
were forbidden from working. He was said to have had women's hands
chopped off, and even a minor violation of his Islamic laws could see
the female offender stoned to death. If it took his fancy, he would place
a woman on the center spot of a soccer field and shoot her dead. Omar's
religious fanaticism was notorious. The destruction of two ancient
statues of Buddha on his orders had left the international community
scandalized.

And here's Aziz telling me that this individual used to live not far from
here? Aziz keeps walking as if nothing momentous has happened. 'It's
really not that long a drive to his old home,' he says breezily.

'Have you ever met him?' I ask.

Aziz nods. 'Yes, a long time ago, of course. You could simply drop by
in those days.'

As I peer in the direction of Mullah Omar's village, beyond a tall
mountain range, I feel surprised to be so close to his former house. I
cannot imagine that it's very accessible. The location must be under
constant surveillance by the Americans and their North Atlantic Treaty
Organization (NATO) allies. There's probably a drone hovering above

at all times to keep watch in case either Mullah Omar or one of his
fighters returns.

———————— ◆ ————————

I knew next to nothing about Afghanistan in 2001, but the war that
erupted after the attacks in the U.S. had made quite an impression on
me. As a twenty-two-year-old studying Communication Science, I had
not yet seen a lot of the world. When 9/11 happened, I didn't even really
know what the Twin Towers were. I grew up in the rural north of Holland
and we would spend our vacations at a Dutch seaside resort about a two-
hour drive away. I had been on a plane a grand total of twice.

Like everyone around me, I had always been in awe of the powerful
United States, the country that had liberated Holland from the Nazis. In
my youth, the U.S. was seen as a strong, shining example, an ally you could
rely on. And this country had enemies? So I understood the urgency of
defending ourselves against these new adversaries in the War on Terror.
After the attacks of 9/11, it was heartwarming to see that nearly every
nation on Earth supported the U.S. in both its grief and its desire to wage
war against these terrorists. That the U.S. would fight in our name, in my
name, made sense to me. I had total faith in the Americans.

When, in 2006, the Dutch Ministry of Defense offered journalists
the opportunity to visit Camp Holland in Uruzgan, I jumped at the
opportunity to see the Dutch contribution to the war effort first-hand.
After obtaining a degree in Political Science in Amsterdam, I had just
started as a journalist at a small Dutch news agency, Novum Nieuws.
The ministry turned me down initially, arguing that our news agency did
not have a big enough readership. In response, I invoked *Libelle*, a high-
circulation Dutch women's magazine I did some freelance work for. After
that, everything moved very quickly and before I knew it I was on my
way to Afghanistan for the first time – for a women's magazine. I sat there
in my khaki pants and Timberland boots carrying my satellite phone,

wedged between soldiers – mostly men – in sandy gray uniforms as we flew in a military transport aircraft from Holland to Tarin Kowt. It was a smooth flight, until the plane had to perform a few evasive maneuvers above Afghanistan to avoid the Taliban's anti-aircraft missiles, as the pilot had announced.

We landed at one of the many well-equipped military bases. I was introduced to NATO officers with stripes and shiny medals on their green, immaculately pressed jackets. These men strode confidently along the neat gravel paths on the base, giving the impression that they had everything under control. When they talked about the war, they spoke in unfamiliar acronyms – I.E.D., I.D.F., T.I.C. – that made me feel stupid and even more in awe of them.[1] At the same time, they would point to the terrain outside the base and describe it as hell on Earth. I should never, that's to say *never*, go out there on my own, they warned. This was territory controlled by the Taliban and Al Qaeda, and therefore a one-way ticket to hell, although they also assured us the army would soon be finishing these guys off. We were told that journalists should always stay with the troops as that would keep them alive. Journalists who wanted to venture outside the camp independently were strongly discouraged from doing so by the Dutch army. Most of us complied.[2]

The army made a deep impression on me. Given the unfamiliarity and impenetrability of Afghanistan, I had no choice but to trust the military. They had what was supposed to be a funny acronym for ignorant civilians like me: 'NuKuBu', from the Dutch for 'Fucking Useless Civilian'.

But the more time I spent on the military base, the more cracks started appearing in my picture of the military in Afghanistan and their control over the situation. An American soldier told me that he always ate lunch with a machine gun next to his plate, because a group of Taliban fighters had once managed to force their way onto a base despite the tight security. A Dutch soldier advised me to give the Afghan cleaner a wide berth since he might blow himself up while cleaning the latrines.

I did indeed experience one incident, when a rocket hit the Dutch camp in Uruzgan. I hurled myself onto the ground, tears welling up from fear. But I was confident that the well-trained Special Forces who were hunting for the assailants outside the base would catch them. It was only when the soldiers came back empty-handed an hour later that I became really scared. All they had found was a wire attached to a light switch that had been used by the attackers. Who had fired the rocket was unclear. Although the perpetrators were often disparagingly described by the soldiers as running around in slippers, they'd still outsmarted us.

After an interview about Operation Medusa with André, a Dutch commando, I was even more skeptical about the mission. The operation was named after the woman in Greek mythology who could turn a man to stone just by looking at him. But the Dutch in Afghanistan were nowhere near as strong as the Greek Medusa. André told me about an incident at a combat station where they had unexpectedly come under siege around lunchtime, with bullets and rockets hailing down on them. His eyes became wild with fear again as he recalled the attack. They had been trapped like rats in a cage, he told me. Unbelievably, none of his team had been killed. What terrified him most, though, was the fact that it was all but impossible to tell the Taliban fighters apart from the rest of the population.

When I was invited to join a patrol outside the base, I shook my head. I felt bad about it, but I'd made up my mind: under no circumstances would I go into that desert. I had lost all confidence in 'our boys'. Despite having the most expensive weaponry in the world, they seemed incapable of defeating the terrorists out there. I was afraid to tell the soldiers this, so I made up an excuse that I was too busy for a patrol outside the gates. When I boarded the plane back to Holland, my head was full of disappointments, concerns, and questions. They were waging a war in my name, I thought to myself. In the name of the West. But did the people 'back home' realize how badly it was going? How was it possible that our

democratically elected leaders, with all the knowledge of the world at
their fingertips, seemed to be so powerless in Afghanistan?

———————◆———————

Back in Holland, I tried to resume my normal life. Yet every day, the
International Herald Tribune landed on my doormat with gory photos
from Afghanistan on the front page. I would read about attacks on
NATO troops, further Afghan casualties, and how strong the Taliban
were. Something in me wanted an answer.

Six months after my return, I met a U.S. commando at a conference
on terrorism in Amsterdam. He told me he had 'done' Afghanistan back
in 2001. At first, I wasn't too keen on hearing yet another story about
how well the Americans were doing in fighting the Taliban. Time and
again I'd hear optimistic noises from that quarter saying that victory over
the insurgents was a matter of months. But there was something unusual
about his story, something that ultimately inspired me to write my first
book about Afghanistan. Jason Amerine told me that he was among the
first commandos to have been dropped in Afghanistan immediately after
9/11 with the aim of toppling the Taliban regime. They were working
closely with the then-unknown Afghan leader Hamid Karzai, who was
to become Afghanistan's new president soon after. Amerine had become
famous in the U.S. as the man whose team was said to have put Karzai in
power. He had even been awarded accolades such as the Purple Heart
by the U.S. army for his efforts. His adventures had been documented
in Eric Blehm's bestseller *The Only Thing Worth Dying For: How Eleven
Green Berets Fought for a New Afghanistan*. This book relied heavily on
interviews with Amerine and his American team, but the author had
barely spoken to any Afghans.

What really piqued my interest was that during his time in Afghanistan,
Amerine had worked intensively with Afghan fighters, mostly members
of Karzai's tribe who still had a lot of power in Uruzgan. I watched him

as he talked on and on. Might those Afghans be able to tell me more about the situation in their country? Did they have any idea who was responsible for those rockets that were fired at Camp Holland? Could they tell me why the Special Forces had felt so despondent that evening?

I was eager to hear more from Amerine so I could see Uruzgan from his perspective, but it occurred to me that I also wanted to know more about the Afghans he had worked with. Only by seeing this story from their point of view as well and coming away with a detailed portrait of Uruzgan would I be able to really understand what was happening in Camp Holland, or so I reasoned.

I clumsily jotted down the Afghan names that Amerine mentioned, with their complicated spellings. They included Mualim Rahmatullah and Rozi Khan as well as Aziz Agha Pir Jan, the man introduced at the start of this chapter. They were members of the local elite in Uruzgan, where they all still lived, Amerine told me. One was a local bureaucrat, another was a mayor, and yet another a key ally of the Dutch army. As I wrote down their names, that daunting desert already started to feel a lot more accessible than it had done a year earlier. There was very little about this local elite in the Dutch media reports, even though it now seemed that Westerners had easy access to them. But perhaps nobody had ever asked to speak to them?[3]

'I'm going back to interview those Afghans about your tour,' I said to Amerine. He didn't really take me seriously. When I sent him the English edition of my book several years later, I hoped he would be proud, but he was actually disappointed because of the role I had ascribed to my Afghan sources.[4] Afghans are good storytellers, was his conclusion about my book. 'But of course I'm not impartial,' he quickly added.

———————◆———————

I emailed the phonetically spelled names to Marten de Boer at the Dutch embassy in Kabul. I had met him at Camp Holland and he struck me as someone who also wanted to know more about what was happening outside the high walls of the military bases. Marten knew instantly who I meant when he read those names. 'These men are all still in power,' he confirmed.

His next email arrived soon after. It mentioned Aziz, the man who would later tell me about Mullah Omar's old house as I stood with him in his garden. According to the email, Aziz was currently in Kabul on a visit. 'You could start your interviews with him. But you'd better be quick, because he's only here for three days,' Marten wrote. I replied that I'd head over at once. I'd now learned that it was possible to travel to Afghanistan on a commercial flight and to interview Afghans without Camp Holland acting as an intermediary. But few journalists were doing so in 2007.

My then boyfriend was worried about me going to Afghanistan without a military escort. 'At least they can offer some protection,' he said as I rushed around packing my bags. I phoned my family in northern Holland to say I was setting off for Afghanistan on my own; that was a long and difficult conversation. When I had gone to Iraq on my own for the first time in 2003, I hadn't told my parents beforehand because I didn't know how to explain it to them. Now I was giving them another shock. Some of my relatives saw Afghanistan as a country full of 'deranged Muslims' intent on hacking one another to pieces. They weren't racist; it's just that they had nothing to go on except newspapers that, too often, tended to focus on belligerent Afghans. Try as I might, I failed to reassure my parents.

The day after Marten emailed me, I flew to Afghanistan for the second time. It turned out to be easier than I had expected to book a last-minute flight to Afghanistan independently. I was able to buy a ticket to Kabul online and pay for it with my credit card. The return trip cost me around $900, which was not unreasonable. And it wasn't as if there was only one flight a week or every other week. Much to my amazement, Afghanistan was more accessible than that, with two civilian flights a day to Kabul from Dubai or Frankfurt. And that number was growing fast. In fact, it turned out there were several Afghan airlines, for example, Kam Air, Pamir Air, and Ariana Air, with daily flights to the Afghan capital from various cities. Even Emirates flew to Kabul, I discovered later. Around the Islamic holidays you had to book well in advance, otherwise you could forget about your trip.

From Amsterdam it was six and a half hours to Dubai, where I had to walk from Terminal 1 to Terminal 2. The latter was known as the war terminal because all the flights to Afghanistan, Iraq, and Kuwait took off from there. It was where the passenger plane that would take me to Kabul in under three hours was waiting. The Kam Air plane – white with an orange stripe and the slogan 'trustable wings' – was built in the 1980s. It was a little old and rickety, but it departed on time. The flight was smooth and, unlike my previous one to Afghanistan, did not involve any nosedives. At Kabul International Airport too, everything went more smoothly than I'd anticipated. The passengers – mostly Afghans – were met at the plane by a shuttle bus and dropped off at the arrivals hall. After I'd had my passport stamped at the customs desk, I could walk straight through to the luggage carousel. It was 2007 – there was hardly any security and nobody seemed interested in scanning baggage.

Before I left Holland, I had booked a room at Le Monde Hotel. I had actually been surprised when someone answered the phone. Not only did people apparently have cell phones in Kabul, but there were also real live receptionists who spoke fluent English. After I had informed the hotel of my arrival date, a certain 'Mohammed' sent me a confirmation email and wrote that he would come and pick me up from the airport. He would be holding up a sign with my name on it.

When I met him at Kabul International Airport, the fear I had felt at Camp Holland came back with a vengeance. I remembered the missile strikes and other attacks, and the Dutch soldier who had warned me to stay away from the latrines while they were being cleaned. Warily, I looked at all the dark-haired, brown-eyed Afghans walking past me. Were they all terrorists? I can still go back, I thought as I slowed my pace. I can simply admit to myself that I had made a mistake, that I was too naïve, that I should have believed the Dutch soldiers when they told me that danger lurks everywhere. I can simply walk back onto that plane and stay there until it leaves for Dubai, back to safety.

I managed to suppress my fear as I walked up to Mohammed, the Le Monde driver, who was holding up a sign saying 'Bette Dam'. But was he the real Mohammed? Suddenly I felt sure the real driver had been kidnapped, dragged out of the airport by a member of the Taliban and forced into a car. My heart skipped a beat. The kidnapper had returned to the arrivals hall with the sign and was now standing quietly among the waiting Afghans. He had been looking out for me with his brown eyes and was using the sign to trap me.

Mohammed was obviously prepared for mistrustful Dutch people; he pulled a business card from his counterfeit Levi's and introduced himself: 'I'm Mohammed. Please come with me.' He looked friendly, so I decided to follow him, although I was still gripped by a cold sweat.

A dusty blue jeep was parked at the busy taxi rank outside the airport. Mohammed pointed to a plastic sticker on the windscreen that said 'Le Monde Hotels'. Had he just stuck that on? Anyone could order a sticker like that. Still fearing the worst, I meekly followed him and sat down in the back of the car. I didn't spot any weapons and the doors weren't armored. The ashtray was full of cigarette butts. 'Everything OK. Welcome!' Mohammed called as he slipped behind the wheel and started the car.

———◆———

I will never forget that drive through Kabul. At first I cowered in the back seat, afraid I was about to be dispatched to the afterlife. I was wearing a headscarf, a long black coat, and loose-fitting trousers in the hope that this outfit would make me inconspicuous. I felt as if I was on a haunted-house ride as I peered nervously out the window. I was convinced something terrible could happen at any moment that would put a premature end to my adventure. We drove off with a U-turn, and then took the second exit on a roundabout that had an old fighter plane in camouflage colors in the middle. Then we negotiated another roundabout and zipped along the chaotic four-lane highway towards Kabul.

'Cigarette?' said Mohammed all of a sudden. While still concentrating on the traffic, he reached back with his right arm and offered me a cigarette. He gave me a friendly nod in the rear-view mirror. 'Please, take?'

I was in the terrorism capital of the world, in the land of Osama bin Laden and Mullah Omar, yet here I was smoking a cigarette in the back of a car. Everything was fine. Slowly, I felt the paralyzing fear drain from my body. I could breathe more easily again. I sat up straight so as not to miss a thing now that we had entered the Afghan capital.

Like any major city, Kabul boasts wide avenues in the suburbs and narrower streets closer to the center. There was the familiar sound of traffic: the honking of Toyotas, the sputtering of mopeds, and the tinkling of bicycle bells. Life went on as usual, even as a white Dutch woman rode through town.

The Afghans took little notice of me, preoccupied as they were with their own daily lives. We passed men pushing red ice-cream carts, women hidden under blue burkas, and boys with big bunches of balloons in all the colors of the rainbow. There were houses of all sizes, some with high walls and some with low walls. I spotted clothing stores, office-supply stores, bookshops, butchers, greengrocers, and restaurants, where Afghans were eating Uzbek, Turkish, or local cuisine.

I cautiously rolled down my window a little. 'My Heart Will Go On', the hit from the film Titanic, was blaring from the ice-cream carts. Shoemakers were chatting to one another on the filthy sidewalks. Beggars who had lost their legs in earlier wars were using skateboards to get around.

Like all buildings in Kabul, the Le Monde Hotel was surrounded by walls so as to shield women from the eyes of passers-by. The hotel vaguely resembled a Swiss chalet, except that it was painted a pale pink. I later learned that the lawn and the pink-and-red roses were Mohammed's obsession; he did everything to prevent them from withering in the summer sun. The care and attention with which he raked the flower beds betrayed his deep love of the country.

Many of the Afghan guests could be found at some point during the day admiring the flowers with Mohammed or one of his gardeners. 'How is it possible for such a beautiful flower to come from such a tiny bulb?' I heard somebody say. Apparently, Afghan children learn in elementary school that Holland is the country of flowers. Ever since I was told this, I have always brought tulip bulbs for my contacts in Afghanistan.

Mohammed made a comment about my clothes, saying they were too masculine. The Timberlands I had worn at Camp Holland were not to his liking at all. 'The women here just wear heels or ankle boots. So if you don't want to stand out, we'll have to buy you some new shoes.' Before I knew it, I was back in his car, on my way to the shoe shop to buy loafers.

I was pleased that I could be myself more in Kabul than I had anticipated. I enthusiastically FaceTimed my then boyfriend and told him Kabul was fine – in fact, we could live there. But while I showed him my comfy room with the deep-red Persian carpets bathed in warm sunlight, I could sense that it wouldn't be that easy to dispel the picture he had of Afghanistan as a scary place.

———— ◆ ————

A day after my arrival, Marten de Boer and I made our way to a hotel in the city to meet Aziz. 'Hello, how are you?' Aziz said to me in Dutch. That took me by surprise. Here I was in this foreign country and suddenly an Afghan was addressing me in my mother tongue? Aziz seemed eager to put me at ease and gave me a friendly look. 'I was in an asylum seekers' center in Holland for a while,' he told me. He had lived there for a year after the Taliban had made Uruzgan too dangerous for him. He used to send his family cassette tapes relating his experiences. 'I wanted to tell everybody that the supermarket had doors that open automatically when you stand in front of them!' he said laughing.

Aziz helped me on my way with his stories about Karzai's rise to power in 2001; he had witnessed it all from beginning to end. I also talked at length with his son Najibullah, who was my age and spoke fluent English. Najibullah was quick to comment on my interpreter, whose Pashto was bad because he was Tajik. 'Do I need to explain to you that half of the people here are Tajik and the other half Pashtun?' he asked. He was referring to the two very different ethnic groups in Afghanistan. We had a good laugh about my mistake with the interpreter. I was sitting on the floor and my first meeting with an Afghan was going really well, yet only recently I'd been terrified of the country. I could get a lot of work done here, I thought with renewed energy. 'I'm going to help you,' Najibullah said as if he could read my mind, and he poured us some tea.

Najibullah soon invited me to visit Uruzgan. This time I could not help but give him a wary look. Kabul was manageable, but a visit to Uruzgan – the province in southern Afghanistan that my experiences at Camp Holland and the Dutch media reports had taught me was incredibly dangerous – struck me as simply impossible. Najibullah was taken aback. When he told me I had the wrong idea, he seemed just as sure of himself as the officers on the NATO bases. He said he would personally vouch for my safety and that I could stay with Aziz.

———— • ————

After my meeting with Aziz and Najibullah, I spoke to several other prominent figures from Uruzgan. I decided that I wanted to meet President Karzai to ask him about his rise to power in Uruzgan. Again, I was surprised at how easily this could be arranged. After only a couple of months, I sat down with him for breakfast at the palace from where he governed. I had brought the list with the names of his Uruzgan friends with me, and I began to read them out. Karzai seemed impressed. It was rare, he said, for a European or an American to speak to his Afghan comrades.

'You really need to visit Uruzgan,' he added. I gave him an incredulous look. 'That's impossible, Mr. President; it's too unsafe there,' I maintained.

After this interview, the invitations from Karzai's Uruzgan connections kept pouring in. Someone I interviewed was prepared to drive me there, a journey that would take at least two days. Another would hire an Afghan army helicopter for me – anything to get me to visit.

In the end, I phoned Najibullah to say that I was coming, but I remained wary. 'Where exactly is your house?' I asked while looking at the roofs of Tarin Kowt on Google Earth. 'Close to that roundabout, you say?' I was trying to figure out how to flee to Camp Holland if I ended up having to fend for myself. The camp is a gray block on Google Earth; for security reasons, NATO does not want to be identifiable. I knew exactly where this gray block was, so with a printout in my hand I'd be able to head for the base, where 'our boys' would protect me. Although I had little faith in the Dutch military, I still thought I'd be better off with them than with the Afghans. 'Right?' Najibullah sniggered. 'You still don't trust me, do you?!' he said.

———— ◆ ————

A ninety-minute domestic flight brought me to Tarin Kowt Airport. It was right beside Camp Holland, where two years earlier I had landed diving and shuddering in a Dutch military transport plane. For a moment, the same uncanny feeling I'd had after landing in Kabul came over me. I hitched my bag onto my back and looked around to see if I could find Najibullah. Now I really was standing outside the high walls of Camp Holland, which I remembered so well. I also remembered the army spokesman telling me after I'd informed him of my plans, 'If you go into the field on your own, we won't do anything for you.'

I recognized the main road through Tarin Kowt from a television report by a colleague who had also been embedded in 2006. Against stirring background music, this journalist had said that the Taliban were 'in total control' of the area and that they were engaged in 'a fanatical guerrilla war.'[5] His report showed Dutch soldiers asking local people whether they had seen any Taliban fighters. If the locals said no, the conclusion was that nobody here could be trusted and that 'the Taliban were definitely in the area'. 'Tapped phone conversations' had revealed as much.

Now I was driving down the exact same road with Najibullah. I drank in the awe-inspiring Afghan scenery with the high, sand-colored mountains in the distance and the perennially pale-blue sky, which would be studded with stars later that evening. We put on music and sang along while filming videos and taking selfies.

At no point throughout my travels around Uruzgan did anybody try to obstruct me, a blue-eyed Western woman over six feet tall. The Afghans saw me going past in the white Toyota, on roads where they could have easily killed me a dozen times over. But they did not.

In fact, I found the people friendly when I was working there. The Afghans I met would talk to me for hours and sometimes days about their lives, and about how Karzai had successfully ousted the Taliban in 2001 to become president. The Afghans enjoyed talking about that era, which had seemed so promising. It dawned on me that I was in the process of making a kind of 'Afghan version' of Jason Amerine's American story, one in which Karzai had been helped into power by Afghans as well as the U.S. commandos.

The American military hadn't played nearly as big a role as Amerine had claimed. Karzai had done most of the legwork long before they arrived on the scene. And he had done so not only by fighting, but also by talking to contacts in his network, whom he tried to lure away from the Taliban.

All in all, the three trips I made to Uruzgan were productive. For the first time, I got a real sense of the Afghan perspective on the conflict. In 2008 I returned to Holland and in 2009 I published my book on Hamid Karzai's road to the presidency. But I knew I wasn't done with this war. At the end of the year, I took up a job as correspondent in Kabul for the NRC, a leading Dutch newspaper. I flew back to Afghanistan, this time with a one-way ticket.

I moved into an $800-a-month room in a bungalow in the Kabul district of Qale Musa (Fortress of Moses). My housemates were Americans. Later, I moved to Street 2 in Taimani in the city center, where I shared a house with a Canadian journalist, a Russian photographer, and a Dutch manager at a microcredit bank. Our two-story house and its circular garden, with three old, bent apple trees in the middle, reminded me of the Le Monde Hotel.

After my experiences in Uruzgan – where I'd mostly stayed with Afghans – expat life in the metropolis of Kabul was a shock. Although Western newspapers depicted the city as a warzone with the smoking remains of recent bomb attacks around every corner, you had to really look hard for that side of Kabul. Life for me was a succession of receptions, dinners, brunches, pool parties, and yoga classes. I had dozens of new friends in no time. And there was alcohol.

My colleagues and I, like most journalists and aid workers, often got $5 rides around town in taxis driven by young Afghans who sported punk hair and listened to sexy Britney Spears songs on the radio or their cell phones. These young taxi drivers put in long hours, on weekends in particular, ferrying hundreds of expats to parties. United Nations (U.N.) diplomats, journalists, staff of non-governmental organizations (N.G.O.) – every weekend they'd host so many parties that you had to pick and choose. They all had guest lists, and if you suffered from FOMO (fear of missing out), you had to register a day or two in advance, or else you'd miss the best events.

Security at these parties was not great. Often there would only be a single guard, holding his weapon and guest list in the same hand; you could just walk straight in. There was always something going on in the restaurants too, where we would dance and drink until the break of dawn. We ate Thai, Italian, Lebanese, Korean, French or Chinese cuisine in Sherpur, which – rumor had it – housed a brothel in the loft. Sushi? Yes, that too.

There were yoga classes in the offices of a think tank, and in our house we made our own vodka with a still imported from Moscow. Receptions were attended by dignitaries such as the Afghan Minister of Foreign Affairs, Abdullah Abdullah, together with former Taliban supporters. There were dining societies and tennis clubs. And we had a lovely doorman who kept us posted about everything that was going on in our neighborhood.

We did the craziest things. When we'd been drinking, we would often forget we were in Afghanistan. The Afghans, who are forbidden by law to consume alcohol, must have felt a vicarious shame at times. I remember driving a car full of weapons that belonged to the Australian Special Forces back to their base in the city one evening, because the men themselves were too drunk. And they didn't know the city very well either, since they spent all of their time in camps.

I also remember a friend sitting in an Afghan taxi at four in the morning and vomiting out of the window because she'd had too much to drink. And then there was the pool party where an ambassador jumped naked into the water. On Fridays – the Afghan equivalent of Sunday – we would spend hours brunching at the French restaurant Le Bistro. Or we'd go for long walks in the Panjshir valley, a six-hour drive from Kabul, where the hero of the Tajiks, Ahmad Shah Massoud, was buried in a tomb the size of a house.

Of course there were explosions in Kabul from time to time. They would shake the city to its foundations. These attacks on the heavily armored cars of U.S. diplomats, for instance, or on NATO military, Afghan army convoys, or occasionally Afghan officials, would often claim a lot of civilian casualties. But they were not an everyday occurrence. You wouldn't get one a week, or even one a month. Sometimes the city would be quiet for three to four months on end. And then – catching us all off guard – a bomb would suddenly explode. With its four million inhabitants, Kabul was about the same size as Los Angeles, the second most populous city in America. It meant there was more than enough space to live a normal life.

———————◆———————

Our fun-filled lives never made the news. I recall a brief chat with an editor shortly after I moved to Kabul. 'How are you?' she shouted, 'are you there?' as if she thought I was at the bottom of a deep hole, held prisoner by the Taliban. 'Listen, I think you've got the wrong idea,' I shouted back. 'Kabul isn't as anti-Western as you imagine,' I added reassuringly. But it had the opposite effect, as I could tell by the editor's reedy voice. She didn't understand what I meant, she said, before adding with a sense of urgency, 'Where's your flak jacket? Where's your flak jacket?! Aren't you wearing it? I'm going to have to call a meeting. We need to talk about this now. You're flouting the rules!'

We worked mostly when there had been an attack. That's when our media outlets wanted to hear from us and when all the editorial teams immediately reached for the phone. I'd pull a headscarf and jacket from the coat rack, tweet that I was on my way to the scene of the attack and, with my notebook in hand, I would traipse after my colleague who had ordered a $5 taxi ride. Some of the attacks took place in Kabul, but even if they happened in Kandahar or the northern city of Kunduz, journalists would still report live from the capital.

It's fair to say that there was a kind of 'global script', a generic template for reporting on terrorist attacks. It always began with footage of the flames, the burned-out car used by the suicide bomber, and police officers and soldiers in action. Then the journalist would give the estimated number of victims and perhaps ask a shocked bystander to say how awful it had been. This was often followed by the Taliban claiming responsibility for the attack – or, in the absence of such a claim, a statement by the journalist that the Taliban were probably to blame. The conclusion was drawn that the Taliban were growing stronger and stronger, which prompted the question of whether more Western troops ought to be deployed.[6]

This was a common scenario. Sometimes I would see colleagues in front of the camera in helmets and flak jackets – in Kabul, where nothing was actually happening. You'd even see them in this attire in hotel rose gardens like that of the Le Monde.

I began to question the journalists about this. Some colleagues in Kabul pointed the finger at their senior editors, who thought this macho getup looked good on screen. But the journalists themselves too were often happy with this image. Besides, reporters working for the big international news outlets were frequently at the mercy of insurers, who would demand excessive precautionary measures lest anything happened to the reporter.

Security personnel too played a key role in this phenomenon. They were remarkably often ex-soldiers, who had been hired for this very reason. 'These guys would say everything was too dangerous for us to do because they didn't feel like doing their job. We have no say in outside reporting and trips to locations around Afghanistan,' an American C.N.N. reporter told me. 'These former soldiers, who often earn up to a thousand dollars a day, decide where we can and can't go as journalists. They prefer to minimize the risks, and that's why we tend to stay as close to home as possible. When it comes to reporting on a story, the editor in New York is more likely to listen to the security staff than to me.'

There were exceptions, especially for background articles or extensive investigative reports for magazines, but generally speaking it seemed that this thinking from a military perspective not only determined the course Afghanistan was taking, but also influenced reporting by journalists working for powerful media outlets.

———◆———

Just how dangerous this 'thinking inside a military box' was, as practiced by both the mainstream media and the nations contributing to the war effort, became clear to me during my research into Hamid Karzai's rise to power. I discovered that the dynamic of the Afghan conflict as depicted by the U.S., NATO and the media – as a battle between the government and the Taliban – was a fiction. It is the accepted account even today, yet after traveling around the country and speaking to a great many Afghans, I realized that the situation is much more an ongoing conflict between many different pragmatic (rather than idealistic) groups that are concerned with safeguarding their positions in this war situation and that frequently switch allegiance.

During my time in Afghanistan, I often wondered where this war was that the Pentagon was waging. I could find no trace of the well-defined enemy that the U.S. could see so clearly. Who were the U.S. (and the Dutch and all the other NATO members) fighting? Was this even the kind of conflict that armies should be involved in at all?

From 2007 onwards, I repeatedly witnessed just how confused Western troops and the mainstream media could (and indeed did) become because of this simplification of the conflict. After each attack or casualty, the U.S. army concluded that it was the work of the Taliban. But was it? I increasingly started to see another dynamic, one that led to bomb explosions and horrific attacks. The Americans created a situation that led to exploitation by their Afghan partners. Local Afghan leaders would send U.S. troops to deal with what they claimed were Taliban fighters, but who in reality were merely their local adversaries. Far too often, this would result in the pointless deaths of both the Afghans in question and the foreign soldiers.

Because I had spent a lot of time with Karzai's supporters, I recognized this deadly pattern. The government was full of figures who also had their own agendas – which the U.S. often ignored – carrying out attacks and then instantly phoning the international media to blame the Taliban. The Western media reporters, who were either embedded with the army or based in Kabul, were incapable of seeing through this charade. Journalists tended to report that the entire conflict revolved around the Taliban, thereby apparently proving NATO and the U.S. army right: there *was* an identifiable enemy in Afghanistan.

Upon closer investigation, the truth behind an attack was often painful. For example, I researched the murder of seven young men not far from Tarin Kowt. 'The Taliban killed the men,' *The New York Times* wrote from Kabul, 'because of their alliance with the Karzai government.' The A.P. news agency (also based in Kabul) reported that the Taliban had killed the young men because they had been 'spying' for the government. The Chinese press agency Xinhua – working from China – said the horrific murders had been committed because the men were 'ex-colleagues of the Taliban'. The Belgian newspaper *De Standaard* quoted local police commander Juma Gul as saying that a group of moderate Taliban had been holding a meeting when a terrorist Taliban group turned up and murdered them.[7]

I needed more time than had been planned for my own article about this incident. 'Can't we just pin it on the Taliban?' my *NRC* editor in Holland would say in cases like this. I understood his frustration. The clock was ticking and journalism is all about timing, speed, and deadlines. I was expected to squeeze the complexity of Afghanistan into this template. But days later, after the news had been reported and everybody had moved on from the murders, I discovered that the Taliban had not been involved at all. My sources told me it had been a personal conflict between the owners of two madrassas that had gotten completely out of hand, and the young men had paid with their lives.[8]

The same was true for the story about the Afghan governor who arranged bomb attacks to eliminate rivals and then phoned the media, claiming they were Taliban attacks. This Asadullah Khalid received a tremendous amount of help from U.S. soldiers in governing his province. At one point, when Khalid was wounded, he received a visit in the hospital from none other than President Barack Obama.[9] And all this time he was stirring up trouble, with the aim of grabbing more land, expanding his power base, and lining his own pockets.

Among other things, in 2007 Asadullah destroyed a U.N. convoy that was about to dismantle his opium poppy fields. It was the first U.N. convoy to be attacked since 9/11. By the Taliban, the shocked mainstream media concluded in its reports on the deadly incident.[10] 'The Taliban have claimed many similar attacks over the past year,' the Reuters journalist added. When the U.N. discovered soon after that a representative of the Afghan government had orchestrated and ordered the attack, the findings were instantly swept under the rug. They did not fit the dominant narrative and would tarnish the reputation of the West's ally.[11] Years later, when the same report was leaked to the Canadian media, it was revealed that by staging this so-called Taliban attack Asadullah Khalid had been able to stop the U.N. team (literally, by killing them) and safeguard his drugs revenue.[12] In the same report, the U.N. wrote something even more alarming: it was Westerners in Afghanistan rather than insurgents (such as the Taliban) who were increasingly falling victim to 'drug interests'.

These new, worrying insights rarely, if ever, made the news, but whenever I could I used them to try and inject some nuance into the prescriptive terrorism script. When filing brief reports on attacks ('We have 30 seconds for you!'), I tried to quickly slip in that the situation in

Kabul was calm and the attack had come as a surprise. And I would add that it might not be the Taliban; warlords or even members of the Afghan government could be responsible.

Every once in a while I managed to attract attention. One day, C.N.N. granted me a longer interview and a column after I had noted this pattern.[13] And I wrote an article for the British newspaper *The Guardian* about an attack in which I stressed just how little we know. 'It is no good asking why Afghan forces did not prevent this attack – the problem is a political one of corruption and patronage.'[14]

———◆———

Soon I was part of a small group of freelancers who all seemed to share the same goal and who were constantly trying to uncover the stories behind the attacks. We wrote about Afghan leaders who were manipulating the U.S. troops, killing one rival after another and pinning the blame on the Taliban.[15] We argued that the mainstream media were talking up the enemy and in doing so were prolonging the war. Their articles appeared in major U.S. newspapers. Time and again, we pointed out that the reports in the big news machines regularly contained factual errors, but we never got a wide hearing.

I became fed up. I'd had enough of the news and wanted to do something different, so in 2012 I quit my job with the NRC. I increasingly found myself thinking back to my conversation with Aziz in the orchard, and to what he told me about Mullah Omar's house. The war had been raging for eleven years and would soon be one of the longest conflicts in American history. It did not look as if either the Americans or their NATO partners would revise their strategies or stop hunting on the basis of false information. And while in 2012 I still considered Afghanistan to be safer than the West's hyped stories of terrorism would have us believe, I was also apprehensive. How much longer would this last? Western military forces were continuing their strikes on 'the Taliban'.

Meanwhile, the Afghan government had become so corrupt that it too was generating violence. Sooner or later things would spiral out of control. Some Afghans were already choosing to flee to Europe because of the precarious situation in their country. They were the vanguard of the millions of refugees that would soon follow.

I kept wondering: If the enemy is such an unknown quantity, who exactly are these Taliban? After 9/11, the Americans enjoyed the support of virtually the entire world in their wish to eradicate this enemy, but did that world have any idea what the military were doing here? Were they asking the necessary critical questions of their powerful ally? Did the Dutch soldiers know who they were shooting dead in Afghanistan? If many of the attacks hadn't actually been carried out by the Taliban, then who were the terrorists? I realized what I had to do: I had to find out who the enemy was. Who was shooting whom? Who was shooting at the Dutch? Wasn't it fairer to the family and friends back home to tell them who had really killed their son or daughter? I suspected that if I understood better who the enemy was, I would be better able to fathom the war too. This enemy was a man of whom there were no photos, a man with only one eye who had disappeared. Why had no one thought of this earlier – giving the enemy a face? I knew it wouldn't be easy but I decided to start a search for the real Taliban, a journalistic hunt for their mysterious leader Mullah Omar, who was in hiding somewhere.

I went back to Aziz and asked him about Mullah Omar's house again. I told him that after my book about Karzai I was ready to start the much more challenging quest for Mullah Omar. To get this difficult job done I would have to draw on the connections I'd made and the experiences I'd had during my travels around Afghanistan. I knew the risk of failure would be considerable. 'But I want to write about him,' I said. Aziz nodded in agreement. 'You should,' he said. 'It's time that people outside Afghanistan learned more about him. I'll take you to the house where he used to live.'

1

In Search of a Terrorist

(2012)

My investigations into Mullah Omar in 2013 were initially quite clueless. Where should I start? I purchased a whiteboard, hung it on the wall in my office in Kabul and wrote 'Mullah Omar' in the middle. My plan was to draw arrows from his name to the people connected with him, and the information they gave me would reveal new leads that would eventually take me to this 'Most Wanted' man. I felt like a real detective, but who exactly was I searching for?

The first thing I did was type 'Mullah Omar' in Google. What was actually known about him? When I pressed Enter, all I saw was the Internet's take on Mullah Omar: lots of photos of dangerous-looking Afghans in black turbans, armed with an impressive arsenal of weapons. There were also pictures taken after attacks by Mullah Omar's men, with bodies in the street and a burned-out car from a suicide mission. I scrolled down the associated newspaper headlines from journalists in Kabul. 'U.S. Might Send Ground Troops to Assist in the Search for

Omar,' wrote *The New York Times* back in 2002.[1] 'Mullah Omar Calls for a Taliban Surge' was written in response to the announcement in 2009 that President Obama was sending additional troops to Afghanistan to put an end to Omar's Taliban.[2] All these reports assumed that Omar continued to lead the rebellion against the Americans and their allies after he had been driven out of Kandahar in 2001.

The Western media also frequently connected Omar to Osama bin Laden. He was rumored to have helped the Saudi Arabian prepare the attack on the Twin Towers, which had been the key reason for the U.S. invasion. Omar was routinely portrayed as a loyal friend of Bin Laden in the mainstream media.[3] I read on the B.B.C. site that they would sometimes go fishing together, and they were married to each other's sisters.[4] The big difference between the two men was that Omar was poverty-stricken and depended on Osama bin Laden for support, whereas Bin Laden himself was said to live 'in a huge mansion' in Kandahar. Apparently he had his 'headquarters' there, a place where Al Qaeda was stationed and where he lived 'with servants and fellow militants'.[5] Mullah Omar's offices to the north of Kandahar City were said to have been built with money from Osama bin Laden.

The fact that Mullah Omar had refused to hand Bin Laden over was proof that the latter had 'a great deal of influence' over him.[6] Omar and his men had essentially joined forces with Al Qaeda and the two groups had merged into one. Some experts even spoke of 'Tal Qaeda', a portmanteau of Taliban and Al Qaeda, as a way of impressing on people in the U.S. and Europe that this was a single group. These were fanatical Islamic extremists, Wahabis or Salafis (these terms were used interchangeably) who hated the West and posed a threat to 'us'.

This supposed close connection between the Taliban and Al Qaeda constituted the legal justification for the presence of foreign troops in Afghanistan and it is still a worry for the U.S. Bruce Riedel, a former Central Intelligence Agency (C.I.A.) officer and one of the key advisers to both George W. Bush and Barack Obama, was for a long time instrumental in pushing the idea of an association between the Taliban and Al Qaeda. He advised the U.S. government to see the two movements as a single, dangerous alliance opposed to America and Europe and easily capable of carrying out new attacks on Paris, Amsterdam, or New York.

Riedel claimed that the Taliban and Al Qaeda had committed a joint attack in the New York subway in 2009. He said the Taliban were actively recruiting for an Al Qaeda attack on U.S. territory.[7] I read in *Directorate S* (2018), the book by the American journalist Steve Coll, that the main demand from the Americans in the first peace negotiations with the Taliban in 2010 (which collapsed soon afterwards) was that the Taliban should abandon its alliance with Al Qaeda. In 2015, the Americans bombed 'probably the largest Al Qaeda camp ever' in the Afghan province of Kandahar. This description went unchallenged in the article that the *Washington Post* printed on the bombing; it was the Pentagon that was the only source for the story of an Al Qaeda camp in Afghanistan.[8]

Even as I read all these self-assured articles and books about the danger posed by the Taliban and Al Qaeda, Mullah Omar remained an enigma. Although he was constantly in the news, there was only one photo of him in circulation. And even that was disputed: no one could be sure whether the man in the picture really was Mullah Omar. Numerous speeches were ascribed to him, yet there was not a single recording to prove this. His whereabouts since 2001 were unknown. The Afghan government, American government, and American mainstream media claimed he was living in Pakistan, but Taliban members refuted this and insisted he was in hiding in Afghanistan. There had also been regular reports of his death since 2001.[9]

Nothing more substantial than speculative newspaper articles had been written about Mullah Omar. Not a single journalist or expert had ever seen him or spoken to him. The picture Western governments and international organizations in Brussels and Washington had of him seemed to be based mainly on the book *Taliban: Islam, Oil, and the New Great Game in Central Asia* (2000) by the Pakistani author Ahmed

Rashid. This book, which describes the rise of the Taliban in the period up to 2000, had rapidly become a kind of Bible for Western policymakers, who had gone into Afghanistan knowing little about the country before 2001. Rashid had never spoken to Mullah Omar for his book either.[10] 'I tried. I hung around his offices endlessly back then but he wouldn't talk to me,' said Rashid when I asked him about this a couple of years ago. According to him, Mullah Omar and the Taliban had essentially been created by Pakistan. Omar was supported financially and protected by the power of Osama bin Laden, whose strict Islamic ideology Mullah Omar had adopted.

———— ◆ ————

I had hoped the U.S. government would have more recent information about Mullah Omar, but the only mention of his name was on *Rewards for Justice*. This website, funded by the U.S. State Department, gives a 'Most Wanted' list of the terrorists sought by America and its Western allies. The hope is that the rest of the world will help the C.I.A. in its efforts to find the terrorists. To encourage them to do so, the U.S. government promises a big financial reward for the golden tip that leads them to the terrorist in question. In 2012, there was a reward of $10 million for Omar.

The profile for Mullah Omar on the site added little more to the information than what I already had.[11]

Hair: black
Height: tall
Nationality: Afghan
Specific features: injury to right eye from grenade

The site did explain why he was wanted:

Mullah Omar's Taliban regime provided shelter to Osama bin Laden and his Al Qaeda network in the years prior to the attacks on September 11. Although Operation Enduring Freedom removed the Taliban from power [...] Mullah Omar is still on the run and he forms a persistent threat to America and its allies.

There were two photos of Mullah Omar on the website. The two portraits were completely different. One showed a man looking up over the top of the camera so that almost all you could see was his throat and beard. He had a round face with thin lips, and both his eyes were intact. I saw someone quite different in the second photograph: an Afghan with a well-defined jawline, a turban, and one damaged eye.

It reminded me of a story in my book about Hamid Karzai: immediately after 9/11, the Americans dropped flyers on the Pakistani city of Quetta with pictures of Mullah Omar, saying he was a wanted man. It gave the city's residents a good laugh because whoever the man in the photo was, he definitely wasn't Omar.[12]

According to leaked C.I.A. documents on WikiLeaks, before 2001 the C.I.A. was using a photograph of a somewhat rotund man, who could not have been Mullah Omar for that reason alone.[13] In 2003, new photos of the Taliban leader were printed in *Vanity Fair* that appeared to show him in a garden full of yellow chrysanthemums. The man had been photographed from the side so you could not see his injured eye, if he had one. He did not look much like Omar. *Vanity Fair* called these photos 'an extraordinary find' and 'published here for the first time', but I was unconvinced. Was this really Mullah Omar, or had the magazine been conned? I tried to get an answer to these questions later on in my investigations.[14]

I also found that Mullah Omar was included in the U.N.'s Sanctions List. For some strange reason, he was listed as Mohammed Omar Ghulam Nabi. No one had ever called him that as far as I knew. The people at the U.N. didn't know much more about him either:

TI.O.4.01. Name: 1: mohammed 2: omar 3: ghulam nabi 4: na w(not available)

Title: Mullah

Designation: Leader of the Faithful ('Amir al-Momenin'), Afghanistan

Date of birth: a) approximately 1966; b) 1960; c) 1953

Place of birth: a) Naw Deh, Deh Rawod District, Uruzgan, Afghanistan; b) Noori, Maiwand District, Kandahar, Afghanistan

Good quality a.k.a.: na

Low quality a.k.a.: na

Nationality: Afghan

Passport number: na

National identification number: na

Address: na

Placed on the list of terrorists: 31 Jan. 2001 (amended on 3 Sep. 2003, 21 Sep. 2007, 29 Nov. 2011, 31 Dec. 2013)

Other information: Father's name is Ghulam Nabi, also known as Mullah Musafir. His left eye is missing. Brother-in-law of Ahmad Jan Akhundzada Shukoor Akhundzada (TI.A.109.01.). Believed to be in the Afghanistan/Pakistan border area. He belongs to the Hotak tribe.

This report/review pursuant to Security Council resolution 1822 (2008) was concluded on 27 July 2010.

———◆———

I knew where Mullah Omar's old house was, thanks to my Uruzgan contact Aziz, as I mentioned in the Prologue. That seemed a better starting point than what I was able to find in all those press reports and archives. Because so little was known about him, I decided the best approach would be to go back to where it all started – his former home. Perhaps he still secretly dropped in from time to time. Or might he have important friends in the region whom he looked up occasionally? They might be able to give me more information about him than I'd found so far. Perhaps I could find out where he was based now.

I called Najibullah, Aziz's son, to ask whether I could visit them again in Uruzgan. This time I flew there with the Dutch photographer Joël van Houdt, who wanted to take pictures of Mullah Omar's house.

We spent one night at Aziz's house to get some rest before setting off on our journey. In the middle of the night, I was woken up by a loud bang on the gate to the house. I heard Najibullah in the room next to me as he hurriedly grabbed his Kalashnikov, loaded the weapon, and rushed to the gate. He had put me in a room with his two sisters, because, he said, Afghan men who were not family would never enter the women's quarters. Not even the Taliban, he added. Now I sat bolt upright in bed. Was that the Taliban at the gate? Had Najibullah misjudged things and were they coming to get me? Najibullah soon returned. He dived into his room without saying a word and went back to sleep. I too crawled back onto my mat on the floor. I managed to relax again and eventually dozed off.

The next day, as we calmly ate breakfast, I told Najibullah that the bang on the door had frightened me. He gave me a teasing grin. 'Nothing will happen to you. Really,' he said. Najibullah suspected that the loud knocking was a tribal rival trying to scare him now that they had two foreign guests staying.

The story behind the banging on the door gave me a glimpse into the world of this family's enemies, who had now perhaps become my enemies too. As Najibullah explained, Aziz was a member of a complex tribal society with disputes both petty and serious. Afghanistan may have had kings in the nineteenth and twentieth centuries, such as Zahir Shah, but most tribes had much older dynasties, and blood relations were still linked by powerful bonds. Each tribe or clan essentially had its own power base, and sometimes its own army. They administered their own laws, arranged strategic marriages between one another, and eliminated any rivals who formed a threat to their blood relatives.

Loyalty could be for sale: if your tribe could obtain money from the government, you took it. If you could get more money from the group opposing the government, you took that too. After 2001, there were plenty of potential donors to choose from: the government in Kabul, the U.S. military, NATO troops, the Taliban, or other tribal leaders.

Each tribe, clan, or even clan-within-a-clan adopted its own stance. Aziz belonged to the prominent Alakozai tribe, which has thousands of members (although no records are kept of the precise size of the Afghan tribes). Possibly the biggest threat to Aziz's family came from the son of Aziz's sister-in-law, a man named Rahimullah.

Rahimullah was Aziz's *turbur*, Najibullah explained. Like I mentioned earlier, in the Afghan tribal world, *turbur* means a rival cousin, nephew, step-brother or half-brother. The term is often used for sons who have the same father but different mothers. They are brought up from birth to believe in a rivalry between them and their half-brothers, which fosters a competitive atmosphere. This was the case in Najibullah's home too.

Before the Taliban arrived, Aziz had been the local police chief for the area and, as such, he had more power than his rival. The situation was reversed when the Taliban came. The *turbur* nephew sided with the Taliban and was therefore in a position to put the screws on Aziz. After the Taliban were driven out in 2001, Aziz was back in business and was now 'on top', as Najibullah explained. Aziz decided to ally himself with the local governor and strongman Jan Mohammed Khan. In the course of my writing this book, Rahimullah was regaining ground because of the failures of the U.S. army and the Afghan government, who lost legitimacy by repeatedly killing the wrong enemy.

It seemed as if Najibullah was privy to a mass of secret family threats I was quite ignorant of. It reminded me of Europe in days of old when the state barely interfered in the lives of its people, and noble families were out for each other's blood. According to Najibullah, you could have long periods of calm, with tribal leaders giving one another friendly greetings, but that could switch in no time to fierce fights or shootouts. Once, a suicide bomber had walked into a teahouse and blown himself up in the vicinity of a notorious local leader. He had been sent by a rival.

———— ◆ ————

I didn't dwell on these stories, but concentrated on the journey ahead instead. I had not yet been in a situation in Afghanistan where I'd had to don the infamous blue burka. None of the expats in Kabul wore one, and Najibullah hadn't thought it necessary for me to cover up in Tarin Kowt either. But now that we were going on a long car journey to remote areas, it would be safer for me to hide under that cloth tent. I pulled the blue veil with matching blue embroidery over my head like a kind of wig. The heavy folds of the fabric fell over my body and I peered through the fabric mesh before me that was designed to obscure my female eyes. When I looked to the left, all I saw was blue cloth, and the same view awaited me when I looked to the right. When I looked straight ahead, I saw the world divided into little squares.

I could bring the net screen closer to my eyes and thus see the world a little more clearly by pulling at the cloth under my chin. I saw all the women doing this, especially when walking along the uneven paths and having to look down constantly to make sure they didn't stumble. Some Afghans told me the burka was a strict Islamic requirement but I found the Quran quite restrained compared with what I encountered in Afghanistan.

In fact, it is also the local tribal rules – collectively known as Pashtunwali – that dictate how women should behave when out in public. These rules are older than Islam, which only arrived in Afghanistan in about 700 AD. They are strictly adhered to by the Pashtun and other ethnic groups in Afghanistan. The Pashtunwali is all about protecting the family by protecting the womenfolk. An unveiled woman walking along the road, exposed to other men, is seen as a threat to the family honor. It is not just a question of wearing a burka either: even robed like that, women rarely leave home, and girls are kept inside from a young age.

When I was visiting Najibullah, I discovered that the women in this remote area had to observe strict rules inside the home as well, rules that went further than the Quran. Even indoors, they had to remain covered up. Once, when one of Najibullah's brothers passed us in the courtyard, Najibullah's wife pulled her veil over her eyes. She peered under it until he had gone and then pushed the black cloth up over her head again.

———— ♦ ————

I wasn't wearing my ordinary clothes under my burka. I had already discovered that people reacted negatively to tight-fitting Western garb. For example, on my first visit to Aziz I wore a long shirt over skinny jeans. Aziz's wife looked at me as if I had turned up in a bikini, and shook her head. The Prophet Muhammad wore loose clothing; according to his followers, he had said that others should also refrain from drawing too much attention to themselves when out and about.

Aziz's wife rushed off and came back with a yellow, loose-fitting *shalwar kameez*, a rather Indian-looking outfit. The long, baggy blouse had slits down the side and was worn over wide pants with a cord around the waist. Men also wear the robe and pants, often in pastel colors. In summer, men frequently go round in a white cotton *shalwar kameez*. Women tend to wear more colorful ones.

My burka was torture because I felt so confined. At the same time, being covered up like this was great for infiltrating Afghan society. No one would notice me, and that made me feel safe. Perfect for my search for the Most Wanted Man. All that could be seen underneath were my flat shoes – I'd swapped my heavy-duty Timberlands for ballerinas – and a flash of yellow from my *shalwar kameez*. Just like every other woman here, really.

The photographer Joël van Houdt sat next to me on the back seat. He couldn't wait to go with me on this first attempt to find Mullah Omar's old house. The Uruzgan trips were always his favorite, he told me. He too had dressed unobtrusively for the occasion. He wore a loose-fitting pastel *shalwar kameez* and had let his beard grow. Atop his head was a black and gray turban made up of no less than six yards of shiny satiny fabric. Wrapping it around his head in the correct way had been quite a challenge. We would not be able to tell people we were just friends on the trip we were about to make, so for the purposes of Uruzgan we became a married couple.

———— ◆ ————

Najibullah and his friend and driver Khairullah had a strategy for 'winning over hearts and minds' for my investigation. It was important for us to approach Mullah Omar's house in a white Toyota. Almost all Afghans drove white Toyotas, so we did too in order to blend in.

When I suggested taking flak jackets with us, Najibullah shook his head. 'That won't help us much here,' he said curtly. 'But...' I stammered, 'what if they shoot at us? What if we drive over a landmine?' In a weary voice, Najibullah explained it to me. If we were to drive over a landmine, the flak jacket wouldn't protect me. What is more, such a thick body-warmer with its metal shields would alienate me from my interviewees. Such a jacket was a sign to the Afghans that you didn't trust them. Najibullah wouldn't approach even the most dangerous Taliban warrior in a flak jacket.

What Najibullah was basically saying was that one hundred thousand Western soldiers in armored tanks named after snakes (such as the Bushmaster), who had been sent to win the Afghans' hearts and minds, actually made them wary. If the Afghans saw a Western convoy, they were on their guard, and if they felt threatened, they wouldn't hesitate to shoot.

It was more than likely that the often ill-informed foreign soldiers were dancing to the tune of a rival, and if so, a villager's fate was no longer in his own hands. The only thing protecting you then was your Kalashnikov.

It was much more common than we Westerners realized for Afghans to shoot at Western soldiers from behind a wall as a precautionary measure, in the hope that they would go away. But that had the opposite effect because the Western soldiers shot back. Sometimes this would turn into a major skirmish that would subsequently be reported in the media as a 'Taliban battle'.

Najibullah did not want to leave in the early morning because that was when the risk of driving over a landmine was highest. If you went later in the day, any newly planted mines would already have been exploded during the morning rush hour.[15] Before we set off, Najibullah made a couple of phone calls to acquaintances who knew the road well. 'Have you seen anything suspicious?' he asked. He had complete faith in the information they gave, and I badly wanted him to be right. 'You always have *khans* [tribal leaders] who are at each other's throats,' he explained. 'Sometimes when a Western military convoy drives over a bomb it might be pure coincidence, while at other times it might have been intentionally for them. It's never really clear who plants the bombs.'

———————— ◆ ————————

So off we set in the hot summer of 2013, without bulletproof jackets, to find Mullah Omar's parental home. It was at least a day's drive from where we were to the place where he had grown up in western Uruzgan – much further than I had assumed from what Aziz had said a couple of years earlier in his orchard.

The long stretch of gravel road slowed us down. This was the road connecting Tarin Kowt to the district of Deh Rawod, where Mullah Omar had once lived. In 2004, work started on upgrading the road, paid for by the U.S., but the job was never finished: the Kuwaiti contractor took off halfway through. 'Is this how America builds roads back home?' asked Najibullah as we zigzagged round the potholes in the road at a snail's pace, our heads banging against the roof every time we ended up in one by mistake. All Najibullah knew was Afghanistan. He had never visited Europe or America.

After we set off, I gave Joël's arm a squeeze. Could we really be in a car on our way to Mullah Omar's house? With no protection other than a Kalashnikov in the trunk? A second car was following us just in case we got a flat tire. If so, we would be able to switch cars, since waiting on the roadside as Europeans was an invitation for someone to rob or kidnap us. Might we have made a miscalculation in our security arrangements, I wondered.

It was one of the most nerve-racking Sunday mornings of my life so far – although I would go on to experience a number of similarly nerve-racking moments in the course of this investigation. As the hot sun stood high in the blue sky, we talked about our friends in Holland and how they would be spending the morning. How they would be getting the kids out of bed, or had already risen and were having breakfast, reading the predictable reports from the journalists in Kabul. If only they knew we were out here in the thick of it at that very moment.

Western Uruzgan stretched out proudly before us as if it wanted to flaunt its stunning beauty. We drove through an endless steppe, with a bush or tree here and there wilting in the heat of the sun. The high, jagged mountains on the horizon were illuminated by that same burning morning sun, which turned them multicolored with reds, oranges, and whites. The sky above us was bright blue.

As I traveled through this unfamiliar territory, I realized how little I knew about the history of Afghanistan and its people. Like many other people, I would not even have been able to identify the country on a map before 9/11. Now I knew that we were taking the same route that Alexander the Great had traveled around 300 BC. He managed to conquer the Persians with the help of armored horses and military elephants that could strangle the enemy with a resolute twist of their trunks.

Six centuries after Alexander the Great, Buddhist monks wrapped in bright red robes traveled along here. They carved thousands of statues of Buddha, both large and small, from the reddish brown and orange Afghan rocks. Two of these massive Buddhas had stood in the central Afghan province of Bamyan. One was no less than 174 feet tall. In the Afghan civil war (1991–96) after the end of the Cold War, rockets destroyed the Buddhas' rectangular faces; then in 2001 the statues were completely demolished by the Taliban. The story goes that Mullah Omar himself gave the orders to attach explosives to the statues and blow them up.

In the sixteenth century, men in brightly colored turbans advanced through this region wielding sharp spears. They were part of the powerful Islamic Mughal Empire that had already spread across much of what is now India and Pakistan and was now about to annex Afghanistan. About sixty miles away, just outside Kandahar, you can still see evidence of how much at home the Mughal Emperor Babur felt here. He had forty steps chiseled out of the mountainside at Chilzina and a throne constructed at the top of this stairway. According to tradition, his wife would regularly climb the stairway to enjoy the spectacular views over southern Afghanistan.

This was also the site of a dusty old cemetery containing victims of the First Anglo-Afghan War, which raged between 1838 and 1842. After many long and bloody battles, the British military eventually managed to exert some influence over the country, but they never for one moment felt safe there. As is still the case today, the tribal leaders had their own dynamics, which the uninformed British generals attempting to colonize the country often failed to understand.

The abandoned, rusting tank was a more recent relic, dating from a struggle in which another foreign army had failed to get a hold on Afghanistan. This vehicle had once belonged to the Soviet army, which had invaded Afghanistan in 1979. The tank's crew must have fled from

Afghan freedom fighters, who were receiving support from the Americans back then.

And then there were the houses that had only recently been flattened by bombs, unmistakable evidence of the U.S. 'War on Terror' against the Taliban and Al Qaeda. I kept hearing Western fighter planes tearing through the sky like race cars and would pop my head out of the window to give a worried look upwards. Aziz had told me that the F-16s and F-18s were even able to spot a box of matches on a table. I hoped they would not be bombing anywhere close to us. I suddenly wondered how they got the information that told them where to drop their bombs. That seemed to me the worst way to die here: killed by a bomb because the Americans had been misled by false reporting from a supposed Afghan ally.

Every now and then, we heard the hum of the latest weapon in the fight against terrorism – the drone. Afghans compared the buzzing drones – unmanned aircraft that might be carrying lethal rockets – to dangerous wasps that sting. Research had soon shown how hazardous this weapon was. The 'precision strikes', as the American government called them, turned out not to be so precise after all: there were missions where 90 per cent missed their target or killed the wrong person. Part of the problem was that the military was often using biased intelligence.[16]

————————◆————————

As we drew closer to Deh Rawod district, our cellphone signal became less and less reliable. By the time we entered the region where Mullah Omar had grown up, we hardly had any way of contacting the outside world anymore.

The last leg of the journey was an overwhelming experience. The village of Rawod lay behind a dense wall of mountains with year-round snow on the summit, rising up above the land like a crown. A road from the east took us over the mountains and led us slowly down into the valley. As soon as we entered the area through the stone gates, we were greeted by the sight of a lush green valley with clusters of mud-brick houses dotted about. The Helmand River, which crosses the entire country, flowed through the valley. The seething sandy waters left a track of green riverbanks and fields in their wake, in which almond trees and hosts of poppies grew.

The first villages we drove through were more like hamlets. Farm laborers could be seen occasionally in the wide expanse of fields, harvesting cereal crops with scythes. People were hard at work in the opium fields too, but there the laborers protected themselves with Kalashnikovs. I imagined that in Omar's youth, Afghans would have traveled by horse or donkey across the gently rolling countryside, along the paths connecting the farms. Now these animals had largely been replaced by white Toyotas.

We soon reached the center of Deh Rawod district, a town of the same name. Vegetable stalls lined a long sand track, along with mud-brick huts with large windows where you could buy cellphones, kitchen equipment, and car parts. The local butcher had the carcass of a cow hanging out the front. The blood-splattered head had been chopped off and was now on the ground, for sale, next to the carcass.

———— ◆ ————

Before driving on to Mullah Omar's house, we stopped for a break in Deh Rawod. We needed to avoid giving the inhabitants of these remote villages the impression that we had come to do them harm. If strangers arrived in the area, everyone knew; there was always some alert Afghan watching on the roadside. I understood now why it was better not to come here with weapons and bulletproof vests. If you didn't want to raise suspicions, you needed a local confidant on your side, preferably one with the time to accompany you constantly as you traveled around.

That was why Najibullah had phoned a friend of the family in Deh Rawod before we got there. This tribal leader was called Mir Hamza and he had known Mullah Omar's family in the old days. Najibullah said he would be able to keep gossipers and people with nefarious intentions away from us. Aziz told us that Mir Hamza also knew a former neighbor of Mullah Omar.[17]

My normal procedure was to phone my sources first to announce my arrival and get an impression of the subject matter we would be discussing. But things were different now. We hadn't dared tell Mir Hamza the real purpose of our quest on the phone. We were not just afraid of a Taliban attack or of fearful, gossiping tribal leaders; we were also worried about the Afghan government and its Western allies. We knew they tapped phones. I was afraid we would be arrested if the National Directorate of Security (the local secret service sponsored by the C.I.A.) were to suspect us of sympathizing with the Taliban. They might easily detain us anyway to interrogate us about their Most Wanted list. What is more, it wasn't fair to our interviewees for us to ask them questions about Omar on the phone. The Afghan secret service and their American colleagues might decide to seize our sources because of alleged 'links with terrorists', or to interrogate them to find out what exactly they knew about Mullah Omar.

Najibullah advised me not to spend too long in one place during our visit. 'That would set tongues wagging,' he explained. I took his advice to heart. When we arrived in Deh Rawod, he parked the Toyota in front of a door in the high mud-brick wall that encircled the town of Deh Rawod. A curtain hung across the small door. I stepped through the opening in my burka.

It turned out to lead to a house. I pushed the blue veil back over my head and Najibullah took us to a windowless mud-brick guestroom where Mir Hamza was sitting, waiting for us. He stood up at once to welcome us. He was small, with long, loose-fitting clothes, a thick beard, and a striped turban, like all the men here. The single oil lamp in the room cast a warm glow on his weathered face. Meanwhile, a child – presumably Mir Hamza's son – ran round in a little yellow shalwar kameez and a small skullcap, the kind that the older men wear under their turbans.

Mir Hamza put out large bowls of rice and lamb, and another little boy – dressed today in pale pink – curled up next to him like a merman as everyone sat down on the carpet. I was the only female in the room. Najibullah had taken off his turban and put it down next to him, so Joël followed suit. Najibullah told Mir Hamza about our plan to visit Mullah Omar's parental home.

'This woman has got guts,' said Mir. 'I appreciate that. I'll help her.' He gave us the names of two men who had known Mullah Omar in the old days and explained to Najibullah where they lived. He told us that the village where Omar had been brought up was called Landi Nawa, and he offered to accompany us on our quest. Then he took me to the women's quarters to introduce me to his wife. The little room was lit by an oil lamp.

'How many children do you have?' asked Mir Hamza's wife as she pushed one of her rings onto my finger.

'None,' I said. She couldn't believe it.

'But how old are you then?' she exclaimed. We laughed, and I explained in my broken Pashto that I was here to find out more about Mullah Omar. 'He was a good man,' she replied.

———————— ◆ ————————

The first man on our little list was Massoum, who had once been Mullah Omar's neighbor. We decided not to interview him at his home as I wanted him to come with us to Omar's house so that I could hear his stories in the setting of Omar's childhood.

When we got to Massoum's home, Najibullah and Mir Hamza went inside first to announce me. A man soon came out and strode towards our car. Through my burka, I saw a tall man with a full black beard, wearing a large black turban and a white *sarwal* (baggy pants). His eyes seemed hostile under his dark, bristly eyebrows. But when I took off my burka so that he could identify me, his stern face softened at once and he grinned in surprise. A Western woman had come all this way?

'Is she carrying weapons?' he asked Najibullah, who shook his head and replied, 'No, of course not.' 'Then it's OK,' he said.

I responded with as cheerful a look as I could manage and told him – with Najibullah interpreting – how pleased I was to see him. This was the man who had known Omar as a little boy. As I sat in the car with him, I felt I was already slightly closer to Omar.

To get to Mullah Omar's childhood village, we had to leave the town of Deh Rawod and continue north. On the way, we passed what I think must be one of the most romantic spots in Afghanistan: a bazaar floating in the air on a rope bridge over the water. Below flowed the Helmand River, which splits in two precisely at that point. The bridge was like a star suspended over the fork in the river. As I peered through the 'window' of my blue burka, I could see the market traders wobbling to and fro as they sat at their stalls. We bumped cautiously over the bridge in our car. At one point I thought we were going to fall through.

Once we reached the other side, we continued past farmland that stretched as far back as the water from the river was able to reach to keep the soil fertile. The land beyond reverted to the barren steppe. Between the jagged rocks lay sheep carcasses, left there by passing nomads. As the track in the direction of Omar's house narrowed, we had to fold in the side mirrors so that we didn't hit any trees. We drove on further until the track became so narrow we had to stop and walk the rest of the way.

'Look, there's the house Omar grew up in,' said Najibullah, pointing. I looked in the direction of his finger but could only see deserted rice fields and arid plains. Then all of a sudden I spotted a lonely house in the corner of a tract of land. 'There?' I asked him in amazement. Najibullah nodded.

Together, we climbed the hill next to Omar's mud-brick house, from where we could look down on the place that had been the scene of that unknown childhood. We had become quite a group by now: Najibullah,

Joël, Mir Hamza, Massoum and me. We were starting to look like a delegation, but fortunately it didn't feel as if we were drawing a lot of unwanted attention. As the place was so sparsely populated, with only a few houses and a mosque, Najibullah had relaxed his burka policy. I pushed back my veil so that I could survey our surroundings properly.

———◆———

While we were standing there, Massoum suddenly tugged at my sleeve. 'Could you do something for me?' he asked. He explained that the Afghan government and the Americans thought that he was a terrorist and that he had only just been released from prison. They had arrested him as an enemy combatant for the same reason that we had looked him up: because he had once been Mullah Omar's neighbor. The Americans thought he might still be in contact with the Taliban leader or even Osama bin Laden.

I knew they had organized major 'clean-up operations' immediately after 9/11, aimed at eliminating 'terrorists', as they were termed by the Western military. The soldiers would come in the middle of the night, burst into suspects' homes, and snatch potential terrorists. U.S. President George W. Bush declared in his State of the Union Address in January 2002 that he had arranged for thousands of known terrorists to be seized. 'The American flag flies again over our embassy in Kabul. Terrorists who once occupied Afghanistan now occupy cells at Guantánamo Bay.'[18] He said this marked the start of a War on Terror.

The American president may have sounded convinced of the success of his hunt for terrorists but no one here shared his confidence. One of the first of those thousands of terrorists was a taxi driver called Delawar. He was picked up by the Americans and taken to Bagram Prison outside Kabul. He soon succumbed to the incessant torture meted out by the Americans. They had hung him upside down from the ceiling, which had made his arms come out of their sockets. When he did not confess, they had beaten his feet to a pulp so that he would never be able to walk again. One foot – or what was left of it – would have had to be amputated but it never got that far, as Delawar died from his injuries.

It was alleged that Delawar had fired a rocket at a military camp in Wardak Province. After his death, the Americans discovered that Delawar had not been the perpetrator after all; it was again a case of false reporting. Their own ally, the local administrator Jan Baz Khan, had wanted to secretly carry out an attack on the Americans and had told his U.S. contact that Delawar was the Taliban behind the assault. (Jan Baz Khan got money from the U.S. for giving in terrorists.) According to a confidential report, the Americans should have done more to verify the information provided by their ally.[19]

Massoum had also been taken to a prison near Kabul. Although he was more fortunate than Delawar and had been released after one year, he had not felt truly free ever since. He could be picked up again at any time. I wasn't sure whether I could do anything for him. I didn't know him and couldn't easily judge whether he was secretly on the enemy side after all. I promised him that I would put in a good word for him with the NATO troops and that I would tell them he had nothing to do with the Taliban. But I was fairly certain they wouldn't listen to me; they preferred to base their intel on their own sources.

———— ◆ ————

A clear blue stream separated us from Mullah Omar's house. To cross the stream and get to the place, I had to do a balancing act in my blue burka on a narrow tree trunk. Najibullah strode ahead of me and held my hand. My Afghan companions laughed heartily at my clumsy efforts to reach the other side. A simple curtain hanging in the small doorway of the mud-brick house served as a door. Not a lockable door – apparently that was not necessary.

The current owner, Said, was suddenly confronted with a five-person delegation in his courtyard. He did not seem very put out by this unannounced visit. Said was small and timid, with an angular face. Like the four men accompanying me, he wore a cotton *shalwar kameez*. His top and pants looked as if they hadn't been washed for days and his hands were covered in mud.

It turned out that even in this conservative corner of Afghanistan, a man like Said was still willing to talk to me. I kept being surprised by this because the country was famous for its misogynistic attitudes. I had been asked innumerable times by friends, colleagues, and strangers whether it wasn't incredibly difficult to operate in a country where women were so oppressed.

We explained why we had looked him up. Said appreciated the effort I had made. 'Did she come all this way to my home, all on her own?' he marveled. He soon asked me if I would like to meet his wife. Najibullah and the other men waited meekly as they knew they were not allowed to meet female strangers. Joël wanted to peep inside but he was only permitted to take photos from the roof. That was actually quite generous of Said. Strange men were often not allowed to come so close at all, let alone take photos. It seemed as if people were more relaxed about the rules in these remote villages than in the crowded towns.

Access to the family quarters in Mullah Omar's old home also turned out to consist of just a doorway with a curtain. I entered the women's area and came upon a scene straight out of the Bible. Said's wife sat in the corner on the sandy floor, a veil covering her long dark hair. With slow strokes, she was weaving a carpet made of red, green, and yellow yarn. She did not look up because strangers must not see her face. A plump white chicken clucked and strutted around the compressed sand floor. A goat lay on its own patch of straw. Dry kindling was stacked in the corner. This fuel was used for cooking over an open fire under a lean-to. The walls of this open-air 'kitchen' were black from the soot of generations of families who had lived and cooked here. Omar's mother too must have cooked rice here and baked flat Afghan *naan* in the oven.

Tree trunks formed a latticework that rested on four clay legs and served as a support for a large cooking pot. Clothes were also hung up to dry on the makeshift table and a burka was stretched out on it. Alcoves had been cut out of the clay on the interior side of the external wall for use as storage space.

When her husband Said explained in a friendly voice that I was a woman and a good person, his wife removed her veil. She smiled and pushed one of her two children towards me. 'Say hello,' she whispered to a girl in a bright pink dress.

I imagined what Omar's life must have been like here as a child. Said's children played with a jerry can and some twigs. They were covered in the dust from the floor; their hair was stiff with the sand. A new-born baby was peacefully rocking in a cloth 'crib' suspended from the ceiling. The baby's eyes were closed but I could see they had been made up with black kohl. Afghans believe fervently that this brings good luck.

Just as Said lived and slept with his wife and children in this little room measuring six square feet, so Omar must have lived when he was young. They slept on the floor, as is still the custom among many families in southern Afghanistan. Sometimes as many as ten people may sleep next to one another on the floor. During the War on Terror, such houses could be hit by mistake during aerial bombardments. The rooms were so small that the damage could seem limited when viewed from a fighter plane. After all, a room that size would just be storage space in the West. But because there were often so many people sleeping in them, one bomb could wipe out an entire family.

A warm ray of sunlight penetrated Omar's old room. 'What was Omar like as a person?' I asked Said.

'I didn't know him as a child, but I've heard that he was an ordinary boy, nothing special,' he replied.

After a while, I left the women's quarters. Outside, my male companions and I chatted further with Said. He and his family had only been living here for a year. He knew Omar had lived in this house in the 1960s and 1970s. The owner lived in Jalalabad, on the other side of Afghanistan. He also knew that Omar's father had made the same deal with the owner that he had now: he farmed the land in return for being allowed to live there. It was a farm laborer's house. You had to work in the fields every day and hand the harvest over to the owner. That was how you paid the rent.

As we stood next to the stream, the men reminisced and I learned some more. Omar's father was not his real father, they told me. No one here had known him, said Massoum. Omar's father died before the boy moved here. Massoum continued, 'I remember Omar used to disappear for days on end sometimes. We'd wonder where he had been and people said he had gone to a cemetery to visit his father. We got the impression that he loved his father a lot. But I don't know any more than that.'

He told us that Omar's mother used to wash their clothes in the stream. Apparently, when she later moved to Kandahar she once said to a friend, 'Wasn't life lovely in the countryside?'[20] 'The nice thing about the countryside is that you can sit and relax next to the water without having to wear a veil,' she was also supposed to have said. I looked around me and it was true; there was no one as far as the eye could see. Women did not have to cover themselves up if there were no strange men around who might see them.

Omar's mother often wore a dark velvet dress, wide skirt, and loose-fitting top. Such sober clothes were worn in particular by the wives of mullahs, the men who led worship in the mosque (just as priests and preachers do in the Christian church). Tribal leaders' wives wore more brightly colored clothes, like the yellow outfit decorated with black flowers that Aziz's wife had given me as a gift.

So I discovered that Omar's stepfather had been a mullah as well as a farm laborer. He led worship in the nearby clay mosque five times a day.

On the other side of the field stood that little mud-brick square building with its Gothic-style doors, and a crooked tree in the sandy yard. Omar's stepfather had studied the Quran. He taught local children about the Quran, lessons somewhat similar to the Catholic catechism.

One of Omar's former neighbors, whom I spoke to in later trips I made to the area, said that he used to have a roadside stall in the 1960s, when Omar was still living here. Omar's stepfather had bought *naans* from him – the cheapest food you could get – on credit. 'They were poor,' he explained. 'But when Omar became the new leader later on, I did think to myself: you could pay that money back now.'

As I stood next to this humble house and listened to all the stories, I realized that the fate of boys like Said and Omar and their families seemed fixed from a young age. Nothing suggested their lives would improve or that they would have careers that took them far away from these remote villages. No one really took any notice of them, said the neighbor. When Omar later came to power in Afghanistan, his former neighbors in this hamlet of five or six houses were amazed. 'Is that our Omar?' the neighbors asked one another.

Omar did return to the village once, in 1995. Not on foot, as in the past, but in his own helicopter. When he disembarked, the astonished locals lined up on either side to honor him. Omar said, 'Peace be with you,' and proceeded towards his parental home to visit his stepfather and mother, who were still living there at the time. There was a conflict between his half-brothers and the boys next door, and Omar had come to resolve it. When he returned to the helicopter, the neighbors lined up again and they all shook his hand. As one of the neighbors explained, 'I just thought: I'm going to shake his hand. Who knows, I might get some benefit from this in the future.'

I had originally pictured Mullah Omar growing up in an ultra-conservative environment, but that picture started to change. I found out from my traveling companions and the people we met en route that Deh Rawod had been better off during Omar's childhood in the 1960s and 1970s. The district where he had grown up had been relatively prosperous and progressive. The region had the rice fields to thank for its prosperity. Deh Rawod supplied all of Afghanistan with this basic food commodity. According to the inhabitants of Deh Rawod, the quality of its rice was without parallel in the country.

Once the crops had been harvested, the summer festivities started. The strumming of the *rabab* – the Afghan guitar – and the long-drawn notes of the Afghan harmonica could be heard everywhere. In the evenings, the tribal leaders met up dressed in the long summer *shalwar kameez* to celebrate the new harvest. They would throw their hands up in the air as they danced round and round.

The musicians were no mere local amateurs but hired Pakistani performers. They slept during the day so that they could carry on playing until deep into the night. Any reason people might have to celebrate was postponed until the harvest festivities. Whether it was a wedding or a baby's first teeth, the occasion was seized as an opportunity to spend the entire evening dancing.

War seemed a distant prospect anyway when Omar was young. The last time the country had been embroiled in a major conflict was when the British had invaded, but that was a century ago. King Zahir Shah, who lived in the far-off modern city of Kabul, kept the peace in the country. There had been no fighting or bloodshed at all in Afghanistan for some thirty years. Moreover, the king had started a process of liberalization.

Zahir Shah introduced the first parliamentary elections in 1949. Under his regime, Islam was the state religion, but an increasingly independent press became more openly critical of the ruling elite and the conservative religious leaders. In Zahir Shah's Afghanistan, you heard female presenters on Kabul Radio and you saw women without a veil. Some even ventured onto the streets in short skirts, something the country had never seen before. Zahir Shah was the first Afghan leader to send a woman to New York to represent Afghanistan at the U.N.[21]

Afghanistan and America were on friendly terms in those days. Omar grew up under a pro-Western government. President Franklin D. Roosevelt paid King Zahir Shah a visit and in 1963 Zahir Shah visited Washington. *The New York Times* described Afghanistan as a buffer state: for a century, it had kept Russian Asia and Indian Asia at arm's length from one another. The king's wife, Princess Humaira, was described in the American press as a 'fancy, statuesque brunette'.

Kabul welcomed American performers, such as the jazz musician Duke Ellington in 1963. I read in an old interview that he had seen the audience suddenly walk out halfway through his performance. Worried, he'd wondered what on earth was happening. But they all returned five minutes later to enjoy the rest of his concert. Afterwards, he heard that people had popped outside to pray.[22]

This was also the period when busloads of Western hippies arrived in Afghanistan. I still come across Europeans who look back affectionately on their trip fifty years ago. Hordes of hash-smoking foreigners reveled in the hospitality of the Afghans. They were welcomed wherever they went; many families invited the tourists into their homes.

Although society remained relatively traditional in the countryside of Omar's childhood, I found a video of laughing Americans in white linen pants sitting among smiling, relaxed Afghans.[23] The clip was filmed in Helmand Province, where the Americans were pumping in millions of dollars to build a 'new society'. They had intensified relations with Afghanistan from the 1950s onwards, mainly in competition with the Soviet Union, which was also heavily involved with aid projects.

If you had asked people in Deh Rawod back then what they thought of America, they were highly likely to have answered with an approving nod. The more conservative lifestyle of the Afghans did not mean America was unpopular. On the contrary, many Afghans looked up to the Americans. 'We thought of America as a superpower,' said one Deh Rawod inhabitant. Without any television to prove otherwise, some even claimed that the streets of far-off America were paved with gold and that the houses were so tall they reached into the sky.

————•————

It wasn't easy to find out where Mullah Omar had been born. My initial idea was to search through the birth certificates in the local government archives, but my Afghan colleagues told me there were no such records. They thought it highly likely that Omar's birth was never registered, as was the case for so many newborns.

We do know that Omar's forebears on his father's side came from Siori, a district in the province of Zabul, which is renowned for its pistachio nuts. It is a day's drive north of central Kandahar and east of Uruzgan. But there are no indications that Mullah Omar was born there. Almost all the Afghans I spoke to thought Omar had been born in Naw Deh. Even people very close to Omar insisted that Mullah Omar had been born in Naw Deh – the mullah himself had told them this.[24] The interviewees I spoke to in Naw Deh itself also told me that the grave of Mullah Omar's father was located there. Naw Deh, which means New Village, is not in Deh Rawod District, as is erroneously stated in the U.N. Sanctions List mentioned earlier; it is in the neighboring province of Kandahar, a good half a day's drive south. Areas such as Uruzgan and Zabul were also once part of Kandahar Province, at a time when it was still known as Great Kandahar. But in 1964, King Zahir Shah divided the region into several provinces as a way of increasing his control over this part of Afghanistan.

Mullah Omar's half-brother Mullah Manan has since added more details to this story. Mullah Omar lived in Naw Deh when he was a toddler, but was born in the village of Chai-i-Himmat in Khakrez, a district of Kandahar that I have never visited.[25] His father was not from there originally, but he worked there as a mullah in a mosque. Mullah

Manan told me that Omar's father married a local girl from Khakrez. This was Mullah Omar's mother, who is still alive and now lives in Pakistan. Omar's mother was his father's second wife, whom he had married because his first wife was unable to have children. This second wife bore him two daughters, who died, according to Mullah Manan. Then Omar was born. After that they moved to Naw Deh, a desert town near the highway leading to Kandahar City. His first wife died there, as did Omar's younger brother. Soon after, Omar's father died in the local hospital.

Mullah Omar was only a couple of years old when he also lost his father. According to my Afghan colleague Ahmad Issa, who is a doctor (and a member of the family who took Mullah Omar in when he was older), early deaths were very common in mullah families. They often did not have access to good food or proper health care. Moreover, mullahs did not (and still do not) believe in 'scientists' (doctors) and preferred to consult other mullahs or a pir (spiritual guide). And they could also be 'careless', as my friend puts it, where women and children were concerned, in particular.

According to Mullah Manan, Omar's father Ghulam Nabi was sick for a long time. I told Manan about the rumors I had heard in Naw Deh, that the brother of Omar's father – Mullah Mohammed Anwar – had killed Omar's father because he wanted his brother's second wife. Manan refuted these stories. Mullah Mohammed Anwar didn't do that: he was much younger, too young to commit such a murder, and was studying in the madrassa in Kandahar when Omar's father was ill with a stomach disease. Also, Manan told me it was Anwar who took his brother to the hospital, where he died. Mullah Omar's father is buried in what is known as the Taliban graveyard, in the center of Kandahar.

Mullah Omar's doctor Baluch had told me that Omar used to visit two graveyards with great regularity. One was the cemetery where his younger brother was buried. The other was the last resting place of his father. As it happens, Mullah Omar was not entirely sure if the grave really was his father's or if it had been a different spot in this graveyard.

The burial ground of a mullah is often marked by nothing more than
a row of stones, which sand, wind, and time can easily efface. Many
Afghans are unable to find family members' graves for this reason. Yet
Omar continued to visit the cemetery. He would park his car next to the
gate and go to pray.[26]

Omar also paid regular visits to the cemetery in Naw Deh where his
baby brother was buried. When I visited the grave later, I saw what Omar
must have seen on all those visits. The graves stood in a jumbled group
in a wide plain surrounded by mountains. Everywhere there were pieces
of green, red, and golden cloth attached to tall, thin poles, flapping in the
wind. Some graves were wrapped in gleaming golden cloth. It was usually
the women who decorated the graves. Pieces of glass, supposed to bring
good luck, were strewn everywhere.

One grave consisted of a mound of carefully smoothed sand some
six or seven feet long. This grave looked more cared for than most of the
others. Long, thin poles draped in red and green cloth stood at the head
of the mound. The gravedigger there, like so many in Kandahar, believed
it was Mullah Omar's father who was buried there. 'If the Americans
discover you've been paying your respects to Mullah Omar's father,
you're in serious trouble.'[27]

———•◦•———

When Omar's father died, Omar was left behind with his mother and a
sister. That only intensified his love for his mother. Mullah Manan told me
that at present his mother doesn't know anything about the whereabouts
and fate of Mullah Omar; she is kept in the dark in order to protect her
feelings. 'She loves him so much – I still bring her presents, and tell her
they are from Omar.'

In 2001, she said that the first years of Omar's life had been the
hardest for her.[28] Immediately after her husband's death, Omar's mother
married his brother, Mullah Mohammed Anwar. This was the rule in

that patriarchal society (although not in Islam). Widows in Afghan tribal society had no money, nor could they own land. These restrictions were deliberate and designed to make sure women always needed a man. Widows also 'posed a threat' to married men, so they were not allowed to remain single for long. It was customary for one of the dead husband's brothers to become the new husband since he was a blood relative.

———————◆———————

Omar must have had a difficult time in tribal society without a father. The Pashtunwali rules were hard on him and the death of his father impacted his social status. He was considered to be an orphan, or *yateem*, which in Afghanistan was the equivalent of being 'uncivilized' or 'half-human'. In fact, the Quran said that a *yateem* should be given extra protection, but local traditions dictated otherwise. Without a father, Omar was defenseless. For example, tribal law said that it was fine to beat a *yateem*. Because of his position, Omar was someone you could insult and ride roughshod over without risk of being punished. A *yateem* was frequently the whipping boy inside the home too. The new father often showed him little respect and openly ridiculed him.

Many *yateem* would spend as much time as possible away from the home where they were treated so badly (Aziz, Najibullah's father and the man who had pointed me towards Mullah Omar's home, was also a *yateem*). A former neighbor of Mullah Omar's once said that Omar had nearly been shot dead with a Kalashnikov when he stole apples from the yard of a tribal leader in the tiny village of Miandow. If the neighbors hadn't intervened, the man would have undoubtedly fired bullets at Omar.[29] I also heard that Omar was once beaten so hard with an iron bar that he was left with permanent scars.[30]

Apparently, Omar's stepfather moved to Deh Rawod with his two brothers, his new wife, and Omar soon after his marriage to Omar's mother. It is not clear why they moved so far away. Some say he wanted to flee Kandahar because he was under suspicion of murder. But it is also possible that the impoverished mullah was offered a job as the cleric for Deh Rawod. Whatever the reason may have been, little Omar and his family did not exactly get a warm welcome from the locals when they arrived in Deh Rawod.

Newcomers were often regarded with suspicion in these small communities. Clans and tribes defined the social structure in places like Deh Rawod. You could see clearly who belonged with whom from their tribal background. Omar's family belonged to the Hotak tribe. It had once been all-powerful and its leader had founded the first Afghanistan state in 1709. But the Hotaki lost power seventy years later; the Durrani tribe seized the throne and was able to remain in control for much longer. King Zahir Shah, who ruled in the 1960s and 1970s, was a descendant of these Durrani, as is the former president Hamid Karzai. The Durrani also held many of the powerful positions in the Deh Rawod of Omar's childhood.

Omar and his family remained outsiders in Deh Rawod. His stepfather was known as Mullah Musafer. That was not his real name; Mullah Musafer means Mullah the Traveler. Life could be tough for local mullahs in this tribal culture. The khans – local tribal leaders who were often major landowners too – were in charge of things. They built mosques on their own land as that was good for their reputation. The mullah had no say in matters; his task was just to preach and lead prayers five times a day. If the tribal leader became tired of him, the mullah could be dismissed without any reason being given, which made the life of a mullah very insecure. Aziz had told me too that mullahs were dirt poor. They had nothing – no house, no land. That was why mullahs were called 'Chennai', after a mythical bird that was always flitting from one branch to the next.

Omar's family was also constantly on the move. I discovered that Omar had only actually spent a couple of years in the house where we had paid a visit to Said. When I asked about Omar's home in Deh

Rawod, people would point in different directions. In addition to Said's house, Omar had lived in Kakar, Dewanawargh, Shangula, Chariaki, and finally in Landi Nawa.

One of the places where Mullah Omar had stayed for quite a while was in southern Deh Rawod, in the Tangi valley. I was fortunate enough to speak to an old childhood friend of his who still lives there. His name is Abdul Koudouz and he comes from a prosperous Deh Rawod tribal family. He is about the same age as Mullah Omar and they lived close by for about five years. 'Mullah Omar was born Mohammad Omar,' he explained. 'I didn't know him as a mullah. He got that title later on, when he started to lead the worship in the mosque. That makes you a mullah. Lots of people called him Mullah Muhammad Omar at first, but that soon changed to Mullah Omar.'

'You know, you're just as tall as Mullah Omar!' he said, and he laughed heartily as he pointed at me. I stood up straight and held my hand about two inches above my head. 'That tall?' Yes, nodded Abdul with a big grin. So Mullah Omar must have been about six foot five.

Abdul's first memory of Omar was of a boy aged about six clinging onto his stepfather's leg as they stood outside the gate to Abdul's family's fort in Tangi. Young Omar had trekked with his family along mountain paths and past steep cliffs to reach the large clay fort next to a stream. All they had with them was a backpack containing some kitchen equipment. Omar's mother held a baby in her arms (one of the oldest of the eight children she would eventually have with her second husband). 'Can I come and work for you?' Omar's stepfather had asked. 'I'd like to be your mullah.'

The family had traveled to Tangi to serve in the mosque housed within the high walls surrounding Abdul's home. Abdul's father asked around and received good reports of Omar's stepfather. First the current mullah had to pack his bags and go, so Omar's stepfather had to wait two months before he could start in his new position. In exchange for his preaching, the mullah's family was given free food.

'Omar was a nice boy. I got on well with him,' said Abdul. In the days when they were neighbors, Omar's family was often to be found sitting in front of their little home like vacationers in front of their tent at a campsite. A mat would be laid out on the sandy ground, always with a pot of tea on it. Omar's stepfather would be studying the Quran, his wife cooking food or looking after the baby.

The mosque was more a mud-brick hut than a house of prayer. A mix of water, straw, and clay had been used to build the walls higher and higher, until there was enough room under the roof to stand upright. Then the walls had been hardened by the sun. Inside, prayer mats lay scattered around and the holy book, the Quran, was stored safely on a shelf up high.

Omar and Abdul were buddies. 'Omar was a loyal friend,' said Abdul. He did not feel the difference in their social status. As a child, you forgot about that. 'You could rely on him. He was dependable.' After morning prayers, Abdul and Omar would remain behind in the mosque, sitting on the ground. That was when their lessons began. Omar's stepfather taught from the Quran. Some of the other children from neighboring mud-brick houses also attended these lessons. In the summer, they would often be taught outdoors, on the small patio in front of the mosque door.

Like many young boys, Omar was not keen on school. 'He played hooky a lot,' said Abdul. He much preferred to go swimming, and Abdul liked to accompany him. Life in this arid region clustered along the banks of the modest rivers. Abdul's family home was built on one such fertile spot next to a river. The water was deep in parts. Abdul avoided those parts as he could not swim. 'But Omar did go there,' laughed Abdul. 'He would pretend he was a skilled swimmer. But he'd always been one of the tallest kids in the village, so while he was pretending to swim, he was secretly touching the bottom with his long legs.'

Abdul also remembered how Omar's stepfather would regularly storm out of the mosque in anger and come and fetch them, especially if they had been sneaking off from class again. The mullah's son came in for the worst punishment, said Abdul. The mullah would find the boy playing, chase after him with a stick and beat his stepson back into the little clay mosque.

'But Omar was also turning into a real comedian,' said Abdul. His big party trick was his imitations – friends I met later confirmed this. As they sat together on the floor in a room around a pot of tea, Omar would often imitate someone. Like an actor, he would play the role of the guest. If an old man exited the room, Omar would limp after him with his back bent, an imaginary stick in his hand, usually to the great amusement of the others.

For a while, little Omar had a pet dog that had been a stray. His stepfather was not happy about this. When the dog was in heat, attracting hordes of potential mates, Omar's stepfather called for a gun. 'I'm going to shoot that dog dead,' he called to Abdul's father. As he prepared to do so, Omar came running, calling: 'I've let her go, I've let her go!' He had saved the dog from being shot but had lost his canine companion as a result.

Omar had to say goodbye to Abdul again far sooner than he would have wanted. That was the way of things for mullahs' sons. They never knew when they would be packing up and moving on. Abdul remained behind. As the son of an affluent tribal leader, he never had to move.

———— • ————

If I have understood correctly, this was when Omar's family moved to Said's house, the place I visited with Najibullah. Omar only lived there for a couple of years, until his stepfather decided it was time for the boy to leave home.[31] The usual procedure would have been for Omar to study the Quran with his stepfather until he was able to support himself. That training was considered the best preparation for a Quran student (known as a *taliban* in the local language) who wanted to become a mullah. But Omar's stepfather now had sons of his own by Omar's mother and he wanted to devote his time to his new family.

It seems that Omar then attended various schools where he could board. Najibullah and I decided to visit one of these schools in Dewanawargh, a half-hour drive north of Deh Rawod, somewhat further than Said's remote home. The road to the village soon turned into a thin strip of sand with a high mud-brick wall on one side and a grayish-blue river on the other side. A dozen white ducks with bright orange beaks bobbed up and down on the water. They swam underneath the crooked overhanging trees towards the water pump that stood in front of the mosque and school. The flapping of their wings was the only sound disturbing the total silence.

The tiny village of Dewanawargh lies in the rolling countryside. A mosque with an adjoining school stands at the point where the river splits in two. I stuck my head through the little door leading into the mosque. The windowless clay building felt cool. The ray of light through the door revealed about five prayer mats on a floor covered in straw. As was customary, the Quran was safely stored on a high shelf.

Opposite the mosque was a tiny building, which I assumed was for laundry. But when I peered inside, I saw a Quran student aged about sixteen, deep in thought. A Quran was placed in front of him on a book rest. 'Is this the school?' I whispered in amazement as I looked round the room, no bigger than a storage shack. Najibullah nodded. The student noticed me and stood up. He greeted us with a soft 'Salaam' and left.

'That could easily have been Mullah Omar,' said Najibullah.

We looked round Omar's former school in Dewanawargh. White sheets covered the clay walls, prints of Mecca were hung up next to a photo of a vase of flowers, another photo of a red sports car and, a little further along, a map of the world. This was a *hujra*, a village hut that served as a classroom. Najibullah told me that in southern Afghanistan, schools like this were typical of the education madrassa students received.

The only person able to tell me more about Omar's time as a student was an old teacher who was nearly eighty. His son was the same age as Omar and he remembered young Omar as a *hujra* pupil of his father's. The son was currently employed as a civil servant in the local agriculture department in Tarin Kowt, and he was not willing to talk about Mullah Omar with me as that could cost him his job. He did imply that Omar was actually quite an ordinary boy who preferred to play hooky rather than go to school. 'He wasn't that special. Quite the opposite.'

Unfortunately, there was no chance of me interviewing his father, the teacher. 'He would never look a strange woman in the eye,' explained the son, for his father was a devout man. I suggested that I could sit behind a tapestry so that he could not see me – an approach regularly used by women in southern Afghanistan as a way of talking to strange men. But that was not an option. It was explained that the father did not want to so much as hear the voice of a strange woman. Even the suggestion of a phone interview, in which he would primarily be speaking to my interpreter and would barely hear my own voice, was rejected. At that point, I gave up.

My only option was to return to Kabul and try and find out more about the *hujras* there. Were these the madrassas featured in the media, with hundreds of little boys wearing white skullcaps and pumping their fists in the air as they shouted 'Allahu Akbar'? Little boys who were being indoctrinated and prepared for jihad against the unbelievers? It seemed unlikely if the little school I'd seen in Dewanawargh was anything to go on. But there was still very little information available about *hujras* such as the ones I had seen in the south and how they operated in practice.[32]

I was fortunate to come into contact with Latif in 2012, early on in my investigations. Latif was an Afghan who was working on a book about his role and experiences in the Taliban regime.[33] He had started out as an employee of Mullah Omar and later became one of his diplomats. I was delighted to discover that his manuscript had a detailed chapter on the *hujras* and that he was willing to tell me more about them.

'A *hujra* is definitely not the same as a madrassa,' explained Latif in my home in Kabul. Unlike the professional madrassas, which tend to both be well organized and teach a broad curriculum to an advanced level in addition to Quran studies, the education pupils receive in the *hujras* is so primitive that it amounts to little more than some rules on how to live your life. There is little serious attempt to transmit knowledge in the *hujras*, according to Latif.

He remembers well what consequences this had when he was working for Mullah Omar. People had no knowledge of geography, for instance. And the mullahs would not accept that the Americans had traveled to the moon in a rocket. They argued that you had to get past seven gates guarded by angels to reach the Prophet Muhammad in Heaven. The angels would never have let a rocket pass. 'I often got into discussions with other people working for the Taliban. They were scared to death about having to walk towards the horizon, for example, because they'd learned in the *hujra* that the Earth was flat. Go on, I'd say then, walk along that river until you get to where it ends. But they wouldn't do that because they were frightened of falling off the Earth.'

The education at the *hujra* schools had nothing to do with hating others. 'It was harmless,' said Latif. 'The schools were actually pretty innocent places, wrapped up in their own little world. It wasn't about shouting anti-American slogans. Political issues in general were seen as sinful, something to be avoided.' According to Latif, the primary purpose of these schools was to transmit the age-old traditions and rituals that you were supposed to abide by as a good Muslim. 'Innovation was a dirty word. Everything had to stay the same as in the past.' The Quran was not seen as a political program for an Islamic state with a religious police, but as a source of norms and values to be embraced by all good Muslims. What mattered were selflessness, humility, patience, forgiveness, purity, honesty, and respect for others.

Latif agreed that the *hujras* appeared unkempt and poorly organized. They didn't have classrooms with students lined up on benches in neat rows. Instead, ten to twenty pupils would sit on the floor. Many of these pupils did not live with their parents; like Omar, they were orphans who lived and slept in the *hujra*. They were fed by local people because it was thought to bring good luck if you gave these students food. After eating, the orphans found a nearby stream where they could wash their pots and pans before returning to the school to study further.

The lighter side of life was celebrated on Thursday evenings. Friday was the day of the week devoted to Allah. On the preceding Thursday evening, poems in the Sufi tradition about God and love would be recited. There would be a lot of singing to the accompaniment of the *thali*, a kind of metal dish that was used for cleaning vegetables during the day and was turned upside down to serve as a drum in the evening. The *thali* was used to accompany plays too.

It was always open house in the *hujra*. Anyone could attend the lessons: travelers, laborers, or lonely old people who had time on their hands. Sometimes these 'pupils' became so enthralled by a particular teacher that they would continue to take his classes. And if a popular mullah left to try his luck somewhere else, students might follow him so that they could continue to be taught by him.

Although the *hujras* did have some textbooks, the mullahs largely did their own thing. There was no fixed time at which classes started, there was no fixed curriculum, and there were certainly no exams. The state had no involvement whatsoever in this form of education, said Latif.

The Quran lessons consisted primarily of phonetically reciting Arabic texts. The pupils did not actually learn Arabic so that they could understand the Quran. They reeled the texts off without knowing what they were saying, not unlike how Catholic children were once taught in Latin. The student who knew the whole Quran by heart was allowed to sit closest to the mullah.

To my surprise, Latif told me that young girls in white headscarves also attended these schools. That would have been the case when Omar was a boy too. It seemed the supposed woman-hater had also gone to 'school' with girls. That is not so strange if you read the Quran, as there are at least four surahs that require Muslims, both men and women, to acquire knowledge.

However, Latif told me that the girls did not go to school for long as in this region they were married off at an early age, which brought the family a dowry in return. The more devout a life the girl had lived – in other words, the more time she had spent hidden from view behind high walls – the more money she fetched. That was an important reason for keeping girls at home and preventing them from coming into contact with men.

Many mullahs struggled with how they should interpret the Quran for their pupils. The Quran was often less strict than the local customs of the Pashtunwali with regard to such issues as women and the veil, the treatment of orphans, and the use of corporal punishment. That tension would come to the fore again when Mullah Omar became leader.

———— ◆ ————

I spent a lot of time trying to discover whether Mullah Omar was educated anywhere else other than in these *hujras*. In his book, the Pakistani author Ahmed Rashid, who is possibly the most quoted expert on the Taliban in the West, claims that Mullah Omar and all the other Taliban leaders studied in Pakistan at what some call 'terrorist universities'.[34] Precisely because he was supposed to have been a student at these Pakistani universities, it was assumed that his emergence as a leader was choreographed by Pakistan and that his regime was, and still is, supported by that country.

Ahmed Rashid goes one step further. He says that because almost everyone in Mullah Omar's Taliban regime had been educated in these Pakistani madrassas, they knew woefully little about Afghan society, a claim that many journalists and academics have subsequently repeated.[35]

I decided to pay a visit to Afghanistan's neighbor to see what I could find out about Omar's time there. He was alleged to have studied at so-called radical Taliban universities, such as Darul Uloom Haqqania in the border area of Akora Khattak. This school has been dubbed the 'University of the Holy War', the 'Taliban factory', and the 'school to all the present Taliban leadership'.[36]

To prepare for my trip, I watched the documentary *I Knew Bin Laden* (2011), in which an Al Jazeera journalist visits one of these schools in Pakistan that is often said to be where Mullah Omar studied. Accompanied by dramatic music that would not have been out of place in a Hollywood movie, the reporter looks rather nervously at the camera as he enters the grounds of the large religious university of Darul Uloom Haqqania. Samiul Haq, the director, appears on screen. A tall man in a white robe and with a graying beard, he has narrow eyes in an elongated face. The documentary seems to be suggesting that this man was an associate of the terrorists – this man admitted Mullah Omar to his school, after which Omar apparently became radicalized. Samiul Haq has often been portrayed in the Western media as a terrorist teacher, or the 'Father of the Taliban'.[37] Even after his death in November 2018, most media were still calling him the Father of the Taliban. The B.B.C. and *The New York Times* repeated the claim that Mullah Omar had studied at his university.

But had anyone checked this claim? When talking to people in Deh Rawod, I heard that there were few Afghan students in Pakistan when Omar was young. There was no war and therefore no reason to flee the country. Sami Yousafzai, a Pakistani journalist, once asked Samiul Haq about Omar's time at his university. He said that Omar had never studied with him. In his book, published at a later date, Haq praises Mullah Omar but also admits that he has never met him.[38] The same argument applies to the claim by Ahmed Rashid that all Taliban leaders had been educated in Pakistan. In 2018, two fellow researchers investigated the educational backgrounds of prominent Taliban members. They came to the conclusion that none of them had studied in the madrassas.[39]

This conclusion is supported by various of Mullah Omar's colleagues. 'Mullah Omar was never a student there,' said Mullah Delawar, a prominent Taliban judge who did actually graduate from a madrassa in Pakistan. Delawar said that Samiul Haq would have been happy to claim Mullah Omar as an alumnus of his school, as Omar was seen by many there as a successful leader. Latif told me that when Mullah Omar became the Taliban leader later on, Samiul Haq of the Haqqania madrassa gave him a kind of honorary degree in Kandahar in gratitude for his services as the leader of the Islamic state in Afghanistan.

I personally visited the Jamia Uloom-ul-Islamia madrassa in Binori Town, Karachi, another school that Western sources say Mullah Omar may have attended. Like Darul Uloom Haqqania, this madrassa was also considered by the Americans to be a place that taught hatred; after 9/11, the school was placed on America's blacklist of terrorist organizations.[40]

The madrassa was not in some dangerous suburb as I'd expected. The impressive deep-red building, where hundreds of young students were immersed in their books, was in the city center next to a police station. I could simply walk in. I met the founder's son, aged about thirty-five and the current director of the Binori madrassa, in his office. He was not particularly friendly. 'Westerners refuse to understand our lives and our ideas,' he said. 'I've had enough of this.'

I told him that I had come to his madrassa to ask him about Mullah Omar and the classes he might have taken. 'I don't know about other madrassas but I do know that the people who are famous in the media for having studied at this school were never students here. That goes for Mullah Omar too. I've never even seen him.'[41]

———— • ————

It became increasingly clear to me during this quest to find out about Omar's early years that the fatherless Omar never left Uruzgan for radicalizing studies in Pakistan. On the contrary, he had stayed in Deh Rawod where, like many other Taliban fighters and the men who went on to be their leaders, he had studied at the *hujras* that are so little known in the West. And there was little hate preaching in these schools.

Omar did not complete his studies and never obtained any qualifications. That was one reason why he was not able to read and write that well, as became clear from conversations with his secretaries and other colleagues. Mullah Omar was not actually a real mullah. He said as much when he was in power: 'Don't call me a mullah because I'm not one.'[42]

2

Omar Fights Alongside America
Against the Soviet Union
(1979)

In the 1970s, when Omar was still studying at a *hujra*, Afghanistan was rocked by a series of major changes. The country had experienced little real unrest since King Zahir Shah had come to power in 1933. However, in 1973 the king was rather unexpectedly usurped by his cousin Mohammed Daoud Khan, who had been his adviser for many years. Daoud Khan was assisted in the coup by the Soviet Union, which wanted Afghanistan as a stable neighbor, endorsing a mild form of Islam along the lines prescribed by the Communist leaders in the Soviet states of Kazakhstan, Turkmenistan, and Tajikistan.

Afghanistan's new leader espoused a political program involving the redistribution of land from large landowners to the landless poor, educational reform with less influence from Islam and local traditions, and equal rights for women in what was still a very patriarchal society.

Daoud met with considerable resistance from mullahs and others, especially outside the cities. With his ungodly plans, he was suspected of wanting to sacrifice Afghanistan's traditional Islamic culture in favor of the Communism of the Soviet Union.

Daoud only lasted a few years. From then on Afghanistan's history becomes chaotic, violent, and in many ways still under-reported. We know that the Afghan Communists split into two factions, the Parcham and the Khalq. By the late 1970s, relations between the two were increasingly bitter and violent, which affected the government of the country. In 1978, there was another coup in Afghanistan, known as the Saur Revolution or April Revolution. It cost the lives of Daoud and many members of his family, and put the Khalq leader Nur Mohammad Taraki in charge.

The new leader, Taraki, is a particular under-reported subject. As far as I understand, Taraki set about changing Afghan society with dangerous haste. His rigorous interventions with 'land reforms' still impact Afghanistan today. If you go to Helmand, for example, you will see that many families continue to fight not because of any ideology, but because their land was taken from them illegally back at that time.[1] The rapid abolition of the traditional Afghan education system also created a lot of unrest and distrust, while at the same time Taraki swiftly proclaimed complete equality between men and women – which was too ambitious. What is more, the new president tolerated no dissent. In the twenty or so months that he was in power, an estimated 50,000 to 100,000 critics disappeared.[2] Anyone opposing Taraki's plans – whether they were rival Communists, moderate modernists, or traditional mullahs – was arrested by his secret police, usually never to be heard of again. In Moscow they called him the Stalin of Afghanistan.

Because of the 'land reforms' that had been set in motion and Taraki's ruthless repression, the people had no other option left but to defend themselves. Soon fierce resistance started to this relentless 'revolution'. The rural mullahs formed an important part of the core resistance against the Communists. They often joined forces with the local *khans* – whose position as major landowners was also under threat – to form a united front in the regions.

In defending their land, traditions, and their *hujras*, the mullahs (and also the *khans*) appealed to the concept of jihad. Jihad means staying close to Allah in your daily life by renouncing worldly temptations and fulfilling your duties as a good Muslim, like praying five times a day. According to many mullahs, this inner, personal jihad had an external, public equivalent that required an Islamic community or country to defend itself against hostile outsiders. The use of force should preferably be avoided, but violence was permitted if negotiations with the opponent did not have the desired result.

It became increasingly clear that the Communists in Taraki's regime were indeed not prepared to negotiate. All over Afghanistan, armed groups started to form to defend their property and country. These men, who were called 'mujahideen' (freedom fighters), were increasingly successful in resisting the harsh treatment meted out by Taraki's troops. Within a year of Taraki's coup, much of Afghanistan was in the throes of an armed rebellion. When Taraki was murdered by a rival party member, the Soviet Union became alarmed. The railroading approach and internal divisions of the Afghan Communists were threatening to turn Afghanistan into a radical Islamic state instead of the Soviet-friendly, stable nation the U.S.S.R. had hoped for. Soviet attempts to influence the state of affairs in Afghanistan had no effect, regardless of how often the Afghan leaders were invited to the Kremlin and instructed to tone things down.

It seems to have been the developments in Iran that finally pushed the Soviet Union into making the decision to invade Afghanistan on Christmas Eve 1979, with about eighty thousand soldiers. The radical Ayatollah Khomeini had recently seized power in Iran after the people had rebelled against their ruler, Shah Mohammad Reza Pahlavi. Up to then, the Soviet leaders had heeded advice not to initiate military action in Afghanistan. Its tribal people and dauntingly difficult mountainous terrain, where as an outsider you never knew who was on your side and who wasn't at any given moment, would have made any military engagement tough and unpredictable. But after the Islamic revolution in Iran, the Kremlin no longer dared to let events take their natural course in Afghanistan.

———————— ◆ ————————

In the context of the ongoing Cold War, the Soviet Union's invasion of Afghanistan and installation of an Afghan Communist in power in Kabul prompted loud condemnation by the international community. The Cold War was still at its height and the U.S. in particular made sweeping and exaggerated assumptions about the intentions of their long-time archenemy. The Americans ignored warnings from their allies, including the British, not to overestimate the aims of the Soviets.[3] But since the dramatic fall of Saigon in 1975, the U.S. had been struggling to deal with the trauma of the Vietnam War, which had ended in victory for the Vietnamese Communists despite many years of fighting and fifty thousand U.S. fatalities. Various American leaders talked openly of how the Soviet invasion of Afghanistan offered no less than an opportunity for revenge. The idea was to make Afghanistan the Soviet Union's Vietnam and to rally the people back home behind that plan by exaggerating the threat.

At the same time, it was virtually unthinkable that the U.S. would send its own soldiers to fight the Soviet army: the pain caused by the Vietnam War, which had resulted in three hundred thousand wounded in addition to the many fatalities, was still too raw. But the Americans' eyes fell on these men in Afghanistan itself who had lost land and family and were willing to fight. To outsiders, it seemed a strange alliance: the mullahs and their students, the tribal leaders who kept their women out of sight whenever possible, and the U.S. administration in Washington, a city where such puritanical rules were unheard of. But their common enemy was formidable enough for them to bridge these huge differences. These Afghan youngsters were delighted to see that Washington understood their suffering and wanted to chase the Soviets out of their country. Over the next few years, the number of Afghan and Pakistani freedom fighters combating the Soviets with U.S. support would rarely drop below two hundred and fifty thousand.

American support for these fighters mainly took the form of weapons. Vast quantities of weaponry were delivered to the freedom fighters through the C.I.A.'s Operation Cyclone. To organize this, the Americans gave Pakistan unprecedented levels of influence – never before had Pakistan had so much power in Afghanistan. This would create even more distrust between Pakistan and Afghanistan, whose leaders had always been wary of their neighbor's intentions. The U.S. was focused on the short term and collaborated closely with Pakistan, in particular the Pakistani secret service, the Inter-Services Intelligence agency (I.S.I.). According to the C.I.A., the I.S.I. staff would easily understand their neighbor and would therefore know which of the many groups fighting in Afghanistan should be allocated weapons. This was a turnaround, as relations between the U.S. and Pakistan had been chilly since President Zia-ul-Haq seized power in a military coup in 1977; the Americans had been horrified by his introduction of tough Shariah punishments such as stoning, amputations, and beatings. It seemed this was no longer a barrier to collaboration.

At the peak of the struggle, dozens of trucks were crossing the Afghan border every day from Peshawar, bringing 'a cyclone of weapons'. From 1985 onwards, those weapons included the famous (and indeed infamous) Stinger rockets that put an end to the Soviet Union's supremacy in Afghan air space. Pakistan's freedom in distributing the American weapons in Afghanistan gave it huge influence over the capabilities of the various groups fighting in Afghanistan. While the jihad against the Soviet Union had its roots in local resistance among mullahs in southern and western Afghanistan, concerned about the threat to their traditions and their apolitical Sufi interpretation of Islam, the Pakistani secret service preferred to give support to the groups commanded by more important religious leaders such as Gulbuddin Hekmatyar and Burhanuddin Rabbani, who were mainly active in the north and east.

These men represented a more political, activist interpretation of Islam, along the lines of the Muslim Brotherhood in Egypt. Both Hekmatyar and Rabbani had fled the country to escape the Afghan Communists a few years earlier. They were both frequent visitors to the government in Islamabad, the capital of Pakistan. After the Soviet invasion of Afghanistan, they returned to their home country. While the Americans were still wrestling with the repercussions of the 1979 Iran hostage crisis, in which U.S. embassy staff were held hostage in Tehran, Hekmatyar was proposing an Islamic state like Ayatollah Khomeini's Iran. These Afghan freedom fighters had a much more internationally oriented, anti-American agenda than most of the mullahs and Quran students; their political Islam was quite alien to the majority of mullahs and Quran students in Afghanistan – people like Mullah Omar – in whose lives the horizon barely extended beyond the village they preached in.

Pakistan brought the various militant groups together in an alliance known as the Peshawar Seven, with the organizations of Hekmatyar, Rabbani, and Abdul Sayyaf (who relied on support from the Saudis) as prominent members. The mullahs and *hujra* students had also banded together into a national organization, the Islamic Revolutionary Movement of Afghanistan, so that their movement too could be part of the Peshawar Seven and receive American weapons. This organization was led by Mullah Mohammad Nabi, who had learned his clerical profession from his father in the village mosque. His sole concern was to make Afghanistan an Islamic state; what happened outside Afghanistan was up to the people there. Mullah Omar belonged to his group for a long time.

In the jihad against the Soviet Union, Nabi's movement was allocated far fewer weapons than other groups of freedom fighters, as the I.S.I.

believed his people were not such skilled combatants. This eventually led to a protest by the *ulema*, a meeting of hundreds of mullahs from all over the country. They felt that Nabi's movement should be in charge of the jihad, rather than the Pakistani secret service.

There was criticism early on in America too of how the U.S. was financing and arming the struggle against the Soviet Union. In an open letter in *The New York Times*, American experts sounded the alarm about the involvement of various Afghan leaders in the widespread cultivation of opium poppies, by far the most lucrative agricultural product in the country. These experts warned that the influx of C.I.A. dollars would probably boost the poppy industry and, as a result, the supply of opium and its derivatives to the U.S. and Europe. Most of the Afghan players talked openly of the cultivation of opium poppies as a key source of funding for the jihad. They argued that it was only forbidden by Islamic law (*haram*) to *use* drugs; producing and trading them was a different matter. Many started fighting over the lucrative poppy fields while claiming to be waging 'holy jihad'. They became the kings of the opium trade. Experts said these men would never have become so powerful if it had not been for this illegal trade.

----------◆----------

The struggle against the Soviet Union in Afghanistan exerted a strong attraction on young Muslims in other parts of the world. As in the more recent jihads in Syria and Iraq, large numbers of them came to Afghanistan to fight.[4] Jihad vacations to Afghanistan were organized in the more affluent Gulf states, with parents donating many petrodollars to the struggle and encouraging their children to take part in the holy war. The C.I.A. even had a program in which some Arab 'jihad heroes' were given U.S. visas to recruit combatants in the Muslim communities of New Jersey and Brooklyn.[5]

American commandos' manuals taught these radical youngsters how to make explosives from aspirins and thermometers. Some returned home and put what they had learned to use in a new jihad against the regime in their own country. I have been struck in the past few years by the similarities between what happened in Afghanistan and the more recent developments in Iraq and Syria.

The Afghan resistance in the early 1980s to one of the two Cold War superpowers also served as a U.S.-sponsored catalyst for a growing self-confidence in the Islamic world, for the first time in a long while. In Islam's initial period in the glorious years of the early Middle Ages, this new religion spread far and wide until the caliphate extended deep into Spain and the Balkans. But the major European powers pushed back and eventually gained control of almost all of North Africa and the Middle East. Then the long-awaited decolonization resulted in authoritarian regimes instead of devout Islamic states, regimes, moreover, that were often propped up by the oil interests of Europe and the U.S. The jihad against the Soviets marked a break with this pattern and fueled a widely felt desire for self-determination.

It should be said, though, that the Arab jihadists (which included a still very young Osama bin Laden) were not universally popular with the Afghans fighting alongside them. I had expected the Afghans and Arabs to be united by the common bond of Islam, but this was not always the case. The locals were not generally keen on foreigners becoming involved, especially Arabs, who had a reputation for looking down on the 'less-civilized' Afghan people. The Arabs' previous experience of Afghans was as low-ranking workers in their home countries who drove their taxis, built their houses, and did other jobs that the Arabs felt were beneath them.[6]

The Islam of Afghanistan was also quite different from the Islam of the Arabs. These big differences reminded me of the division between the Protestants and Catholics that I had grown up with in Holland. The Islam of the Afghans has always been more influenced by Sufism and is both more traditional and more mystical. Dancing at the graveside and praying for the dead is very important to many Afghans, for instance. What's more, many Afghans draw a lot of hope from superstitious beliefs. The Islam of the Arabs is inspired more by Salafism; it is sober and strict. They abhor superstitions and praying at gravesides to such an extent that when in Afghanistan, they would even destroy the graves worshiped by the Afghans.

When I interviewed the important Taliban judge Mullah Delawar and told him about my recent trip to Saudi Arabia, he looked at me in great surprise and warned, ostensibly as a joke but with a serious undertone, 'Don't turn into a Wahabi, Bette.' 'Wahabi' is an insult among the Taliban – in most of Afghanistan, in fact. It is therefore a gross exaggeration to say the Afghans and Arabs fought side by side as brothers on the frontline. In fact, many Arabs operated in isolated groups in eastern Afghanistan, fighting for warlords such as Sayyaf and Hekmatyar who were ideologically closer to the Arabs.[7]

The chaos on the Afghan battlefields led to increasing concerns among American diplomats about the radicalization fueled by a war aided by the C.I.A. and Pakistan. What would these Arab jihadists do when the fight against the Soviets in Afghanistan ended? What if an Islamic fundamentalist like Gulbuddin Hekmatyar became the country's new president? He would undoubtedly be an anti-Western leader, another Khomeini, enjoying the full support of the Islamic parties in Pakistan that were only too keen to see more Islamic states in the region.

———•———

Mullah Omar was twenty-two or twenty-three when the jihad started. The *hujras* emptied everywhere as the students left to take part in the fight against the Soviet invasion. Omar joined a group of resistance fighters but he soon had to leave Deh Rawod when the Russians gained the upper hand there.[8] In the early 1980s, he popped up in Maiwand

District, in the west of Kandahar Province, not far from where his father was buried. There was also a direct route from this part of Kandahar to Deh Rawod.

———————— ◆ ————————

In the hope of finding people who had known Omar when he was in his twenties, I resumed my quest in 2013, concentrating on Maiwand District in Kandahar. When I mentioned the place, my friends in Kabul looked worried. At that time, many journalists visited Maiwand primarily on an embedded basis, accompanied by international military forces. It was rare for journalists to work there independently; if they did, it was mainly on background stories.[9] As far as the Americans were concerned, the town was 'the birthplace of the Taliban'. They believed many warriors were still in hiding there, waiting for 'better times', and that perhaps Mullah Omar was among them. Even in 2013, thousands of soldiers were still hunting down alleged terrorists there on a daily basis. If the stories of my fellow journalists were to be believed, I was crazy to be heading off in that direction. But wasn't that precisely what I had thought previously about Kabul? And Deh Rawod?

This time I flew from Kabul to the civilian airfield in Kandahar, which had been virtually taken over by the large NATO camp next to it. At that point, there were 30,000 soldiers based at the camp. They spent their free time on the so-called Boardwalk, which had restaurants, stores, and a hockey rink. I had bought a one-way ticket as I had no idea how much time this investigation into the next phase of Omar's life would take.

I left the military base with the husband of an Afghan friend of mine. He was waiting at the entrance to the base with his Toyota. I was wearing my burka and took a seat in the back. We turned onto the main road to the city. This Highway 1, as the Americans called the road connecting Pakistan, Afghanistan, Iran, and Tajikistan, was bustling, full of cars and freight vehicles going in both directions. Brightly painted trucks raced past, loaded with car parts, washing machines, or crates with pomegranates, and with poems and bells on the tailgate – the famous jingle trucks of South Asia.[10]

My Afghan friend's home was in the center of Kandahar. It turned out to be an excellent place to start my investigation. At the back of the house, widows were embroidering goods to sell in the market. Whenever I received men for interviews, I had to warn these ladies so that they could make sure they were not seen. There was no barbed wire on the walls surrounding the house, and no guards with machine guns at the door. My Afghan friend's knowledge of the local situation was all the security I needed during my stay.

———◆———

It was much easier than I had expected to find people who had known Mullah Omar in the time of the Soviet invasion. I had a photo with me of a mosque that he might have visited during that period.[11] It was not long before I was sitting face to face with the businessman Issa (the name Jesus in Arabic). The friendly, diffident Issa was Omar's age. He was a *khan* – a major landowner – from Maiwand who lived in the little village of Haji Ibrahim, named after his father, who was buried there.

Contacts in Kandahar had put me onto Issa as they thought the little mosque in my photograph was in the vicinity of his land. This turned out to be correct. Issa clearly remembered the arrival of Omar, with a group of anti-Soviet fighters from Uruzgan. At the time, his father had a large family fort that had been turned into a command post for the jihad against the occupying Soviet forces. Omar and his group settled there.

When I told Issa that I would like to visit Haji Ibrahim, he introduced me to his son Ahmad. His son was in his early thirties and spoke fluent English. Ahmad had tried to flee to Europe in around 2001 in the hope of studying there, but he had been caught with false travel documents in Pakistan and had spent some time in prison there. He was keen to help me. Ahmad had also known Omar in the days when he was in Haji Ibrahim, and as a teenager Ahmad had paid visits to Mullah Omar.

So there I was, traveling to Haji Ibrahim with the best translator I could wish for. Ahmad sat in the front of the white Toyota with a cousin, while I sat in the back, hidden again under my burka.

Haji Ibrahim is a small village in the Sangisar area. Sangisar is not exactly in the middle of nowhere as Highway 1 runs through it. This road is an important transport route connecting Kandahar to Herat, and continuing into Iran and Pakistan to connect Afghanistan to the ports in these two countries. This route, which has existed for more than two millennia, is used to transport not only food crops such as pomegranates (Afghanistan's national pride) but also numerous other products, including the opium poppy.

The word 'Sangisar' means 'defense fortress' and the area has been fought over by rival parties since time immemorial. This was where the British fought the Afghans in the famous Battle of Maiwand in 1880, which is commemorated in imposing paintings on display in London's museums. After the Soviets invaded Afghanistan, they soon gained control of the road, and reconquering it became a priority for the jihad parties in their fight against the invading forces.

The place was still unstable when I traveled there with Ahmad and his cousin some twenty-five years later. There were regular battles, with U.S. and Canadian troops fighting various Afghan groups. But Issa assured me that we would be OK today: there was no war for now.

After weaving in and out around the trucks for about twenty minutes, we turned left in the direction of Haji Ibrahim. A man standing at the side of the road put up his hand. He was wearing a blue policeman's cap and had on an Afghan National Army (A.N.A.) jacket and ordinary civilian pants. He was an *arbaki*, one of the armed militiamen who were part of the latest American program aimed at winning the war in Afghanistan. The Americans were spending millions of dollars on weapons for what they considered to be the strongest and most loyal tribes in the area in the hope that they would help the local Afghan police. People were keeping a wary watch on the program as everyone here knew that once a tribe got ahold of money and weapons, it would inevitably attack rival tribes.

I said nothing when the *arbaki* stuck his head through the car window. I always kept my mouth shut anyway whenever we were stopped on the road in southern Afghanistan. I knew this man was not allowed to look under my burka and no one in this tribal area would violate that rule. But just to be certain, I cast my eyes downward behind the grille of my burka. Ahmad had impressed on me the importance of doing this as the militiaman could become suspicious if he caught sight of my blue eyes.

So far, I had been able to go wherever I wanted as long as I followed the instructions given by my guides. 'We're here on a family visit,' I heard Ahmad say in a friendly voice. The *arbaki* apparently believed this distorted version of the truth. He let us pass and we continued on our journey. At one point, we had to drive through a shallow river because the bridge had been blown up in fighting.

It was quiet in Haji Ibrahim. I saw that despite the persistent fighting, the extensive estates owned by Issa were planted with grapevines, although the adjoining mud-brick houses were deserted. The largest house stood at a point where two sand tracks met. This was the family fort that Issa had already told me about. The walls were a good ten feet tall.

When I pushed aside the curtain that served as the door to the fort, I saw a house that looked just like Said's place (Omar's former home), only five times the size. It had a courtyard measuring about sixty by sixty feet, with a well in the corner. Here and there were a few mud-brick huts. On the right were a couple of sheds with tractors. At least a hundred mujahideen must have lived in this complex during the ten-year jihad, including Omar.

In Haji Ibrahim, I interviewed two men about Omar's time in the jihad. They had stayed on in Haji Ibrahim and still had many memories of Omar. Later, I met four more men in Kandahar City who had been in Haji Ibrahim at that time. One was Sheik Hotak, whose sister is married to a father-in-law of Mullah Omar's (Mullah Omar married four women, one of whom came from the Haji Ibrahim locality). Another interviewee was Haji Ghausedin, an important tribal leader who Mullah Omar had helped resolve conflicts in the jihad. The last two were former militants who now worked in Kandahar, one as a car mechanic and the other as a truck driver. The last source was Mullah Manan, Mullah Omar's half-brother. He is the youngest son of Mullah Omar's mother and Mullah Mohammed Anwar (Omar's step-father). There is a fifteen-year age gap between the two half-brothers. After the jihad, Mullah Omar took this little brother to Haji Ibrahim to live with him. Together, these men helped me piece together the next phase in Omar's life.

———————•◆•———————

At some point in the 1980s, the *hujra* student Omar turned up at the command post in Haji Ibrahim. Before that, he had been fighting in Deh Rawod with a local jihadi leader, a young man of Omar's age named Mir Hamza. That was where he learned how to use a weapon. Soon Deh Rawod fell into the hands of the Communists, and Mullah Omar left together with Mir Hamza. (Mir Hamza went on to become the governor of Helmand, Gereshk District, during the Taliban regime and he is now an active Taliban member in Helmand Province.) The people in Deh Rawod and also Mullah Manan told me that Mullah Omar was wounded in Deh Rawod.

The Deh Rawod group went to Haji Ibrahim as Mir Hamza is a Nuurzai tribesman and Haji Ibrahim was an area led predominantly by the Nuurzai. They joined up with the group of another Nuurzai tribesman from Deh Rawod, Nek Muhammad. This locally famous jihadi had already joined a group of his own tribe in Haji Ibrahim, who were even more important in that area than Issa's family. His large and wealthy family had big estates with orchards and grapevines (their young son Bashar would play a big role in setting up the Taliban in 1994, as discussed later in this chapter). They also owned three bazaars in Kandahar City, with about three hundred stalls. But all their property had been nationalized by their rivals, who were now part of the Communist government of Afghanistan. This setback in the family rivalry was why the family was prepared to join the rebellion. Once again, I discovered that personal motivations (rather than ideology) played a dominant role in choosing whether or not to support a particular government. Issa's family is another example of this: they became jihadists fighting the Communist regime because a local rival in Haji Ibrahim sided with the Communists (Mohammed Issa's father was killed by this rival).

Nek Muhammad was soon killed, on Highway 1, where he had been firing rockets at the Soviets. The Russians are alleged to have taken his head as a trophy. His followers from Uruzgan fought on and it was not long before they were being called the 'Uruzgan band'. They formed a loyal network of people who trusted one another, and one that would go on to play an important role in Afghan history. With fellow students such as Mullah Berader (first the main negotiator with the U.S. and now an official in the cabinet of the Islamic Emirate), Omar formed a kind of fraternity of jihadists who jointly led the Taliban until they were driven out in 2001.

But back in the 1980s, Omar and his Uruzgan band were just some of the many fighters based in Haji Ibrahim. The hundred or so warriors in this command post belonged to various Peshawar Seven jihad groups. Omar must have been a striking figure at six foot five, which is tall for an Afghan. He was described by some of the fighters as a handsome man with his wide mouth and high cheekbones. His bluish-green eyes made him stand out too; almost everyone in Afghanistan has brown eyes.

In 2016, an old passport photo of Omar suddenly turned up. It shows him when he was still young, possibly about twenty-five, the age he would have been when fighting in the jihad. The young man in the photograph exudes self-confidence with his long face, pale skin, and clearly delineated dark eyebrows above bluish-green eyes. A black beard curves round the elongated, rather languid face. Interestingly, his turban is not black or white as was customary for Quran students, but a green silk one with gray stripes. These turbans were often worn by tribal leaders. He may have put on this turban specifically for the purpose of the photo as it looked more luxurious than the black or white turbans 'of the poor' worn by the jihad fighters.

In the resistance, Omar was given the nickname Rocketi after he successfully deployed a couple of the U.S.-supplied rockets. The young fighters often missed their targets and many innocent civilians were killed as a result. His fame brought him to the attention of the enemy, the Soviets. According to Wakil Mutawakil, who later became the Taliban Minister of Foreign Affairs, at one point they even announced his elimination on the radio: 'The tall guy is dead!' 'But that was wishful thinking because the tall guy wasn't dead at all,' said Mutawakil.[12]

As in his childhood, Omar acquired a reputation for being a comedian in Haji Ibrahim too. Yet he was a quiet, even shy man with people he didn't know, I learned from his former fellow fighters. Students were taught in the *hujra* that a future mullah should be modest and deferential. But when among good friends, Omar liked to act out scenes, and his impersonations often caused great hilarity.

One former militant still had to laugh at the memory of the time Mullah Omar suddenly plastered thick, white yogurt soup on his face, saying, 'Look at us, always having to eat the food of the poor.' Such evenings soon got out of hand, and would end with a group of Pashtun men wrestling and horsing around on the floor. Then Omar would call, 'All pile in!' and before they knew it, everyone would be piled on top of one another.

During lulls in the fighting, the combatants would play games. Many were reluctant to challenge Omar as he was so strong. He always won the cow game, for example. This involved the head of a cow or sheep being placed on the ground and two groups of men standing on either side. The aim was to hop closer and be the first to get your knee close to the head. If someone looked like he was about to win, Omar would bite his shoulder and hop past him. Omar hated to lose.

———•———

The longer the war continued, the more strain there was on the religious values that the resistance fighters were supposed to be defending. The insurgents were increasingly motivated by power and material gain. In particular, the opium and hashish available in Afghanistan formed an irresistible temptation for the fighters. Incidentally, they were quite happy to sell the drugs on to the Soviet soldiers, who had also developed a taste for the narcotics. Meanwhile, people increasingly fought for control of the fields where the opium poppies were grown. Other leaders gambled large sums on dog fights or the popular age-old Afghan sport of *buzkashi*, a kind of polo played with a goat carcass.

Boys like Omar had learned at the *hujra,* however, that you could not just fight a jihad as if it were a bar-room brawl. It was a holy war that could only be waged if your religion was being threatened and there was no other way of dealing with that threat. Strict rules of conduct applied: civilian casualties must be avoided at all times, and if the enemy surrendered, you had to forgive him and offer him a place of safety. You should also never use excessive violence unless absolutely necessary.

It was important too to fight the jihad for God in as 'pure' a state as possible. You had to have a beard grown to fist length, and keep your hair cut and your clothes as neat as possible – however dirty they might get in the fighting. You were obviously not allowed to drink or smoke when fighting for the restoration of God's rules, and drugs were also out of the question. The same applied to listening to music. You were allowed to listen to the radio for news about the war, but if music was played in between the news reports, you had to turn it off. Settling internal conflicts between the jihad groups themselves with arms was not permitted. And even if you were in the midst of a fierce battle, if there was time to pray you had to put down your weapons and bow towards Mecca. I still see this today: in large-scale fighting, the entire Afghan platoon will suddenly put down their weapons to fulfill their duty to pray. It irritates the Americans immensely.

Hujra students such as Omar were increasingly demanding a role as guardians of the holiness of the jihad. In Haji Ibrahim, Omar acquired a reputation for reminding his fellow fighters of the strict rules they should be following. He made combatants cut their hair if it looked untidy and he would speak to them about their dirty clothes. If they were listening to the wrong things, he would personally destroy their radios. On one occasion, Omar discovered that *bacha bazi* – a widespread phenomenon in Afghanistan whereby young boys are used for sex – was being practiced at a certain command post. Omar saw a group of boys standing around the cooking pots, but he realized what was going on. 'Let them go,' he ordered. 'Everyone knows they aren't cooks.' He didn't just lecture his own fighters on how to fight the jihad, he also held other groups to account. 'Where is your mullah?' he would ask.

In 1989, the final year of the jihad, Omar became embroiled in a serious conflict with his commander, Mullah Abdul Khan Abdul Hakim. For years, the Soviets had tried to undermine the resistance in Afghanistan by bribing jihad commanders. They were often unsuccessful because the commanders had already amassed great wealth through their share in the opium trade. Others, however, were happy to switch sides. When Omar saw his own commander receive visits twice from a known Afghan Communist, he was furious and fired a rocket at the commander (which missed, as it happened). In response, Mullah Abdul Khan Abdul Hakim ordered Omar to hand over his weapons, but he stubbornly refused.

Even the previously mentioned Haji Ghausedin, who was assigned by the higher authorities to mediate in the affair, had no success initially.[13] 'Let's split the weapons so that you each get a few, and then you can both go your separate ways,' he suggested. But Omar turned down that offer too, apparently saying, 'Why should I give up my weapons? I captured them myself in the jihad. Lots of my friends died for them. Why should I hand them over?' He felt that he was making every effort to win the war and he owed nothing to a boss who wanted to betray them all. Eventually Omar had to give in. He handed his weapons over, adding in outrage, 'Here, have my blankets, mat, and mattress too. Take everything. I don't need anything more from you.' He didn't leave, but retreated to the mosque adjoining the command post, where he was able to stay with the support of Haji Ibrahim's inhabitants.

'It was a strange situation as all of a sudden I had two mullahs,' laughed Issa as he recalled that period. 'Omar refused to leave. And Mullah Abdul Khan Abdul Hakim also insisted on keeping his position in the mosque.'

Prayers were now being led by two mullahs in the same mosque, which was no bigger than about thirteen by sixteen feet. This situation continued for months, until the end of the jihad. Mullah Abdul Khan Abdul Hakim would sit at one end of the room and Omar at the other end. Each would bow towards Mecca; each would lead their supporters in worship. Some were seated behind Omar's opponent, others bowed down behind Omar's long body.

———————◆———————

At the end of the 1980s, when the Soviet Union had been losing ground for some time, Omar lost his right eye. There are probably several hundred people in Afghanistan who claim they witnessed the event.[14] For many Afghans, the loss of that eye is one of the most heroic incidents in the life of Omar the war hero, which is what he was for them at that point. In Europe and America, his missing eye is often the only thing people know about the Taliban leader. 'Wasn't he the guy with a pirate's eyepatch?' a radio program editor once asked me.

I have based my account on the information I was given by two of his fellow fighters from that period. They took me to the site of the accident:

the *hujra* next to the mosque that Mullah Omar had occupied after his quarrel with Mullah Abdul Khan Abdul Hakim.

One day, Mullah Omar and his supporters were hiding in this little *hujra* because they were expecting an air raid by Soviet troops. Of course, they didn't know exactly when it would take place. Just when Omar popped outside to survey the skies, a bomb fell, followed by a huge explosion. The mud-brick mosque was badly damaged but still standing. Shards, branches, stones from the little burial ground – everything flew through the air. In the process, Omar's right eye was hit by flying debris. It took a day for medical help to arrive. Dr. Baluch was the man who treated Omar. This wasn't the first time; he had previously had to remove a bullet from Omar's back.

'I was the only doctor in the area,' Baluch explained when I met him in his pharmacy in Kandahar City in 2014. 'I rode here, there, and everywhere on my scooter, with a bag full of bandages and dressings, a couple of pairs of scissors, a saw, and some painkillers, all the brands I could find.' The C.I.A. may have been pumping loads of U.S. dollars into the jihad, but there was no money for medical aid. Whenever a mine exploded or a rocket or bomb landed, Dr. Baluch would rush off to the scene of the incident on his scooter to see what he could do. 'There were days when I had to saw off as many as eighteen legs.' Despite Baluch's lack of resources, his work as a doctor was appreciated by the jihadists; he was like a father to them.

When Baluch arrived to treat the wounded Omar after the Soviet air raid, the Taliban fighter had already removed the shard from his eye and used his turban to stop the bleeding. The doctor found that almost the entire eyeball was gone. After Baluch had given some limited assistance, a friend took Omar to a hospital in the Pakistani border city of Quetta. Mullah Omar made no fuss during the journey across the bumpy desert terrain. He groaned occasionally, but mainly from anger as he was afraid he would no longer be able to aim a rocket properly with just one eye.[15]

Omar's wound was photographed in the Makkah Al-Mukarramah Saudi hospital in Quetta. This black-and-white image (also part of the cover of this book) ended up in a pile of similar black-and-white photos of victims of the war who had lost eyes, legs, or arms. The photograph only resurfaced after the 9/11 attacks. For a long while, this was the only known definite picture of Mullah Omar.[16] Omar must have been in his early thirties when this snapshot was taken, but his jihad experiences had aged him. Other Taliban fighters said the same thing to me. His face, previously so symmetrical, was now uneven with one bluish-green eye and one closed eye socket with a few protruding eyelashes. His beard was twice as thick and twice as long in the hospital photo compared to the photo taken when he was about twenty-five. Like in the other photo, Mullah Omar wore a turban in the style of a tribal leader rather than the typical black 'Taliban turban'. Both photos show hair peeping out from under the turban over his forehead, suggesting bangs neatly combed to one side.

———————— • ————————

There are few written sources about the fighting in Haji Ibrahim. I was, however, lucky enough in the course of my investigations to meet a man who had been a pupil of Omar's uncle. His father had a soft-drink crate full of old cassette tapes with recordings of radio shows from the jihad days. Songs praising various warriors were sung on these shows. One of the cassettes bore Omar's name. When I asked the man to play the cassette, he looked outside nervously, afraid that his neighbors would hear this old song about Omar and inform on him as a traitor. So he turned the volume down to almost nothing before pressing 'Play'.

Various jihad militants were mentioned in the song. All had fought or lived in and around Haji Ibrahim. I heard Mullah Nek Muhammad's name, in an account of how he was beheaded in an attack on the road between Kandahar and Herat. Another man who turned up in the song was Mullah Rabbani; he was already highly regarded by the jihadists in Kandahar and went on to collaborate closely with Omar during the Taliban period. Finally, praises were sung of Mullah Muhammad Omar Mujahid. The singer gave his full name, including the title of 'freedom fighter'. Omar's rocket-firing skills came in for lavish praise, and the singer added that this was why he was called Mullah Rocketi.

3

Back to the Mosque
as Chaos Reigns
(1991)

THE struggle against the Soviet Union came to an end in early 1989, when the last Soviet tank crossed the border out of northern Afghanistan on February 15. The mujahideen's victory over the superpower had cost the fighting forces somewhere between 75,000 and 90,000 lives, compared with over 15,000 fatalities on the Soviet side. It was the Afghan civilian population that had suffered most from the fighting. An estimated half a million to perhaps two million civilians died as a result of the war. Five million Afghans fled the country, most going to Pakistan. A further three million Afghans were injured, many of them incurring permanent damage such as a lost arm or leg.

The departure of the Red Army did not mean an end to the fighting. The Soviets had left behind Najibullah, the Communist who had become president in 1986, in Kabul. To everyone's surprise, he had been able to hold off various belligerent jihadist groups with the help of the regular Afghan army for a number of years, at any rate around the capital. This was partly because once the Soviet troops had withdrawn, the U.S. almost immediately lost interest in the Afghans' jihad and abruptly ceased the financial and military support that the combatants had enjoyed up to then.

In the final years of the jihad, the Americans had started to worry about what would happen once the fight against the Soviet Union in Afghanistan ended. It looked as if Gulbuddin Hekmatyar would emerge from the confusion of Afghan rebel groups as the strongest leader. The U.S. was increasingly concerned that he would turn Afghanistan into a second Iran, along the lines of Ayatollah Khomeini, with the support of his Pakistani backers. There were now quite a few U.S. functionaries who regretted the support America had given the warlord Hekmatyar. They included Milton Bearden, the former C.I.A. chief in Pakistan, who openly lamented not having personally shot the man dead. The American diplomat Peter Tomsen also said in his book *The Wars of Afghanistan* that he had tried to put a stop to the support for Hekmatyar.[1]

The joy felt in Afghanistan at the departure of the Soviet Union soldiers did not last long. The fighting continued almost unabated. Not only was there continuous conflict between the mujahideen and the surprisingly intransigent troops of President Najibullah, but the mujahideen groups were also increasingly fighting one another. Now that they were no longer united by the common enemy of the Red Army, they were unable to agree about the future direction of the country. Many Afghans blamed the continuing crisis in their country – there were still no airlines flying to Kabul, for example – in part on the withdrawal of American support. As C.I.A. analyst Bruce Riedel put it, the Americans were concerned about the Cold War and the Soviet Union, not about a better future for the Afghans.

———————◆———————

With the collapse of the Soviet Union in 1991, the financial and military support President Najibullah's regime had been receiving from the Russians also came to an end. Najibullah agreed to plans for a new government of national unity, with all the belligerent parties on board. In April 1992, this resulted in a complex and fragile agreement between all the parties that had been part of the Peshawar Seven during the jihad.

The smallest party, which was actually advocating the return of the aging King Zahir Shah, would be put in charge for the first four months to calm things down a little. Then it would be the turn of the Tajik Islamic theologian Burhanuddin Rabbani. He would be given four months to draw up a new constitution, after which a *shura* (a national gathering of tribal leaders) would appoint an interim president for a term of eighteen months. This president would then be required to prepare elections for a democratically elected new president.

The complicated agreement was arranged with the help of the U.N. The only person not to accept it was Gulbuddin Hekmatyar. He thought the role he had been assigned was not commensurate with his military strength. He refused to sign the agreement and threatened to block its implementation with 'unsheathed swords'. Osama bin Laden was one of the people who tried to calm Hekmatyar down at the time. Bin Laden – not yet a prominent figure at this point – advised Hekmatyar to accede to the U.N. agreement in the interests of Afghanistan, because otherwise it would be Muslims fighting other Muslims. Bin Laden also spoke to other leaders in the hope of resolving the many disagreements between them.[2] But Hekmatyar preferred to put his faith in his unsheathed swords.

As had been agreed, the representative of the monarchist party took charge in the presidential palace for his allotted four months. But then his plane was shot down, with the man only just surviving the assault. He accused Hekmatyar of orchestrating the attack, but the latter's party denied any involvement. However, Hekmatyar was still continually firing rockets at Kabul. When Rabbani was appointed interim president by the *shura* in a poorly organized election, Hekmatyar's attacks gave Rabbani the excuse he needed to seize power in Kabul and establish himself as the new permanent president. He managed this thanks to the military support provided by Ahmad Massoud, a man who had enjoyed the respect of both the American and European diplomats as well as the Soviet generals in the 1980s. This would be the first time a Tajik held this position in Afghanistan, a country where Pashtuns make up the majority.

The diplomats and aid workers of the U.N. nurtured a hope that Rabbani, who spoke excellent English and was familiar with the world beyond Afghanistan, and Massoud, who had built up a reputation as a skilled, disciplined soldier among the often rather 'wild' Afghan warlords, would bring stability to Afghanistan. Kabul might once again become the modern city that it had been before President Najibullah took over (at least, when it was not the scene of fighting). A place where women could work outside the home and walk down the street without wearing a burka or veil.

Meanwhile, the city was filling up with fighters affiliated with the various warlords. They found it difficult to reconcile the modern way of life in Kabul with the local traditions and age-old Islamic values they had been brought up with. That gulf between the two was most obvious in their attitudes to women in the capital. Many mujahideen thought women were 'good' if they stayed at home and 'bad' if they dressed immodestly or appeared in public without a male chaperone.

It soon became clear what the president, and indeed most of the other parties in the Peshawar Seven, had in mind when they said they wanted to establish the ideal Islamic state. Rabbani sought to restore order in Kabul by setting up a Committee for the Promotion of Virtue and the Prevention of Vice, based on the motto taken from the Quran that you should 'enjoy what is good and is permitted, and do nothing that is of the devil and is prohibited'. Believers were explicitly called upon to promote virtue and prevent vice in others, and to make sure others were fulfilling their duties as good Muslims, such as praying five times a day and, in the case of women, covering up. To ensure that the rules were enforced, in

1992 plans were made in Kabul for a religious police force. Restrictions were placed on women's freedom of movement in particular. They were barred from working in some places, such as foreign aid organizations, or else they had to comply with very detailed clothing requirements.[3]

Rabbani was far from alone in advocating a strict Islamic society. The introduction and enforcement of these rules were supported by other leaders of the Peshawar Seven parties, including the traditionalist Mullah Mohammad Nabi and the Wahabi Sayyaf, who leaned towards Saudi Arabia. Many of the rules had little to do with the Quran; they stemmed from local traditions in the more rural parts of Afghanistan, the burka being a typical example. What women wore under the burka was subject to requirements too. Those clothes could not be brightly colored and should not make a noise. Stiletto heels and perfume were prohibited. Women were only allowed to walk along the edge of the street, not down the middle. What is more, women had to talk quietly, and laughing was a sin. These are just a few examples of the numerous rules and regulations that Rabbani's Committee for the Promotion of Virtue and the Prevention of Vice had planned.[4]

However, he was not able to introduce them in their entirety as Rabbani's rule was soon being questioned by other jihad parties. Different parts of Kabul were controlled by different parties and insurgent groups, which often decided to apply their own rules and regulations. An example is the ban on keeping pigeons, a popular pastime in Afghanistan. In the western city of Herat, it occurred to a local leader that men who kept pigeons on their roof had a good view of their neighbors, and consequently of neighboring women. This led to the wholesale massacre of pigeons by the religious police in Herat – and later in Kabul.

Despite all the rules and regulations, everyday life in Kabul soon became more dangerous as disagreements between the various groups in the city were often settled by violence. While in principle the groups shared the common aim of fighting for Islamic values, in practice that unity was sabotaged again and again in a fanatical and bitter struggle for power. President Rabbani was unable to prevent or put a stop to the internecine feuding and it was not long before he was just one of the battling parties, despite occupying the presidential palace.

Hekmatyar, supported by Pakistan's I.S.I., continued to rain rockets on Kabul.[5] Other insurgent groups, often divided along ethnic lines such as the Uzbeks and Hazaras, waged countless battles. There was no lack of weapons as there were still plentiful stocks of the weaponry that the U.S. had once supplied to Afghanistan, including large quantities of heavy-duty rockets.

Afghanistan was suffering a major humanitarian crisis. Yet this largely took place out of sight of the international media, who lost interest the moment the American government decided to stop funding this 'jihad'. Once again, there was a major exodus of refugees in the direction of the Pakistani border. Occasional food convoys organized by the U.N. reached the hungry citizens who had been left behind in Kabul. But the convoys were often intercepted by one or another of the belligerent parties. These factions were all violating human rights on a wide scale, according to organizations such as Human Rights Watch. The list of violations was endless: random murders, summary executions, rapes, the use of landmines against civilians, air raids on civilian targets, and so forth.

———— ◆ ————

Without a doubt, women suffered the most during this period. The young men fighting in the various militia groups ran wild in the anarchy of the capital. Young girls – and boys too – were sold to warlords as sex slaves. The warlords no longer kept to the maximum limit of four wives, either; they were just as likely to marry eight or ten women.

Some people say the situation was worst in Kandahar, mainly because the fiercely divided tribes there all had their own militias and gangs. Indeed, the new governor in Kandahar City, Gul Agha Sherzai, was unable to keep the members of his administration united. The situation rapidly deteriorated into civil war, with Gulbuddin Hekmatyar's men now constantly firing rockets on this city as well.

Even today, you still hear horror stories in Kandahar about the years from 1992 to 1994. One such story concerns an old jihadi commander in Spin Boldak who was in the government. When he didn't get his way at a meeting with tribal leaders, he shot everyone dead. As there was no functional justice system anymore, he was never punished for his crime.

Many of the stories about Kandahar point to women as the biggest victims of the civil war. It was as if the war had dumped a mass of young men onto the city to prowl the streets in search of a woman. Some waited for women in their homes or lured them into their cars, in some cases for them never to be seen again. The civil war forced women to spend months hiding in the darkest corners of the home in the hope that they would be left alone. Their skin turned yellow from the lack of sunlight.

Everyone in Kandahar tells the story of two women who were abducted near the airport, just outside the city. They were grabbed off the street and pushed into the back of a car. They knew what was in store for them: they would be raped by the jihadi commander behind the wheel. When they saw a hand grenade between the two passenger seats, they detonated it. They assumed they wouldn't survive, but anything was better than ending up with this man. As it happens, one of the women did survive the explosion.

During this period, tribal leaders and commanders increasingly took young boys as sex slaves. At the time of the jihad, young Quran students (including Omar) had agitated against this practice. But during the civil war, some men went one step further just for kicks, 'marrying' these boys in extravagant fake wedding ceremonies.

By contrast, it appears as if little of note happened in Omar's life during this period. After the victory over the Soviets, he tried to pick up the thread of his normal life again, like many *hujra* students. There was much heroic reminiscing about the successful war they had waged. Fighters liked to tell one another that they could have captured Moscow if they had wanted to, concluding with, 'But the Americans wanted us to stop, so that's what we did.'

Omar continued to live with his small 'Uruzgan band' in Haji Ibrahim. Issa still clearly remembers how Omar came to him for a talk. 'Could I be the mullah here?' Omar asked, pointing to the mosque where he had lost his eye. The mosque belonged to Issa's family, as did the now abandoned command post next to it. Issa did not have to consider the request for long. He thought Omar would make an excellent mullah for their mosque. Omar had already been leading the worship, along with his rival Abdul Khan Abdul Hakim. But now that the rival mullah had left for Pakistan, Omar was given responsibility of the whole mosque.

Issa was sure he would perform his duty well as he had a calm personality and was good with people. 'Whatever your problem, you could go to him and discuss it for hours. Then he'd give you some advice, just a couple of sentences that would really help you,' said Issa, laughing at the memory. Although Omar still did not have all the requisite certificates and had only attended the *hujra* in Deh Rawod for a couple of years, that didn't matter – the young *yateem* was now a genuine mullah.

Mullah Omar was in his early thirties at this point. His life settled into a routine in Haji Ibrahim. He led prayers in the mosque five times a day, starting at sunrise (surrounded by desert, they could literally see the sun rise). About twenty believers would walk over to the tiny mosque in white plaster, wash themselves under the cold stream of water and sit down on the colorful carpets to pray with the man they now informally called Mullah Omar. Without clocks, they used the sun's shadow to determine the right time for midday prayers: if the shadow was two hands wide, it was time. When the sun turned into a big red ball and started to sink quickly behind the skyline of Kandahar City, these men would saunter towards the mosque for the fifth time in the day through the desert landscape dotted with fields of grapes.

Mullah Omar also occasionally gave lessons in the tiny *hujra* with the straw roof. The school was attended on a daily basis by young boys – and a few girls in white headscarves as well. In the evenings, the students who slept in the small dormitory heated up the food they had been given by neighbors over a blazing fire. I saw the blackened wall behind the fireplace when I paid a second visit, with Issa's son Ahmad. The little books that were used until September 2001 in this mosque lay scattered everywhere. When I tried to pick one up, Ahmad became nervous. It felt a bit like being on an archeological site: I must not touch anything.

Omar returned only once or twice to Deh Rawod to pick up some old things that he had left there all those years ago. During one of those visits 'home', he married his first wife, who belonged to the powerful local Babuzai tribe.[6] His new wife and his mother accompanied Mullah Omar on his return to Haji Ibrahim, but his stepfather remained behind. Omar's stepfather worked in the north of Deh Rawod in one of the many Islamic courts and provided for his second family, which included at least three sons with whom Mullah Omar was on good terms.[7]

————•◆•————

On my second visit to Haji Ibrahim, we set off from the mosque and walked across a field. We came upon a row of square mud-brick huts. They were uninhabited now but Ahmad pointed out one of them and told me that it had been Omar's home from 1989 to about 1997. He lived there with his mother, his two sisters, and his first wife. Omar soon invited Abdul Manan, fifteen years his junior, to Haji Ibrahim as well. Ahmad Issa remembers the teenager helping Mullah Omar. They got along very well. Manan now speaks highly of this invitation and feels honored, but that is mainly because of Mullah Omar's current status. At the time he was essentially a helping hand for his big brother Omar. He collected the bread from the neighbors for the mosque.

Mullah Omar's wife soon had a baby. This first-born son was still a toddler when Ahmad saw him wandering around here. The little boy was considered beautiful, says Ahmad, because he had blonde, auburn hair, which is most unusual in Afghanistan. He was called Yaqub, after the son of Abraham who is seen as the forefather of both Jesus and the Prophet Muhammad. (Yaqub studied in Pakistan and is now one of the most prominent Taliban leaders. I exchanged letters with him when I was seeking the release of Najibullah, who was kidnapped by the Taliban. Yaqub was willing to help, but was not able to overrule the kidnapper Mullah Shereen, who was a trusted bodyguard of Mullah Omar. Najibullah eventually escaped after one and a half years in custody in terrible conditions.)

Ahmad said Omar's first wife was a mild-mannered woman who did not say much, but she came across as kind. She spent most of the time sitting in the hut, where there was no daylight, on a cheap straw mat, wearing a purple or black velvet dress and a veil. The belief was that Allah watched you as you ate, which was why Mullah Omar's wife kept her veil on indoors, even though no strange men could see her in there.

As I stood in front of the hut, I was struck once again by what a simple life this man had lived, the man who would become one of the most feared enemies of the U.S. The building had just two rooms measuring six by six feet. The roof consisted of wooden beams covered with straw. I stood in front of the tiny door and tried to imagine how the tall Mullah Omar squeezed through it.

When I bent down to take a look inside, Ahmad held me back. There could well be an unexploded landmine in the hut. The floor was covered in garbage and a pile of straw. There was an alcove in the wall, probably intended for a brush and mirror. I imagined how Mullah Omar would have stood in front of the mirror, slightly bent over, combing his hair before rushing off to the mosque. (Ahmad later told me the tiny shack was destroyed in 2020.)

Omar's new neighbors were three friends from his Uruzgan group. Two steps to the left took you to another hut. This was the home of Mullah Berader, whom Mullah Omar had already met in Deh Rawod, where they both lived, according to Mullah Manan. Berader never left the side of his friend Omar, though he would become politically milder than Omar. After the Taliban was toppled he surrendered and went back to Deh Rawod, but the U.S. chased him out of his house. He then became the Taliban's number two until 2009, when he was arrested in Pakistan. The U.S. got him released because of his capabilities to negotiate and he became the main Taliban negotiator with the U.S. in talks that would soon fail. Now he is a member of the Taliban cabinet.

Next to him in Haji Ibrahim lived Mullah Ghazi, who stayed on as a good friend of Omar during the movement and shifted to Karachi after 9/11. There he left the movement, joined a network of mafia, and made money from kidnapping Afghan businessemen. Mullah Qayoom lived in the last of these huts with his family. In the Taliban years, he got into a conflict with Mullah Omar when he acted on his own in Deh Rawod, where he became very harsh to the people in the name of Islam. He was removed from the movement. After 9/11 and with the arrival of the foreign troops, he escaped and died in hiding.

I came across a former neighbor of Omar not far from his hut. He was an in-law, an uncle of Omar's second wife. Omar married for the second time in 1996, this time to a local woman from near Haji Ibrahim. Everyone around here knows the gossip that this was supposed to have been a love match. Apparently Omar fell in love with her when she attended the Quran classes in his *hujra*. It is quite possible that the girl did join the *hujra* classes as she only lived around the corner. However, her uncle denied that it was a love match. According to him, the girl's family had gotten into financial trouble. Their financial problems were resolved by her marriage to Omar, who was an important leader by that time.[8]

The old neighbor remembered Yaqub well. He told me that young 'Jacob' always accompanied Mullah Omar when he left the house, holding onto his father's hand. Indoors, Yaqub would run around in just a shirt so that he could answer a call of nature wherever he was without dirtying his pants. 'Mullah Omar was crazy about his son. They went everywhere together.'

The neighbor did wonder whether Omar and his wife had any other children or whether there was a 'problem'. In this rural area where large families were the norm, it was unusual for a four-year-old to be the only child. 'You didn't pry,' said the neighbor. 'That wasn't done. But we reckoned something was up. We pitied him a little. It would have been awful if he couldn't have any more sons.'

In addition to his job as a mullah, Omar soon had a sideline in Haji Ibrahim, helping out with the sowing and harvesting. His friend Mullah Ghazi always joined him when laboring in the fields. Together they would sow the land. At harvest time, they would carry baskets full of grapes back to the drying rooms. Grapes were not the only crop they harvested. In April they would cut the pale-red flowers off the poppies and then use a knife to scrape the opium latex off the seed pods. Opium production had risen all over Afghanistan during the jihad. Any tribal leader could grow whatever he wanted and it seems that mullahs such as Omar had no objection either to working in the poppy fields.

Omar used the money he earned to buy four sheep. When he put them out to graze, he used to enjoy chatting to passing neighbors. The neighbor I spoke to told me that Omar still relished boyish pranks even though he was now a full-grown adult. For example, he could suddenly take hold of your arm and bend it across your back the way police officers do with a criminal. He hoped that would lead to some playful wrestling in the field. 'I don't want to fight you!' the neighbor would call, shrieking from pain, if that happened, as he was much smaller than the mullah. Sometimes Omar would throw his opponent through the air. 'Hey, guys,'

Omar would say as he wandered back towards his sheep, 'I just need to keep in shape.' The neighbor smiled at the memory.

Although Omar hardly had any possessions, he once bought a Chinese-made bike – to everyone's great surprise. It was quite something (Issa's family now has the bike). The bicycle was his pride and joy because it was very rare for a mullah to ride around on one. He often cycled along the bumpy sand tracks, which were quite unsuited for bicycles. If he came across an obstacle, such as an irrigation channel that had flooded and didn't have a bridge, he would lift the bike onto his shoulders. Every time he went out on his bike, Omar would clean it afterwards. He wrapped a colorful handkerchief around the front light, partly for decoration but also to protect it from the dust because a generator-powered light was something precious that you had to take good care of.

In Haji Ibrahim, Mullah Omar continued with his studies. He was a more serious student now than during his childhood days in Deh Rawod, where he had preferred playing outdoors to going to school. In his own *hujra*, Mullah Abdul Rahman gave him lessons in Sufism.[9] Abdul Rahman later married Omar's sister. As far as applying tribal rules was concerned, Mullah Abdul Rahman was, if anything, even stricter than Mullah Omar. On car journeys, his wife had to lie down on the back seat even though she was wearing a burka, as otherwise men could stare at her eyes through the grille of her burka.[10]

———◆———

Until 1993, there was little sign in Haji Ibrahim of the civil war that had plunged cities such as Kabul and Kandahar into total chaos since the departure of the Soviets. But even the people here were increasingly impacted by the constant blockades and tolls being levied on the highway near Sangisar, which passed close by the village. There were at least six roadblocks on the twenty-five-mile road between Haji Ibrahim and the city of Kandahar, including one organized by the notorious commander Saleh, who was nicknamed 'the Child Rapist'.

The men who had led the jihad against the Soviets in Haji Ibrahim, which included Mullah Omar and his small Uruzgan group as well as Haji Ghausedin, discussed this growing problem and how to tackle it. During the jihad, calling the fighters to account and pointing out their bad behavior could still work. But those fighters had now become ruthless warlords who earned a great deal of money with their roadblocks. The men of Haji Ibrahim decided to send a large delegation of mullahs in the hope that they would be able to get the reprobate warlords back on the right track. 'Do you remember what we were all fighting for in the jihadi days?' they said to the men who had set up the roadblocks. The men gave the mullahs a friendly reception and listened to what they had to say, despite the fact that they could just as easily have shot them. But the intervention had little effect: as soon as the delegation had left, the toll collectors returned to their bad old ways. 'We went to see them three times,' said Haji Ghausedin. 'They refused to listen, and at that point we didn't know what else we could do. How do you get the upper hand again with men like that?'

4

No Taliban Without the Drugs Mafia
(1994)

T HE sudden rise of the Taliban and their leader Mullah Omar in Afghanistan has often been seen as the work of Pakistan and its secret service, the I.S.I. Authoritative publications such as the book *Bush at War* by Bob Woodward have repeatedly claimed that Pakistan and its powerful I.S.I. played a 'massive role' in 'creating the Taliban and keeping the Taliban in power.'[1] This is also the tenor of *Taliban* by Ahmed Rashid. He presents Mullah Omar as an Afghan Robin Hood who suddenly decided to take up the cudgels against the powerful warlords and their injustices. But in his account, he was largely a tool of the Pakistani secret service.[2]

Some Kabul residents have talked to me about their memories of the rise of Mullah Omar. People in the schools and streets of a city filled with many opponents of the Taliban were saying that Omar did not really exist; he was merely a Pakistani fabrication, part of an attempt to control the chaotic situation in neighboring Afghanistan. If Kabul was increasingly prepared to believe these rumors, it was largely due to the mystery surrounding Mullah Omar throughout his life. He was an almost illiterate mullah from what was then an insignificant tribe, a man of whom there were no pictures and whose voice most Afghans only heard occasionally on the radio.

It is difficult to crosscheck what impact the Pakistani government and its secret services had, but my impression from the interviews with the people in Haji Ibrahim is that the I.S.I. was not involved in the efforts by the delegation from Haji Ibrahim to deal with the toll collectors on the highway by talking to them (see the previous chapter). Those actions were local and attracted little attention. Mullah Omar was barely known back then outside Haji Ibrahim. He was only involved because, as the mullah for the local mosque, it was to be expected that he would play a role, like other mullahs from neighboring mosques.

However, the failure of these efforts *did* attract the attention of one powerful family who had businesses, both legal and illegal, in Pakistan.[3] This was the same family that had helped Nek Muhammad and the Uruzgan group in the Haji Ibrahim command post at the start of the jihad. In particular, the oldest son of this very wealthy family, a young man in his thirties called Haji Bashar, was alert to the possibilities. After the Soviets left, Haji Bashar became governor of Maiwand, the district that included Haji Ibrahim. This scion of the family had fought alongside Omar against the Soviets in his younger days, and they had spent weeks and months together at the command post in Haji Ibrahim. In his capacity as governor, he had also accompanied the group of men from Haji Ibrahim to the road blocks a couple of times.

Haji Bashar, who was not on good terms with the incumbent leaders of Kandahar, was interested in getting rid of the toll collectors on the route between Kandahar and Herat not just as a matter of good government – he also had a private agenda. His family belonged to the locally extremely powerful trade mafia, doing business in used cars, car tires, and consumer goods such as washing machines. But, like almost all other middling and senior tribal leaders in Kandahar, his father had also profited from the large quantities of opium being produced in Afghanistan during the jihad. The extremely rich family owned a number of heroin labs in the region and was part of the drugs cartel that reached deep into Pakistan, where opium production was also rampant. This network was called the 'Quetta Alliance' by the U.S., after the Pakistani city of Quetta just over the border from Afghanistan. The U.S. government talked about arresting these kingpins in the early nineties, but eventually decided against this.[4] Instead, Haji Bashar and his comrades could operate freely in the region and beyond. With offices in Singapore and Dubai, they had been earning millions of dollars from this lucrative trade for a number of years now.[5]

The toll collectors blocking the road to Kandahar were causing Haji Bashar's family big problems. They were losing thousands of dollars a day in income and were afraid that their armed militias would rise up against them if the family was no longer able to pay the men's salaries.[6] Other drug barons in Quetta and Kandahar were in the same position.[7] While their trade was at a standstill, their competitors' businesses were flourishing in Peshawar in the north, where the transport routes to Uzbekistan had remained open despite the civil war raging around Kabul.[8]

Haji Bashar had tried everything to get the trade route moving again. But agreements with the toll collectors to at least open the road for a short period every week were disregarded because of internecine conflicts among them. Desperate attempts to send the convoys across the sandy Red Desert rather than along the highway also came to nothing.

By the summer of 1994, Haji Bashar had had enough. During my investigations in 2013, I spoke to his deputy in a hotel in Kandahar. 'Haji Bashar called a large meeting to which he invited various people in the district, including Mullah Omar and his Uruzgan group, and Haji Ghausedin and his landlord Issa.' Mullah Omar came on his bicycle, bringing it inside with him so that it wouldn't be stolen, Mohammed Issa told me.

The meeting in the district capital got off to a turbulent start. The men attending – twenty to twenty-five in total – were furious with the toll collectors. 'Let's get rid of those bastards!' shouted one. 'We're tired of being their slaves!' called another. 'We're nothing anymore, we don't even own our own possessions, not even our own bodies. We must take action.'

Then Haji Bashar addressed the meeting. According to him, the crux of the problem was the tribes' loss of power. In the days of King Zahir Shah, they had held meetings with one another where they reached agreements to resolve conflicts in a way that kept everyone happy. Now, with the civil war, it was every man for himself in Kandahar. That was why they were unable to make a united show of force against the toll collectors. Everything was at a standstill.

'The only neutral party we still have,' continued Haji Bashar, 'are the *hujra* students.' The men nodded in agreement. Up to this point, the students had stayed out of politics and the permanent civil war since the departure of the Soviets and the Americans. But they had also demonstrated their fighting prowess in the jihad against the Communists. If the main tribal leaders in Maiwand were to join forces and give their support to a 'holy' *hujra* student, that would make a big impression on the toll collectors and their commanders.

No one else in the meeting room seemed to have been informed beforehand, but Haji Bashar already knew who he wanted for this role. All of a sudden, he turned towards the tall figure of Mullah Omar sitting at the back. Would he be prepared to show the way and lead an armed rebellion against the toll collectors?

Before Omar could answer, an outraged murmur ran round the room. 'Him? No way!' said one man. 'I definitely won't be handing my weapons to a nobody like this mullah!' cried another. 'We should at least appoint an influential mullah,' suggested someone else. 'Mullah Rabbani, for example. Or Mullah Borjan.' Both these mullahs were well known locally as they had led large groups of combatants during the jihad and enjoyed considerable success. (Mullah Rabbani would later become Mullah Omar's deputy, and Mullah Borjan the commander-in-chief of the 'Taliban Army'). As a result, their status was much higher than Mullah Omar's. While he might have been skilled in firing rockets, he had never been made a commander during the jihad against the Soviets, simply because he was not important enough.

Everyone now turned to look at Mullah Omar, who was sitting at the back of the room and had not yet uttered a word.

Haji Bashar shook his head as he listened to the comments. He knew mullahs such as Rabbani and Borjan had strong reputations but he believed that was precisely the problem: they were too powerful to have an effect. Local administrators saw them as a threat because they enjoyed just as much power as the tribal leaders. The solution was to find someone who would not be perceived as threatening by anyone. In his opinion, it was to Omar's advantage that he was an insignificant mullah.

But Haji Bashar was unable to convince his audience. Or Mullah Omar, for that matter. Omar had sat quietly in the corner for the entire meeting, not saying a word. Now he shook his head. How could he ever stand up to such powerful and cruel commanders, he asked the people at the meeting. Without saying another word, he cycled home.

Haji Bashar did not give up. At a subsequent meeting that Omar and his group also attended, Haji Bashar improved his offer. 'If you and your *hujra* students are prepared to take the lead, I'll give you my militia's weapons and cars.'[9] He did not want to send his militiamen, though, as he was afraid those men would then become the face of the rebellion. He preferred to keep his family in the background, in the shadow of the *hujra* students, who would then be the moral face of the rebellion. His offer to give Mullah Omar his weapons was intended as an example to other local leaders.[10]

In the end, Mullah Omar promised that he would consider Haji Bashar's offer. After consulting with Haji Bashar, he spent the next few weeks visiting numerous *hujras* in the area and recruiting students to join the campaign against the toll collectors.

The mood at the next meeting was suddenly a lot more optimistic. *Hujra* students from all over the district descended on the place. Some were wearing black or white turbans. Many came on foot or dumped their motorcycles haphazardly outside the house. The mullahs and their students sat in Haji Ghausedin's large yard, right opposite Mullah Omar's hut (this house was destroyed in the post-9/11 fighting). Haji Ghausedin had slaughtered a sheep but one sheep was never going to be enough for such a large group.[11] The *hujra* students had to wait in the yard while Mullah Omar and his fellow mullahs such as Berader discussed matters in Haji Ghausedin's house with Haji Bashar and Bur Gate, another trader and rich businessman. Like Haji Bashar, this powerful businessman and drug lord was prepared to give Mullah Omar cars, weapons, and money.

When everything had been arranged, Haji Bashar walked out to address the students, who were in the yard awaiting further instructions. Mullah Omar stood next to him but said nothing. They made an unlikely pair: the short Haji Bashar, a powerful businessman whose life revolved around earning money, and standing quietly next to him, the much taller Mullah Omar, for whom removing the roadblocks was a religious duty.[12]

Later, Mohammed Issa and Haji Bashar's deputy both drew the same conclusion in conversations with me: without the drugs mafia the Taliban would not have existed.

———— ◆ ————

Some time later, I accidentally came across a cassette tape from 1996 with a recording of Mullah Omar himself talking about these early days in front of a big crowd of mullahs. My Pashto teacher had been there when Omar spoke, reflecting on this period, and the teacher had recorded the speech. This was the first documented recording that I found of Mullah Omar speaking.

When I pressed 'Play', I heard a dark voice speaking slowly. It was the first time I had heard Omar's voice. Everyone in my office in Kabul was very excited. I had been investigating this man for two years by that point but we had never heard him or seen him on film. We knew that there were audio recordings in the archives of the national radio and television organization Ariana in Kabul, but the archivists did not dare give us access. They were afraid that the recordings would be leaked and become popular among the Afghan people.

Mullah Omar spoke like an old man, talking at an unhurried, even sluggish pace. In his pronunciation, the Pashto vowels were longer than they needed to be. He sounded like a mix between an aging, uneducated villager with a bit of a stutter – he would repeat words like 'I' (I, I, I) as if he had forgotten what he wanted to say – and a Southern Baptist preacher addressing his flock with long-drawn-out arguments. It was as if he would much rather not be standing behind the lectern with my Pashto teacher's microphone and tape recorder in front of his nose. He sounded like a man who did not enjoy speaking at formal occasions like this one.

'So this is how the Taliban began,' said the dark voice. He was clearly not reading from a printed or handwritten text in front of him. He talked as if he were standing in front of his house in Haji Ibrahim and telling a passing neighbor the story of how he became the leader.

Mullah Omar spoke of the immorality that was rampant in Haji Ibrahim in 1994. There were some bad people around then and the situation was unstable, he said. People were plundering and stealing, murders were committed for no reason, and the bodies could not be buried afterwards. He mentioned the roadblocks set up by the toll collectors. In his speech, he admitted that he had doubts about whether *he* should be the one tackling this. 'Allah tells us that no one is responsible for more than he can cope with,' he said, quoting the Quran. But he also said that he had no option other than to trust in Allah. Then he gave a detailed account of how the Taliban came into being.

'Some people wonder how this movement started, under what "secret circumstances". Who supported us? Who organized us? And who trained us?' Without answering these questions, Mullah Omar related how he visited the *hujras* on a scooter to mobilize students for the campaign against the toll collectors. 'We students,' Omar said, using the word *taliban*, 'need to rise up. If we want to serve Allah, we have to stop studying and start fighting.'

According to Mullah Omar, the students at the first *hujras* he went to were reluctant and he could not rely on their support. They would say, 'We could manage Friday evening,' for instance, but he thought that was not enough. In the end, a few students – he said literally 'five to seven' – agreed to join him. After this, the movement soon grew to over fifty students. They gathered in his mosque in Haji Ibrahim. That was how it all started, according to Mullah Omar.

At the end of his speech, Mullah Omar referred to a dream he'd had of angels with soft hands. We don't take dreams very seriously in the West but I have discovered that many in Kandahar believe in them. Even my Afghan friend who has often been to America did, as I found out to my surprise. She once asked advice in her dreams on whether she should marry the man she was in love with, a request known as *istikhara*.

As the tape played, I heard Omar fall silent after describing the angels in his dream. A moment later, I heard him fighting back his tears. My Pashto teacher confirmed that he had seen Mullah Omar become emotional as he talked about his dream. The room was deathly quiet. But Omar regained control of himself and continued, 'Then I said the angels should touch me.' At these words, the audience jumped up and cheered as if he had told them that these angels were a sign Allah himself had chosen him. The audience started to chant rallying cries such as 'Allah is great' and 'long live Islam'. Mullah Omar called on them to be silent and concluded his talk: 'So that was the start of the movement, and everything got going within twenty-four hours. That's what happened.'

When the fighters – a mix of *hujra* students recruited by Mullah Omar and men from Haji Bashar's militias – gathered to prepare for the confrontation with the toll collectors, they were in for a surprise. Mullah Omar thought Haji Bashar's men in particular were not in a fit state for his religious battle. Their hair had not been cut or washed, their robes were dirty and full of holes, and most of them smoked hashish non-stop as well.

'If I'm going to be leading this uprising, your men will need to look sharper,' said Mullah Omar when he arrived at Haji Bashar's command post. Surrounded by militiamen, Omar announced that everyone with unkempt hair would have to have it cut. The fighters were amazed. Who on earth did this man think he was? One of Haji Bashar's commanders said he heard horrified voices on his walkie-talkie that day. 'We've got some crazy guy here who wants to cut our hair,' the young men had said. 'What should we do?' 'He's one of us,' replied the commander.

Haji Bashar had to go first.[13] Once he had had his hair cut, the other young militants underwent the process without further protest. Incidentally, the knife was so blunt that it left the fighters with spiky hair. One of them was so disgusted by what he saw in the mirror that he grabbed a sharper razor blade and shaved all his hair off.

Omar wanted the fight to be in accordance with strict rules of conduct, as became clear from another incident. Just before the fighting was about to start, Haji Bashar saw an opportunity to settle a tribal dispute in which his family's honor was at stake. He had a rival in his district hanged. Mullah Omar was furious. Honor killings were against the rules of Islam and it was even more important in this particular fight for everyone to set a good example, including Haji Bashar. It didn't matter to Mullah Omar that Bashar's rival had probably been an accomplice of the Communists; the man had never been tried for that.[14]

In fact, the clean-cut, neatly dressed fighters brought together by Haji Bashar and Mullah Omar would not be seeing action for a while yet, as the first task was to secure the support of one of the key leaders in Kandahar

Province: Naqibullah.[15] He was an influential and opportunistic strongman from the days of the civil war. In 1979 he had supported the Communists, but he later joined the jihad. Now he supported Rabbani, the president clinging to power in the distant capital Kabul. Naqibullah was the local Minister of Defense, which meant he controlled all the weapons in Kandahar Province. Haji Bashar and Mullah Omar soon managed to get Naqibullah on their side. He endorsed their holy fight and gave Haji Bashar large quantities of weapons and cash.

According to the Quran, if a conflict arises, you must first try to resolve it by talking, and only use violence if all else fails. I have also read this in Michael Griffin's book *Reaping the Whirlwind*, which says that a lot of what the movement achieved in its early days was done by talking to people.[16] But it wasn't Mullah Omar who did the talking; it was mostly Haji Bashar. He had the money, the power and the necessary connections for this uprising. As Haji Bashar's deputy said to me, without Haji Bashar there would have been no Taliban. Mullah Omar sat in on the discussions mainly to lend religious legitimacy to the endeavor. Haji Bashar would point to the silent man next to him and say, 'He's the leader of the movement.'

Naqibullah's support had a positive effect on the negotiations with the first few toll collectors and their commanders. One after another, they surrendered without a shot being fired. The first real challenge for Omar's movement was the warlord Amir Lalai. He was one of the most powerful tribal leaders in Kandahar, with at least a hundred toll collectors in his employ on the road traversing the province.[17]

Amir Lalai was not impressed by the alliance that Haji Bashar and Mullah Omar had forged with Naqibullah. He was one of Naqibullah's rivals and was determined to hold out against the alliance. Mullah Omar responded to his resistance by turning up at his house with a large group of combatants. 'Join us,' he warned Amir Lalai.[18] The large group of men he had brought made clear that he was starting to lose patience.

Amir Lalai did not yield, saying, 'Try your luck with the others first.' At which point Mullah Omar's students went on the attack. Amir Lalai's local men soon fled and his toll collectors deserted their posts on the route from Haji Ibrahim to Kandahar. Omar's students planted their first makeshift white flags, pieces of cloth attached to broken-off branches and bearing the hastily written Arabic words: *La ilaha illallah Muhammadur Rasulullah* – 'There is no god but Allah and Muhammad is his Prophet.'

The most notorious toll commander on the road, known as Saleh the Child Rapist because he owned underage sex slaves, was dealt with in a similar way to Amir Lalai.[19] Omar held talks with the man at least three times and asked him to withdraw voluntarily. Saleh too refused to surrender initially. He was not in awe of the new movement, which he thought weak and easy to defeat. Mullah Omar had his men surround the roadblock and gave orders for them to shoot. Saleh fought fire with fire but eventually had to admit defeat.

Both these victories were followed by the discovery of cases full of weapons that Omar's men took with them to add to their stockpiles. The movement was turning into an army that could no longer be seen as a band of well-meaning mullahs and students fighting the good fight without weapons or violence.

More and more people in the province heard about what was happening along the highway. Mullahs called out through their mosques' loudspeakers: 'Listen, everyone: a *talib*, one of our own, is advancing.' If the mosque didn't have a loudspeaker, the mullah would just stand outside and shout out the words. Amidst all the turmoil caused by the civil war, now there were young men in the area organizing a righteous rebellion. The movement was automatically dubbed the Taliban after the word *taliban*, which means 'Quran students'. (Later on, it took on the more formal name of the Islamic Emirate of Afghanistan.)

In the early days of the movement's rise, Mullah Omar still returned to his little home in Haji Ibrahim every evening, but now his humble abode was never quiet for one moment as a steady stream of visitors came, curious to find out how the uprising was going. There were no radio reports in those days informing people of what was happening in the district, so news traveled by word of mouth.

Omar felt the weight of responsibility; people noticed he was no longer the prankster he had once been.[20] He would often sit in front of his house, with his hands in his hair, staring into space. He believed that he was Allah's servant, and looked to Allah for support. He became very nervous at times now that he was taking risks that could get people killed – after which he would have to appear before Allah.[21]

The prominent tribal leaders in Kandahar kept a close watch on Omar's movement during this period. One such leader was Abdul Ahad Karzai, the father of Hamid Karzai. During the jihad, Abdul had lost his position as a leader of the Popalzai tribe to Amir Lalai, the intransigent leader whose toll collectors had blocked the road from Haji Ibrahim to Kandahar. After the jihad, Amir Lalai had been given a dominant role in Kandahar's local government, again at the expense of Abdul Ahad Karzai.

This made the victory achieved by Haji Bashar and Mullah Omar a very interesting development from Abdul Ahad Karzai's point of view.[22] The Karzais already knew a few members of the old Uruzgan group, in particular Mullah Berader (they were from the same tribe). They let it be known that they believed in the new movement, and Abdul Ahad soon sent messengers to his fellow tribesmen elsewhere in Kandahar, and in the provinces of Uruzgan and Helmand, telling them that they too should give their support to Mullah Omar. The Karzais saw a chance of the situation returning to how it was before the jihad. Perhaps they could even bring back King Zahir Shah – who had by this point been living in exile in Rome for twenty years.

Eminent *khans* from other regions were also keen to find out more about Omar's movement, and they came to size up the situation. The police commander Aziz in Uruzgan, the father of my friend Najibullah, had received one of Karzai's messengers saying he should support the new Taliban.

'I was curious. Who was this Mullah Omar exactly?' Aziz said. 'Did he have any land? Did he have any property? In fact he had nothing, and yet he'd had so much success. I had to find out more about him.'

Within a few weeks, the government of Uruzgan Province surrendered without putting up a fight. Najibullah and Aziz were there. Aziz walked out and left his police station behind unmanned. There was little resistance in the rest of Uruzgan Province. Najibullah told me that a few chopped-off hands were soon on display in a square in Tarin Kowt. 'That was gruesome, but it did mean no one dared steal anything, so we didn't have to lock our houses. Even the stores left their doors open.'

Not much later, it turned out, news of Haji Bashar's successful plan had reached as far as Kabul. President Rabbani himself decided to give his support to the local movement.[23] Mullah Omar did not know Kabul. In fact, he had probably never visited the capital at that point, let alone met the president. But no one worried about that. 'Give them weapons. Give them whatever they need,' the president had previously said to Naqibullah in Kandahar.[24] He was thinking partly of his own interests. In Kabul, the president was embroiled in a fierce armed conflict with his great rival Gulbuddin Hekmatyar, and he saw Omar's movement as a way of getting at Hekmatyar in southern Afghanistan.[25]

Now, thanks to the support of the president of Afghanistan, Mullah Omar had fighter planes at his disposal. The palace had them delivered to Kandahar Airport and Omar was allowed to use them for as long as he wanted. Rabbani's Minister of Defense, Ahmad Shah Massoud (the man whom the Soviet Union had feared most during the jihad), was another Taliban supporter; he called them 'the angels of peace'.[26] Omar was also sent a group of mechanics by the Uzbek warlord Abdul Rashid Dostum – another long-standing enemy of Hekmatyar. They were able to fix some old Soviet planes that had been left behind in Kandahar.

Thus, a national alliance of opponents of Gulbuddin Hekmatyar hoped the Taliban would defeat him in Kandahar. When I met President Rabbani years later, after he had been deposed, in his spacious mansion in Kabul, and asked him about his alliance with Mullah Omar in 1994, he reacted as if he had been found out. After all, by then he was an established ally of the Americans, someone who saw the Taliban as barbarians and fumed about them in his conversations with journalists.

———— ◆ ————

In the course of my investigations in Kabul, I met Abdul, a former Communist who spoke fluent English and Russian and who had obtained his pilot's license in Moscow. I went out for a meal with him at a restaurant named Sufi. Abdul just wanted to talk in a quiet place in the restaurant because, like many of my sources, he was afraid people would criticize him for his past Taliban connections. He hadn't had any problems with the rise of the Taliban at the time. He thought they offered a good alternative to the civil war. With the Taliban in charge, many Communists were able to stay on in their old government jobs.

Back then, Abdul was managing Kandahar Airport. Quite unexpectedly, seven MiG fighter planes and eight Mil Mi-8 transport helicopters were delivered.[27] He still clearly remembers Mullah Omar driving up to the airport (the mullah himself was behind the wheel). 'Hello, Mullah Saib [literally Mr. Mullah],' Abdul said politely, somewhat ill at ease in the presence of this visitor. Mullah Omar immediately strode over to one of the fighter planes that Rabbani had sent. He stared in amazement at the gray aircraft with the red stars on its wings. 'He had never seen an airplane from close before,' explained the pilot Abdul. For ten years, planes had raced through the skies above him; one had dropped a bomb that had cost him his right eye. Now he was finally getting to examine these dangerous aircraft from close up.

Of course Mullah Omar was pleased with the planes that had unexpectedly been donated to him. However, Abdul was sorry to have to tell him that not all the planes on the ground were in working order. He explained to Mullah Omar that certain batteries were impossible to get hold of in Afghanistan. They soon agreed this would need to change after the war. Then everything would be better, Omar assured him. The Taliban would rebuild Afghanistan and the country would function normally again.

'Would you fly one of them a bit for me?' Mullah Omar suddenly asked Abdul. Without a moment's hesitation, the pilot took a seat in one of the functioning aircraft. He took Rabbani's fighter plane into the air and circled in the sky above Mullah Omar a couple of times. Abdul told me Mullah Omar looked absolutely delighted.

———— ◆ ————

Meanwhile, the struggle to free up the roads around Kandahar continued. Now that the toll collectors on the west side of the city had been chased off, the Taliban's focus shifted to the east side and the road to Spin Boldak, a town on the border with Pakistan. Some important jihad leaders in that area – Mullah Rabbani, Mullah Mohammed, and Mullah Borjan – joined the movement. The Taliban also still depended heavily on support from the powerful Quetta traders, whose colorful trucks were parked along the side of the blocked roads in their hundreds. Their support for change took the form of large amounts of money rather than weapons.[28]

The powerful truck mafia hoped not only that the toll collectors would be driven off the highway on both sides of Kandahar but also that much more of the highway would be cleared of roadblocks. This trade route crossed southern Afghanistan from east to west: it started at the Pakistan border in Spin Boldak, ran west to Kandahar City and continued to the neighboring province of Helmand via Sangisar – which includes Haji Ibrahim. The town of Gereshk in Helmand was an important stopping point for the transfer of goods destined for the neighboring countries of Iran and Turkmenistan via the city of Herat. Many businessmen in Quetta were eager to open up the route as soon as possible.

It was not just the truck mafia who had a particular interest in freeing up this important trade route; the Pakistani government also suffered from the blockades and wanted to be able to trade again with nearby countries such as Turkmenistan, now that the jihad had ended. The blockage of the flow of goods to the Central Asian Republics – largely medicines, in return for cement and cotton – was costing the Pakistani economy millions of dollars a year. All attempts to get this trade moving again by working with President Rabbani's government in Kabul had failed.

In the same year that the Taliban first had success in their campaign around Kandahar, Pakistan decided – coincidentally or not – to attempt to send a convoy of trucks with goods to Herat and beyond, this time without consulting President Rabbani.[29] This was part of a larger plan. Back in 1994 the Pakistan government had sought Western aid to help reopen the road as a boost to the economy. This convoy would prove to the world that the donations would be used effectively. But the Pakistani Minister of the Interior had to postpone the convoy's trip because fighting had broken out in the Spin Boldak area, with the Taliban taking over the town and large quantities of weapons.

A couple of weeks later, the long line of trucks set off but had barely got going before the operation turned into a fiasco. Amir Lalai, the leader who had lost to Mullah Omar in a fight over his roadblocks to the west of Kandahar, was still operating to the east of Kandahar. Lalai had his toll collectors hijack the Pakistani convoy the moment they got into Afghan territory. He claimed he had done so because they were carrying weapons for Mullah Omar's movement.[30]

The sixty or so Pakistani drivers and their co-drivers were badly treated. Colonel Iman was among them. He had only recently been appointed Pakistan's consul in Herat and had earlier that summer given receptions for the potential Western donors, together with the governor appointed by the Rabbani government (Colonel Imam would stay on in this position during the Taliban regime). Now the colonel was punished particularly harshly because he had shared out the C.I.A. money among the mujahideen parties during the Soviet–Afghan War. He was seen by Amir Lalai as a powerful Pakistani player who was manipulating the Afghans. Amir Lalai was convinced this colonel was behind Pakistan's plan to help the Taliban gain power. Colonel Iman was raped and held captive for days in a tiny latrine, according to Lalai's deputy. Amir Lalai demanded that the Taliban be ejected from all the roads around Kandahar. In vain, Pakistan called on President Rabbani's government to persuade Lalai to change his mind. Instead, the leader escalated the situation and even threatened to set fire to the trucks.

In the end, the Pakistani convoy was rescued by Mullah Omar's new ally, the prominent jihadist Mullah Borjan. While Amir Lalai fled to Iran, two of his commanders who had tried to escape were murdered by the Taliban and hung from the barrel of an old Soviet tank at the entrance to Kandahar Airport as a warning to others. No one should defy the will of this movement of mullahs and truck mafia, was the message. Amir Lalai's deputy, whom I interviewed, also tried to slip away but when he arrived in Pakistan, he was imprisoned for eight months as an accomplice of Amir Lalai.

Amir Lalai's claim that the Pakistani convoy was mainly transporting weapons for the Taliban has often been cited as important evidence that Pakistan was instrumental in the Taliban's rise to power. Ahmed Rashid in particular refers to this accusation by Lalai as proof for that claim in his book. However, it is not clear what the Pakistan government's relationship was with the Taliban at that time. For sure, Islamic parties in Pakistan openly supported the rise of the Taliban. Several witnesses told me that the black-and-white Taliban flags were seen on the highway in Kandahar. Pakistani Pashtun businessmen did not hide their enthusiasm for the new movement either and helped the Taliban wherever they could, mainly through the truck mafia of Afghanistan. But in 1994, the I.S.I. was formally still close to the Taliban's key rival, Gulbuddin Hekmatyar, their ally from the jihad. Also, the Pakistani government had already communicated plans to open the highway for economic reasons in press releases before the rise of the Taliban.[31] Amir Lalai's deputy denied the presence of Pakistani weapons and said that the convoy contained goods such as medicines. Those goods were stolen after the hijack. To me it is far from clear that this convoy was a Pakistani political move to demonstrate the strength of the Taliban, as some American authors claim.[32]

For what it is worth, the Taliban themselves acted surprised and far from pleased with the arrival of the Pakistani convoy. They saw these uninvited 'guests' as yet more evidence of the arrogance in Pakistan's attitude to Afghanistan, treating the country as if it was just one of Pakistan's provinces.[33] An American cable from America's Islamabad office quotes a Taliban 'spokesman' who refers to the local Kandahar governor Gul Agha Sherzai, who was loyal to President Rabbani in Kabul. 'He should vet convoys from Pakistan,' the Taliban spokesman is quoted as saying, in support of the Rabbani government.[34] After the incident, the Taliban wanted to ban the use of Pakistani trucks on Afghan territory with immediate effect.[35]

One thing was clear: by that point the Taliban were no longer suffering from a shortage of weapons. Every time they seized a checkpoint on the roads around Kandahar, they were able to lay their hands on large quantities of weaponry. In October 1994 alone, Mullah Omar's fighters confiscated 18,000 Kalashnikovs and other munitions when they took control of Spin Boldak. These weapons had belonged to Hekmatyar. 'We don't need any weapons from Pakistan,' said a Taliban spokesman at the time. 'There are enough weapons in Afghanistan at the moment to conquer the whole world.'[36]

Mullah Omar's movement became increasingly well known. News of their victories reached the madrassas in the Pakistani city of Quetta, where many Afghans had fled during the jihad. Those Afghans' sons were now studying at the many madrassas, which had been financed with American money during the jihad. When the jihad ended, the truck mafia had taken over the task of funding the madrassas as they were afraid the youths would otherwise turn to crime.

The uprising by fellow students in Kandahar was a magnet for these Quran students. Busloads of students, both Afghans and Pakistanis, crossed the border at Spin Boldak – some voluntarily, others under duress – to join the movement in Afghanistan. The Quran student Abdul Rahman Hotaki, a war orphan aged about twenty, voluntarily boarded a bus to Kandahar in 1994, like many around him.[37] Having heard about the new role of the students in Kandahar, he hoped he would be able to earn some money there. Already during the bus journey, he could see the hated toll collectors had gone. All the traffic – cars, buses, the traditional Afghan jingle trucks – flowed smoothly as if there had never been a war. There were even women in burkas walking down the streets again. Abdul Rahman said the fact that men were prepared to let their womenfolk out (albeit wearing burkas) was a huge advance on the situation during all those years of savage civil war when almost nobody ventured out onto the streets.

I met Abdul Rahman during my investigations in Kabul, where he now lives and worked as a member of the Afghan Independent Human Rights Commission. Shortly after he joined the Taliban at the end of 1994, he became an informal employee of Mullah Omar, mainly because they were from the same tribe. Initially, he was primarily responsible for the movement's contacts with the press. He shared that task with Tayyab Agha, who went on to become one of Mullah Omar's most important secretaries (Tayyab Agha refused at least ten requests from me for an interview). Another man who worked for Mullah Omar from an early stage, as his communications expert and secretary, was Mullah Mutawakil. He was soon promoted to Minister of Foreign Affairs.

I don't know why, but Mullah Mutawakil did not want to say anything about Abdul Rahman Hotaki's position in the early days of the Taliban. Perhaps this was because of a personal conflict, or perhaps Abdul Rahman had already left when Mutawakil was given a more prominent position. Abdul Rahman himself said he was transferred at the end of 1995 because Mullah Omar didn't want someone from the same tribe working in his office. This was a sensitive matter, as the Taliban were opposed to tribalism. Abdul Rahman became a government official working in the local Education Department, and then an administrator in Nimroz Province after it had been captured by the mullahs. Later, he returned to Kandahar to manage the Department of Transport, a job he also had in Kabul after that city fell to the Taliban in 1996. He remained in the service of Mullah Omar until 2000, when he quit.

After the fall of the Taliban at the end of 2001, Abdul Rahman was arrested by the Americans and detained in the notorious Bagram prison. 'I was put in the freezer room on a number of occasions, and interrogated with icicles hanging off my arms,' he said. Hamid Karzai, the Afghan president at the time, eventually got him released. 'The good news is that I learned to speak English in Bagram,' Abdul Rahman laughed.

When Abdul Rahman arrived in Kandahar in 1994, he had no problem finding the grand governor's house. After the governor of the province had done a vanishing act, Mullah Omar and Mullah Hassan – Kandahar's new governor, who was known for being direct and even rude at times – moved in. The building, with its Gothic-style windows and wide balconies, was by far the most impressive structure in the city. There was a time when the governor would stand on the verandah waving at the people. Now, young students in black or white turbans were wandering around the building that had until recently seemed an impregnable fortress to most of them.

An eight-member informal council made up of all the mullahs and one businessman (Haji Bashar) had now taken up residence in the governor's building.[38] It was in charge of the administration in all areas controlled by the Taliban, and its plan was to rapidly implement the Prophet Muhammad's law – the Shariah.[39] Abdul Rahman said 'council' was actually a fancy name for a few men meeting up. 'It was all really accessible and informal. I was usually there too. We often met up in the evenings, and anyone who came along was allowed to give his opinion and take part in decision-making.' He said that Mullah Omar did not always attend these meetings. Omar was focusing on his fast-growing army and he left the political aspects to men he trusted such as Mullah Jalil – who would have many talks with the C.I.A. on Mullah Omar's behalf at a later stage – and the new governor Mullah Hassan, who was even more puritanical than Mullah Omar himself and would often clash with international visitors.

To prevent paralysis in government functions, many civil servants and other public officials were allowed to stay on in their jobs, even if they had worked for the Communists.[40] The Taliban were quite happy to reap the benefits of the solid education these people had received in Moscow, such as the pilot Abdul who managed Kandahar Airport. However, they also ordered these government officials and public servants to let their beards grow. Some Afghans were irritated by this requirement but most did not see it as a problem; after all, many men in Kandahar already had thick beards (as is still the case today).

An Afghan friend of mine told me that in the mid-1990s, when he was sixteen years old, he was desperate to put the IT skills that he had acquired in Pakistan to good use. He drew a thick mustache and an embryonic beard on his face, applied for a job, and got accepted. He was soon working in Mullah Omar's office, typing speeches for the mullah on one of the few computers.

During these exciting early days, Abdul Rahman and his media people resurrected the newspaper *Tolo Afghan*, which had closed down during the civil war. While he was trying to get the old printing presses working again, some strict mullahs came along and asked him, 'What if the word of Allah is printed in the newspaper and a copy falls on the ground? Wouldn't that be a stain on his name?' Abdul Rahman didn't take them particularly seriously. 'You always get some mullahs who take their religious beliefs to extremes,' he said.

As it happened, there was not much news in the paper at first. With no experience in the business, Abdul Rahman mainly selected and printed popular local poems. The verse below appeared in one of the first issues of *Tolo Afghan*. It describes the pain caused by the devastation in Afghanistan.

> Black crows bring bad news to the land of the nightingales.
> I see it as a wounded hand after an accident.
> It is a red flame that you see in my besmirched land.
> My beautiful white *shalwar kameez* is sullied.
> And my honor has been taken into the river of the land of the privileged.
> The face of the dark wreckage has arisen from the black hair.
> This is the sound of crying that I hear coming from the land of poetry.[41]

———— ◆ ————

Mullah Omar spent more and more time on his rapidly growing 'army' of Quran students from the *hujras* and madrassas. A lot of deserters from the militias of the defeated leaders were also joining his army. An American diplomat who visited Kandahar was impressed with the discipline in Mullah Omar's army. He reported back to the U.S. Government that the Taliban were doing much better than the militias, who had been in control up to that point.[42]

Mullah Omar, though, was worried about whether these youngsters would stick to the rules of his holy struggle. Omar often reminded his fighters that if they misbehaved, so would the general populace.

Omar had limited facilities for communicating with his army. The devastating civil war in Kandahar had left only three functioning phone lines. Number 1 was Mullah Omar's number; Number 2 connected you to the governor's compound in the city; Number 3 was functional but was not used. So Mullah Omar and his men communicated mainly by walkie-talkie.

Omar went around permanently with one of those walkie-talkies held to his ear, giving instructions to his commanders in the field. Those instructions were not just military orders; time and time again, he reminded them of the Taliban's rules of conduct. Mullah Omar's people made lists summarizing these rules and distributed them locally (the Taliban is doing this again now). It was not uncommon for Mullah Omar to give even his most senior commanders a loud dressing down, telling them they were not allowed to curse the enemy on the walkie-talkie, even if the opponent had started it.

The priority for Omar was always that his army should set an example to society at large. Take the following decree:

> Honored ministers, governors, all district governors and Taliban platoon commanders [...] Beardless youths who want to join a platoon or wish for a position in my movement shall be barred categorically, even if they are accompanied by a family member. Shariah law says that we must protect ourselves so that we cannot be accused of child labor.

Anyone who failed to take all these rules seriously was punished ruthlessly. People in Kandahar regularly saw men being driven around with their faces painted black. Sometimes signs would be hung round their necks saying what it was they had done wrong. Or there might be someone with a loudspeaker who let the condemned man list his offenses himself so that the people watching could learn from his example. These public punishments were often for accepting bribes. Stealing was punished even more severely, by the amputation of one or both hands. Little attention was paid to legal niceties in these punishments. In Herat, one militant was beaten up by his fellow militiamen purely because he had opened the wrong drawer in a bank.[43] There was no mercy at all for deserters, who were executed without any trial or due process.[44]

———— ◆ ————

It was during this period that Mullah Omar was approached for the first time by a major international media outlet. Rahimullah Yousafzai worked for the B.B.C.'s Pashto-language radio station, which many Afghans used to listen to, including Omar. In spring 1995, Yousafzai was given permission by the Taliban leader to visit him in Kandahar.[45] Years later, I spoke to Rahimullah Yousafzai in his home in the Pakistani border city of Peshawar.

'Omar's reputation in Pakistan was already almost legendary,' Yousafzai told me. 'Many people were full of praise for this new, incredibly mysterious leader who'd been able to establish what seemed to be a stable Islamic state in the south of Afghanistan, a country ravaged by civil war. Various Islamic parties in Pakistan wanted to work with him; they often visited him and wanted to do the same in their homeland, but they hadn't managed it as yet. What Mullah Omar had achieved in Afghanistan was something Pakistani Islamic fundamentalists could only dream of, so lots of people in Pakistan assumed he must be an imposing, forceful figure.'

As he traveled to Kandahar, Yousafzai noticed that the toll collectors had indeed all gone. Another surprise was awaiting him when he got to the governor's building where Mullah Omar was based. He found the mullah taking a midday nap, sleeping on the grass using his turban as a blanket. 'He clearly hadn't been expecting me yet,' laughed Yousafzai.

The B.B.C. journalist was amazed at what he found in the governor's building. Mullah Omar's office was in a cubicle that bore a distinct similarity to a broom closet. Yousafzai had already heard about this from other Taliban leaders, who complained about the spartan conditions that Mullah Omar operated in. The building actually had ballrooms, but he preferred a windowless room under the stairs. Omar would hold meetings about the uprising with the other Taliban leaders in which they all sat on an old carpet around cups of tea. A metal box stood in the corner; this was where he kept the new regime's money. Some people wondered later whether Mullah Omar had ever changed his clothes because he always wore the same *shalwar kameez*. His diet was plain too – often just soup and some potatoes that he wolfed down as if he was permanently hungry.[46] One of his wives would frequently complain about this spartan diet, and she asked her brother to take him some meat from time to time.[47]

Mullah Omar gave Yousafzai a respectful welcome. He had often heard him on the radio and said he was honored by the visit. But the Taliban leader insisted there could be no interview. 'I can't talk to you with a microphone on. I've never given an interview in my life,' he said. Besides Omar's lack of experience, Yousafzai suspects humility was also a factor in his refusal of an interview. He didn't want to be portrayed as the head of the Taliban as that was such a big responsibility. Omar told Yousafzai about the concept of *andiwal*, the notion of an egalitarian group of friends working together. 'I would never have managed this alone,' said Mullah Omar, and he pointed to the friends seated around him.

As an alternative, Yousafzai suggested making radio recordings in Haji Ibrahim, the village where Mullah Omar still lived. The Taliban leader would not have to go with him. That made Mullah Omar laugh. 'The famous B.B.C. journalist wants to go to my home so that he can understand the Taliban? Who the heck cares about my home or my village?'

After persevering for three days, Yousafzai finally got permission to visit Haji Ibrahim. Once again, he was struck by the sober conditions in which Mullah Omar had lived. Back in Kandahar, he joked about it to the mullah. 'Heh, look at how far you've come! There was virtually nothing in Haji Ibrahim – a tiny house and a tiny mosque – and look at how big your house is here! You didn't have a car back there, not even a scooter, but now you're driving around in a Land Cruiser. In fact, you've got so many of them that there isn't even enough room in the parking lot.'

Yousafzai did eventually get his interview. At any rate, he was allowed to leave his tape recorder plus a list of questions with Mullah Omar's press officer Abdul Rahman Hotaki. He was able to pick up the recorder one day later – with Mullah Omar's answers on the tape. When Yousafzai listened to the recording, he could tell Omar had struggled with his answers. Abdul Rahman was there that evening and he told me that they had had to re-record some sections perhaps a dozen times. Rahman had written the answers down for Omar but he had trouble reading them. Yousafzai said the answers were not very surprising. Unfortunately the tape has been lost; the B.B.C. Pashto station was unable to find it anywhere either.[48]

———— ◆ ————

In the summer of 1995, Omar's movement had gained control of at least four neighboring provinces that were all very strict and devoutly Islamic. It was then that the movement experienced its first serious setback. One group of militants and drug traders split off and pushed through to Wardak Province in central Afghanistan while another group set off westwards to Helmand – where it all went wrong. In Helmand, Mullah Omar's men came up against the powerful drug baron and Haji Bashar's rival Mullah Abdul Ghaffour Akhundzada, who was not prepared to submit to the demand that he should withdraw his toll collectors and give up his drug empire.[49]

Although Mullah Omar had sent one of his best commanders, Mullah Muhammad, to lead the attack on the western front, the number of fatalities continued to rise. The drug baron Mullah Ghaffour had put together a coalition of expelled commanders to defend the position against the Quran students. His allies included Naqibullah, the man who only a few months earlier had been collaborating with the Taliban but ended up on the opposite side.[50] They won and managed to take Gereshk, the city about halfway between Kandahar and Herat that all the drug transports passed through. After a couple of days of intense fighting, the Taliban were able to re-capture Gereshk. But they never got any further. Mullah Omar received a message that the fighters attached to his ally Mullah Rabbani – not to be confused with President Rabbani – were refusing to care for the wounded in Omar's army because they thought they had been such hopeless soldiers.

Worse news was to follow. Mullah Muhammad, one of the men who had been with the movement from the start and Omar's most important commander, had been killed in the fighting. The Taliban army's leader was dead.[51]

Abdul Rahman was with Mullah Omar in the car on their way to the governor's building when they heard the news. Omar had lost one of his best friends and was in the midst of a crisis. He started to cry from fear. 'I made a mistake, I made a mistake,' he said with tears in his eyes. 'Allah will ask me later, "What did you mean by making that mistake?"' Then Omar became angry. 'I thought everyone wanted an Islamic state! So why am I getting so much resistance?' he cried.

Other Taliban leaders were standing outside the governor's building waiting for Mullah Omar. When he arrived, he refused to get out of the car and stayed in the back seat, mourning his loss. The men ran up to the car and asked him who he was appointing to replace Mullah Muhammad. But Omar was too upset by the news of his death.

'Choose someone, I don't care who,' he said to Abdul Rahman, who conveyed this message to the other leaders. But the men refused to accept this and sent Abdul back to his boss, who was still weeping in the back seat of the car. Omar said, 'I can't make any decisions right now. Please go away.' Omar slammed the car door, nearly shutting it on Abdul Rahman's leg.

Panic-stricken by the threat of defeat, Mullah Omar set off shortly afterwards on his own and drove to Kandahar Airport. Abdul the pilot, promoted a few months earlier to commander of the airport, knew at once what Omar had come for. The news of Mullah Muhammad's death had affected Abdul deeply too.

Mullah Omar walked straight up to the only fighter plane on the airstrip. 'We need this plane now. Do something,' he instructed Abdul. As the pilot sat in the cockpit, he started to explain that a number of essential components were not working properly, including the batteries. Mullah Omar didn't quite roll his eyes but he was desperate and he repeated, 'Do something. Do something. We need it for the fighting in Gereshk and Herat.' When he saw that Abdul's tinkering was not having any effect and he couldn't get the engine to start, Omar quietly crept round the back of the plane, knelt on the ground and started to pray, using his turban as a makeshift prayer mat. Abdul couldn't believe his eyes. When Abdul told me this story, he was surprised by the simplicity of this man.

'Pray for it, pray for it so that Allah can help us,' Mullah Omar said to the astounded pilot. 'Allah will help us if we pray for it.' Meanwhile, the pilot continued with his tests on the plane. He managed to get the engine to start, but it stalled again. Abdul replaced the batteries with some old ones. While Mullah Omar was still praying, the plane's engine started up again, this time properly. 'This is Allah helping us, this is Allah helping us!' cried Mullah Omar. Abdul was dumbfounded. It had to be a coincidence, nothing more. The batteries must have had some life in them after all. Abdul had disconnected everything, so there was less of a load on the batteries when starting up. Or perhaps the batteries had needed to cool down a bit as well. They would have been able to do that while Mullah Omar was on his knees praying.

Abdul started to laugh again as he told this story. 'Well, anyway, the plane suddenly started to work again after all that praying.' He gave me a meaningful look. 'I just thought: hang on, what happened there?'

He had gotten the plane running and hoped fervently that it wouldn't crash right away. 'It was an urgent situation, we were in trouble, so off I went. I flew one hundred miles westward and dropped just five or six bombs. I had the impression that I'd arrived in the final stage of the battle and that my bombs broke the frontline.'

After Abdul had left in the plane, Mullah Omar got back in the car to head straight off to the western front.[52] This was against the wishes of the other Taliban leaders, who were afraid he would be risking his life. 'You need to stay alive!' they urged. But the stubborn Mullah Omar had already gone.

He stopped for a break in his home village of Haji Ibrahim and ordered a few neighbors to take the last remaining Stinger rockets left over from the jihad and use them in the battle in the west. By pure coincidence, he also saw a man named Nader Jan in the village, who Omar knew had been on the side of his enemies in Gereshk. Nader Jan had in fact been arrested by Taliban militants for collaborating with the enemy.

When Mullah Omar saw him, it was as if he was seized by panic all over again. As if his own life was in danger, he grabbed a gun off a bystander and shot Nader Jan dead, breaking his own rule of only punishing people after they have been tried in court. The local villagers told me about this incident but most Taliban are reluctant to discuss it. Some, like Mullah Zaeef, the Taliban's ambassador in Pakistan, deny it ever happened, knowing it meant their leader had violated their own strict Shariah.

Mullah Omar did eventually appoint a new army commander for the conflict in the west, and the tide turned. Within a few days, the Taliban had gained control not just of Helmand Province but also of the Province of Herat further west still. 'Now, all of the west has been brought under the command of the butterflies of the Taliban,' wrote Omar in an upbeat mood in the *Tolo Afghan*.[53]

———— ◆ ————

While they might not have had political support, the Taliban were raising more and more revenue themselves. In one day in March alone the Taliban collected $150,000 from Pakistani and Afghan transporters. The customs duties from these trucks would soon become a formal source of income.[54]

Some sources claim that in the battle in Herat, the Taliban were helped by the Pakistani secret service.[55] Abdul Rahman Hotaki says that there were indeed 'many Pakistani Talibs' from the madrassas in the border areas who helped them in the fighting. This would continue to be the case until the fall of the Taliban in 2001. Nobody in the Taliban objected to that, says Hotaki. But Hotaki is not aware of a donation of 1,500 Toyota Hiluxes, for example, by the I.S.I.[56] 'We were very suspicious of the I.S.I.,' he said. 'We always distrusted their interference.'

U.S. diplomats in conversation with the Pakistani Minister of Foreign Affairs were told that Pakistan did not deny significant contact with the Taliban and that they gave 'some' assistance to the Taliban. However, little outside material aid was necessary as, according to the minister, the Taliban had widespread support throughout the Pashtun areas of Afghanistan. The minister said that most of the money came from the traders. He also said that it was very difficult to influence the Taliban. He called them 'hard-headed' and said, 'We tried to bring them from the fourteenth century to the twentieth century,' because in some cities the Taliban were alienating the population – but the Afghans didn't listen. The minister explained that he supported the parties that opposed Rabbani, the incumbent president, and encouraged them to work together so that the U.N. could take over and start peace talks.

After the fall of Herat, the Pakistani embassy in Kabul was attacked, and its ambassador Qazi Humayun was severely beaten. This incident soured the relationship between President Rabbani and Pakistan, Ambassador Humayun told American diplomats.[57] 'This made our policy more opposed to the Kabul government,' he said. He was also worried that the Taliban government in Kabul would start a war because their ideas clashed with the views of the people of Kabul. Having such a conservative state as a neighbor was not in the interest of the Islamabad leadership, he said. 'But there is no way back. The Taliban think they can do it all alone.'

The struggle to capture Herat had shown Mullah Omar that he could no longer rely on the support of President Rabbani in Kabul. Mullah Omar realized that the greatest resistance in Herat had come from the president and his troops. It seemed that Rabbani now feared that Haji Bashar's mullahs were advancing too close to his city and annexing land too quickly, and he was afraid that he would be ousted.

Omar thought it was hypocritical of the president to act in his own interest rather than in the interests of an Islamic state. While ministers from his government were defecting to the Taliban to help it set up an Islamic state, the president didn't want to give up Kabul. 'There will be no place for villains like President Rabbani in the future Islamic state,' wrote the *Tolo Afghan*. 'Inshallah, the only people who can achieve this are the Taliban, not the so-called government of Rabbani and Massoud.'[58]

The fighting in the west had caused dissent within the Taliban's ranks too. Mullah Rabbani blamed Omar and his lack of experience in military matters for the debacle and the many fatalities. He argued that Mullah Omar was not fit to lead the movement anymore and claimed that role for himself. But at a meeting in a school in Kandahar, Mullah Omar's position as leader was eventually confirmed after much pleading. Many Taliban leaders acknowledged his inexperience but were afraid of internal divisions, so they stuck with the man who had started the movement that promised to improve life in Afghanistan.[59]

While Mullah Omar retained leadership of the Taliban, the advance on Kabul was running into more and more trouble. The struggle for Kabul, the real center of power in Afghanistan, was taking place far from the Taliban's home base of Kandahar, and that made it difficult to wage war in accordance with the rules of jihad. While Mullah Omar still tried to spare the civilian population on paper and in his instructions, numbers of civilian casualties were increasing as Taliban rockets hit the wrong targets in Kabul. Amnesty International reported that the movement was regularly responsible for the deaths of dozens of innocent civilians.[60]

————— ◆ —————

According to the Peshawar Accords that had been concluded under the auspices of the U.N., President Rabbani should have called an election back in 1994 and then transferred power to the winner. However, he had disregarded those agreements because it was impossible to hold elections. Now he was embroiled in a bitter struggle for the capital, in a constantly changing constellation of alliances. Numerous leaders and their militias were involved in this conflict, including Gulbuddin Hekmatyar, Abdul Rashid Dostum, and Hazara leaders. They too were responsible for large numbers of civilian casualties in Kabul.

The stalemate around Kabul led to intense debate within the Taliban. Could there be alternatives to the military solution to break the deadlock? While it had not yet proved possible to dislodge President Rabbani from his palace in Kabul, the Taliban were convinced that Mullah Omar and his Islamic state were already shaping the future of Afghanistan. It was time to give the leader of that state an appropriate title. That was one way of further undermining the legitimacy of President Rabbani, who was still recognized by the U.N. as the country's leader.

In April 1996, hundreds of mullahs were invited for a meeting in a technical school in Kandahar. There is an audio recording of that meeting that I was able to listen to during my investigations. The man who made the recording also gave me a personal report of what happened.

At that meeting, Mullah Omar hung around next to a wall in the classroom, with an air of slight detachment. He had wrapped a large shawl around his head and was clearly uncomfortable with the fact that he had to sit at the front, with the eyes of about four hundred mullahs on him. Many of them had never seen him before and they stared frankly at the man under that shawl.

Mullah Ehsanullah Ehsan, one of Omar's confidants, opened the meeting. 'I have something very important to say. We all know that the land, the water, and the air belong to Allah. So whose rules should govern Allah's country? The Americans' rules? The Russians' rules? [referring to the countries involved in the jihad, B.D.].'

Rejecting such foreign intervention, everyone in the room called out in unison: 'No, Allah's rules!'

The man at the microphone continued. 'The Prophet said, "If anyone is able to bring back the rules of the Quran in my name, what rank will that person then be given?"'

'The rank of one hundred martyrs!' cried the mullahs.

Then Mullah Ehsanullah Ehsan announced that he wanted to give Mullah Omar the highest title available in Islam, that of Amir al-Mu'minin – comparable to the Pope in the Catholic Church. According to the rules of Islam, you were granted this title either directly by the Prophet Muhammad or by a full *ulema*, a meeting of all mullahs.

The mullah continued. 'By making him the Amir, we are restoring our connection with the Quran, are we not? Do you too want the hundred martyrs? Do you too want the Quran restored? Will you make a pact with this Amir to achieve that? Or not?'

Again, while Mullah Omar sat there uncomfortably on the floor, many of the mullahs called out in unison: 'Yes, that's what we want!'

Mullah Ehsanullah Ehsan concluded his speech with some words about the Taliban's leadership. 'Do you agree it's time to get rid of [President] Rabbani?' he asked the audience. Everyone answered in unison: 'Yes!' 'Is His Excellency Mullah Muhammad Akhund the general Amir of the Muslims?'[61] They replied with one voice once again: 'Yes!'

At this point, Mullah Omar came forward rather slowly to be congratulated by all the mullahs at the meeting, each of whom had to shake his hand. This was not just a handshake; it was seen by many as a *ba'yath*, an oath to the Amir, a promise of infinite support. 'With this oath,' Abdul Rahman Hotaki said, 'any possibility of negotiations with the other groups like Massoud or Rabbani was finished. Now the Taliban had an Amir al Momineen, and they all wanted to be in his presence, near him. He was like an angel.' The only thing the Taliban offered the other parties in the conflict was the possibility of a *ba'yath* for them too, so that they could also become part of the Taliban. Shortly afterwards, the U.N. negotiator Mestiri would propose peace talks, but that went nowhere.

In the school, the first to come up to Mullah Omar was his opponent Mullah Rabbani. He gave his oath and even kissed Mullah Omar's hand. That was a political statement: the idea was that if he bowed down before Mullah Omar, the two would be reconciled once and for all. After his rival had bowed, Mullah Omar said loud and clear, 'From now on you are my deputy.'

Omar went up to the microphone and spoke. 'Now that we've started this movement, we have a big responsibility. If a journalist, an enemy, or an ordinary citizen asks us what our goal is, we tell them that we want to bring back the religion of Allah. That we want the Shariah back.' He continued, 'We have taken on a big responsibility. Today we live as Taliban, tomorrow we may be wounded and the next day we're martyrs. But it is our responsibility to rid our country of corruption and irresponsibility.'

A few weeks later, it turned out the Taliban was not yet done with claiming authority when there was an unexpected follow-up to this meeting. An announcement on the radio told everyone to come to the Eid Gah mosque in Kandahar. What the listeners didn't know was that preparations had already been underway for several weeks for the ceremony that was to take place there. Accompanied by some of the Taliban faithful, Mullah Omar had taken the holy Cloak of the Prophet from a silver chest in another mosque, where the relic had been kept for hundreds of years, and transported it in the trunk of his white Lexus to the Eid Gah mosque.[62]

This was not the first time the cloak had been exploited for political ends. In the 1970s, King Zahir Shah had traveled from Kabul to Kandahar with the plan of showing the Prophet's Cloak to the people as a sign that would bring the country prosperity. However, when the elegantly dressed king stood in front of the silver chest containing the holy Cloak, he was so overcome with emotion that he walked out of the mosque without actually opening the chest.[63]

Fortunately for me, a B.B.C. cameraman was driving around Kandahar on the day of the gathering at the Eid Gah mosque. He hadn't heard the radio announcement and was mystified as to why so many people were at the mosque, standing and cheering. He surreptitiously recorded the scenes. Sitting in his car, he zoomed in on a tall man who stood on the roof of the mosque holding a cloth in front of his face. The cameraman couldn't make out who it was from his car.[64]

This almost accidental film clip is still the only video recording available of Mullah Omar. It shows a tall thin man in a grayish-brown robe holding up the Prophet's Cloak in his hands. For the first time, I was able to get a better look at Omar's narrow face, his wide mouth and his thick, long beard. I couldn't tell from the images whether he was missing an eye. The clip did, however, show the spectators' ecstatic response on seeing Mullah Omar with the Cloak. Men threw their turbans at the stage and tried to touch the holy Cloak. It looked as if some spectators fainted.

———— • ————

President Rabbani in Kabul responded almost immediately. Via the medium of the main radio station in the capital – which he still controlled at that point – he proclaimed that as the president, *he* was the only true leader of the Islamic state in Afghanistan, not Mullah Omar.[65] According to Rabbani, Islamic rules excluded anyone with a disability from such an exalted title. Rabbani therefore concluded that the designation of the Taliban leader as Amir al-Mu'minin should be declared invalid.

That same day, President Rabbani drove to the luxury Continental Hotel in western Kabul where a ceremony was being held for the confirmation of his presidency. The plan was also to announce officially that his archrival Gulbuddin Hekmatyar had accepted the vice presidency. Together, the two men would take on the Taliban. But just as Rabbani and Hekmatyar were presenting themselves under the chandeliers of the Continental Hotel, the Taliban made their presence felt. Explosives rained down on the city. At least sixty rockets hit strategic targets in Kabul, including Rabbani's home. There were fifteen fatalities and dozens of civilian casualties, something Mullah Omar said he wanted to avoid at all costs.

5

An Inexperienced Leader of an 'Islamic State'
(1996)

Dʊʀɪɴɢ their drives between the office in Haji Ibrahim and Mullah Omar's office in Kandahar in the months before Kabul fell into the hands of the Taliban in September 1996, Mullah Omar had had long conversations with his close colleague Mutasim Agha Jan about what they could expect in Kabul.[1]

Mutasim had joined the movement early on when he was just a young Quran student, and would later go on to become the Taliban's Finance Minister. In 2001 he went into exile in the city of Quetta in Pakistan and tried to surrender to the new president, Hamid Karzai, only to turn up a few years later as the Taliban's financial man. In 2009, Mutasim became embroiled in a conflict with another Taliban member, possibly over a money matter. Snipers were sent after him and he was severely wounded. He was evacuated to a hospital in the Turkish capital

Ankara with the help of the U.N., which saw him as a potential peace negotiator.[2]

I wanted to interview this Mutasim and find out more about Omar's ambitions, but I didn't hold out much hope of that ever happening. He had never met with a Western journalist. When this prominent Taliban member ended up in the hospital in Ankara, journalists waited by the entrance in the hope of speaking to him. It took me six months and the help of several intermediaries to finally get access to him. He eventually agreed to talk to me because he trusted these intermediaries and they had urged him to do so. 'It's a really important book! It's the first book about Mullah Omar – and the last one!' they had told him. I set off for Ankara along with an Italian friend who would be my interpreter. Neither of us knew exactly what to expect. I felt a pang of fear when we were picked up by a brand-new black Mercedes without a license plate. The fear intensified when the Afghan chauffeur started to drive around in circles in the city. What if he was planning to kidnap me? After the interview, when I told the chauffeur about my fears, he said he had also only just arrived in Ankara, did not know the way, and had even briefly gotten completely lost.

My misgivings evaporated when we arrived at Mutasim's luxury home. He came to the gate to let us in. And instead of the one-hour interview we had agreed upon, we talked for two days about his experiences with Mullah Omar. He spoke enthusiastically of his memories of the mullah. He recalled in particular those trips commuting between Haji Ibrahim and Kandahar City. Mullah Omar would pick him up every morning from the hamlet near Haji Ibrahim where he lived. During these journeys, Omar was his old self, making lots of jokes. Once he deliberately almost drove into an electric pole in order to give Mutasim a fright.

I eagerly produced a photo that I had gotten ahold of through strange circumstances and that I thought might be of Mullah Omar. A Dutch photographer who had approached me through Twitter had sent me a snap he had taken during a visit to Jalalabad in 2001, immediately after 9/11. In an Afghan home, he had seen a framed photograph that his Afghan host had rapidly tried to remove once he realized the photographer was examining it. The Dutchman was curious about the mysterious man in the picture, so he had taken a quick snapshot.

When I opened the image in my inbox, I saw a man getting into a pickup truck. He was wearing a *shalwar kameez* under a jacket with large pockets. Although the picture showed him from the side, I thought at once this must be Omar. When I heard Mutasim's stories about Omar, I knew it for certain. This was the second photo of Mullah Omar to have surfaced anywhere that I could consider to be the genuine article.

Mutasim grinned when I showed him the picture. The man getting behind the wheel was undoubtedly Mullah Omar, he said. Mutasim remembered the car. And the fact that Mullah Omar always pushed his seat up close to the steering wheel because he felt more in control of the vehicle that way. 'Driving was his big hobby. He didn't have a driver's license and he had an awful lot of accidents. We didn't want him behind the wheel but, stubborn as he was, he refused to have a chauffeur simply because he enjoyed driving so much. He could often be seen after yet another one of his accidents, waiting impatiently at a garage while they repaired the worst of the damage so that he could continue on his way.'

During their many trips in Omar's car in the months before Kabul was captured, Mutasim repeatedly asked Mullah Omar, 'Are you sure you want to be the leader of Afghanistan?' Neither of them knew Kabul well. The capital had suffered heavily from the lengthy civil war, but it still had a million inhabitants.

'Doesn't the thought of such a big city and all the responsibilities that come with that worry you?' Mutasim asked his boss. By then, Mutasim had already been the Taliban's 'treasurer' for a year and he'd found even that hard going. Yet he did not see the slightest hint of doubt in Mullah Omar, sitting behind the wheel as always.

'Since the jihad, no one has been able to create the Islamic state we were promised,' Omar said to him. Now Mullah Omar felt it was up to him to demonstrate that this could be done. He still hoped back then that he would not have to do this alone, that he would eventually get the support of someone like President Rabbani. He thought Muslims should be united in their beliefs. Disunity was not a good thing. But if Rabbani were to put his personal interests before a state in the name of Allah, then the Taliban would have to go it alone, thought Omar.

In the course of their long conversations, Mutasim and Mullah Omar regularly discussed the meaning of dreams. Mutasim told me Europeans often make fun of this. He personally did not believe that *all* dreams have a meaning, but you had to be alert to that possibility: they could be a message from on high. 'Your Jesus also got his supernatural powers in a dream,' said Mutasim, trying to explain it in a way I would understand.

Mullah Omar had a number of dreams. At the start of each day as they met for morning prayers, the Taliban leaders would briefly discuss their dreams.[3] Like many Afghans, Mullah Omar took these dreams seriously.[4] He would ask his Taliban friends for an explanation. Sometimes he brought in a specialist in the interpretation of dreams, such as the respected Mullah Deobandi, one of the few men in Kandahar to have studied at the Deobandi madrassa in far-off India – which was how he got his name. Now he was one of Mullah Omar's most important advisers.[5]

Along with Pir Sahibzada, another prominent figure, Mullah Deobandi had been at the meeting in the school in Kandahar when Mullah Omar's leadership had been questioned by Mullah Rabbani. Emotions ran high at that meeting and the members were divided, but Mullah Deobandi's vote had been the deciding factor and it was partly thanks to him that Mullah Omar was able to remain leader. Mullah Deobandi soon had his own phone-in radio program at Radio Shariat. Afghans would call in about all kinds of dreams, asking, for example, whether they should get a divorce because that night they had dreamed they would divorce their wife. (We also listened to some of these programs, which are stored in the archives of a radio and television station in Kabul.) Mullah Deobandi used the dream interpretation booklets that were incredibly popular in Afghanistan. They explained what it meant if you had seen a river of milk in your dream, for example, or a red rooster or a barefoot man.[6]

Mutasim told me that the battle for the cities of Gereshk and Herat in 1995 was initiated after Mullah Omar had a dream about it. At first the Taliban strategists' plan had been to advance north and capture Kabul, but because of Mullah Omar's dream the army was sent westwards towards the city of Herat instead. As described in the previous chapter, the troops became embroiled in heavy fighting in which Mullah Omar lost his close friend and important military commander Mullah Muhammad. He was very upset by this incident, possibly in part because he had decided to obey his dream and advance on Herat first.

Mutasim also said that Mullah Omar had dreamed about his rise to power: angels with amazingly soft hands had touched him, thereby indicating that he was on the right path. Another dream was about a plump red rooster. It had been given to Omar by his favorite Sufi teacher, Abdul Rahman. A red rooster is an omen that you will achieve a high-ranking position. Mullah Omar saw this dream as a sign that he had been sent by Allah to be Afghanistan's leader. According to Mutasim, he was quite convinced of this.

———— ♦ ————

The craziest stories were told in Kandahar about Kabul, the city where King Zahir Shah had allowed all kinds of alien customs in the 1970s. In their view, little trace remained in Kabul of the devout Afghan society that Mullah Omar had grown up with in the south of the country. Kabul was thought to constitute the biggest challenge for the Taliban, the city that had strayed furthest from the ideals of Islam.[7] Mullah Omar imagined a place that had degenerated into complete decadence, an infidel stronghold. He had heard that students were not even allowed to pray any more during class at the university and that girls would make fun of boys.[8] Moreover, the city was becoming toxic with different political parties constantly obstructing one another rather than working together. This discord had led to the bloody civil war of the past few years and was completely at odds with the ideal of an Islamic state united under one leader – Allah. That is why Omar said the Taliban would never become a political party, but would always remain a movement.[9]

The advance on Kabul did not progress as rapidly as had been the case elsewhere in Afghanistan. In fact, the new alliance of President Rabbani and Gulbuddin Hekmatyar regularly managed to force the Taliban to retreat. This removed any doubt from Mullah Omar's mind that President Rabbani was an apostate: Muslims were not supposed to fight other Muslims. Mullah Omar repeatedly rejected pleas by his highly respected Sufi leaders to cease fighting for the capital and start negotiations with President Rabbani instead.[10]

Impatient at the lack of progress, Mullah Omar decided to show up at the battlefront from time to time and fight in person for his ideals alongside the other Taliban. He would have preferred to have been stationed permanently next to his boys in a trench, as in the days of the struggle against the Soviets, but his commanders would not allow it. They were dismayed to see how he would sometimes run huge risks. 'We need you as a leader, not as a soldier,' they would say after they had brought him back to safety again.

The Taliban entered Kabul on Thursday, September 26, 1996. After months of fighting, their entry met with very little resistance.[11] Radios throughout the city relayed the Taliban's message: 'Now Afghanistan is the home of all Afghans. No foreign power can rule Afghanistan anymore.' This announcement was followed by a long series of Quran verses.[12]

Although hardly any of the Taliban soldiers knew their way around Kabul, that didn't stop them marching through the largely deserted streets carrying their white flags. They were heading for Gul Khana, the presidential palace at the heart of the city, but some of the soldiers lost their way and had to ask for directions: 'Where's the palace?' Others made for the key government offices, the national radio station and other strategic buildings, which they occupied. American journalists reported mixed reactions. Some people cheered while others looked very worried. What did these strangers from the villages want in the city? What were these fundamentalists doing here? An American reporter interviewed one woman out on the streets in a burka, who said she was glad the fighting had stopped. 'Right now I don't care what they [the Taliban] make me wear,' she added.[13] According to the Taliban's own newspaper, the capital's inhabitants were so overjoyed to see the victors that they showered the soldiers with flowers, as is the custom when pilgrims return from the hajj, the sacred pilgrimage to Mecca.

What is undisputed is that the Taliban gave the Red Cross permission that same day to bring food convoys into the badly battered city. By then, long queues of traffic had built up heading north as government officials and President Rabbani's militias fled Kabul. They were heading for the verdant valleys of Istalif and Panjshir, which Rabbani's Northern Alliance still controlled.

The capture of Kabul was not really a day of celebration for Mullah Omar as shortly before then he had received a message that another one of his key army commanders had been killed. This time it was Mullah Borjan, who he considered one of his best friends. He had spoken to Borjan every day on his walkie-talkie, discussing the fighting and instructing this senior military commander to behave himself.[14] He said that with good reason.

Earlier that year, Haji Bashar had picked Borjan up from the hospital in Quetta and given him a lift to Kandahar. The B.B.C. Pashto journalist Daud Junbish was in the car with them. While Haji Bashar spoke with deep respect about Mullah Omar as their 'spiritual leader', the loudspeakers blasted out music, which was forbidden by the mullah. 'You're from Europe, so I'm playing some music for you,' Haji Bashar told the journalist. 'I know you find it pretty boring here in Kandahar.' Only when it was time to pray did Haji Bashar turn the volume down slightly. Mullah Borjan did nothing to stop this; he just sat there relaxing with his feet up on the dashboard.

Six months later, the Taliban were close to capturing Kabul when Mullah Borjan was hit by a sniper on the road to Jalalabad. He died on the spot. Mullah Omar was in such deep mourning that he didn't eat for three days, according to one of his ministers.[15] I still see people visiting Borjan's grave in Kandahar (in the cemetery where Mullah Omar's father is also buried). A woman driven to desperation because her baby wouldn't stop crying hoped that if she prayed at the grave of 'the strong, good commander' Borjan, her baby would be cured.

International reports on the fall of the Afghan capital were dominated by stories of a gruesome murder allegedly committed by the Taliban: the death of the former Communist Najibullah, who had become president of Afghanistan in 1986. After the Soviet withdrawal, he had held onto power until 1992, when he was deposed by President Rabbani. Since then, he had been staying in the basement of the U.N. office, where he was left in peace. Now he and his brother had been hanged from a lamppost in the city center. For many in the West, the video images of this grisly execution soon came to epitomize the barbaric nature of the fundamentalist Taliban regime.

Abdul Rahman was with Mullah Omar when the news of Najibullah's death reached the 'Amir'. That night Mullah Omar was feeling ill, and he lay on a bed in his office with his back turned towards the other men in the room with him. Abdul Rahman had been ordered against his will to leave his job at the Department of Transport in Kandahar for a position at the Ministry of Transport in Kabul. He wanted to discuss this with Omar, so he went to his office. There he heard what had happened in Kabul. 'As I walked to Mullah Omar's room, the initial reaction from the men hanging around there was that this murder must be the work of the Pakistani secret service. There was a lot of mistrust among the Taliban about Pakistan interfering in our country,' Abdul Rahman told me.

Mullah Omar, who was still mourning his friend Borjan, distanced himself from what had happened, Abdul Rahman saw. 'I didn't do it. Who did it?' he lamented as he reclined on his bed. 'Nobody at the office seemed to know what had happened in Kabul,' said Abdul Rahman. Was this the work of one of their fighters or of one of President Rabbani's 'heretics'? Mullah Omar was no fan of Najibullah but he hadn't wanted the man bumped off like this by a bunch of soldiers.

'Get the head of the law court to do what he is supposed to do, please,' Abdul Rahman heard Mullah Omar say; perhaps legal arguments could be used to legitimize the murder. Shariah law would never allow a man to be killed who had not shown any resistance (though Mullah Omar himself had committed a crime by shooting Nadir Shah in 1994). One week after Najibullah's murder, Mullah Omar's Minister of Foreign Affairs announced in the local media that a judicial investigation would be started to find the perpetrators. However, I have never been able to find the results of that investigation. Later on, Abdul Rahman spoke to the judge, who told him that he had had no idea what he should do.

Afterwards, several sources claimed that Najibullah had already been in contact with the Taliban. A U.N. guard who had visited Najibullah shortly before he had been killed confirmed to me that Najibullah had not been afraid of the Taliban and had not wanted to flee Kabul either. A colleague of his, Eckart Schiewek, who worked for the U.N. in Kabul at the time, told me that Najibullah himself had admitted that he had a deal with the Taliban. Later, the bodyguards Tokhi and Jakfar, who had protected the former president for years, saw how Najibullah and his brother left with the Taliban without putting up a struggle.

Some said Najibullah had made a deal with Mullah Omar's most important commander Mullah Borjan, who was then on the point of capturing the capital. Telegrams sent by the U.S. embassy in Islamabad report that Borjan had apparently told Mullah Rabbani that the former president Najibullah should 'just' be arrested and then be brought to trial. Abdul Rahman Hotaki's story suggests that this was what Mullah Omar had expected as well.

It was also suggested that Mullah Rabbani, Mullah Omar's eternal rival within the Taliban, was behind Najibullah's execution. People said that he'd ordered the execution because of a long-standing family vendetta.[16] The American diplomatic telegrams also mention this: one stated that Mullah Rabbani did not want a judicial procedure for Najibullah because the Communist had killed both Rabbani's brother and his father. He wanted revenge. The Americans claim that the conflict between Rabbani and Borjan ended in a fierce argument about the former president. It was even alleged that Mullah Rabbani was behind the death of Mullah Borjan because Rabbani wanted to prevent former president Najibullah from being brought to trial.[17]

———— • ————

The capture of the ravaged city of Kabul did not bring an end to the fighting in Afghanistan. The fighting could only stop once every Afghan was a subject of the Islamic state as far as Mullah Omar was concerned (some would say it was an obsession of his). And that was not the case. President Rabbani and Gulbuddin Hekmatyar may have been driven out of Kabul, but Rabbani still controlled five provinces in the north and he was based only thirty miles outside of the capital. Massoud, his Defense Minister, still presented a formidable military challenge for the Taliban and was constantly threatening to drive them out of Kabul.[18] As long as that threat persisted, the Taliban maintained a state of emergency.

Meanwhile, Mullah Omar stayed behind in Kandahar. He initially left the day-to-day management of affairs in Kabul to his deputy, Mullah Rabbani, who moved into the presidential palace vacated by his namesake, the expelled President Rabbani. Nearly all the mullahs who had led the Taliban movement in Kandahar over the past few years were now also abruptly sent to Kabul. On the whole, these mullahs, many of whom had little experience in government and some of whom were very young, were not keen on a new job as minister. All they knew was how to teach the Quran and how to fight in the trenches around Kandahar; they were barely able to write their own signature. But they had little choice.[19]

These newly appointed ministers brought with them a more informal atmosphere, as the government officials (most of whom stayed on at the ministries under the new regime) were soon to discover. The civil servants were surprised to see their new turbaned bosses remove the chairs from meeting rooms and chuck cushions into a corner. From now on, meetings would be held sitting on those cushions. Many of the mullahs were moving to Kabul for the first time, so they slept and ate at the ministries as well. Others preferred to meet their colleagues at home rather than at the office. They also walked around Kabul rather than use an official car, because there were so few vehicles available in the devastated city and the price of gas had skyrocketed. Many Kandahari mullahs were skeptical about the wild metropolis of Kabul, as they saw it. But others were more hypocritical: they abused their power and forced city girls (famous for their reputed beauty) to marry them.

The first government officials to notice a more significant change of course were the employees in the Ministry of Defense. The new minister here was Mullah Obaidullah, who came from distant Uruzgan. One of the first decisions he had to take concerned the new army uniforms. He immediately rejected the proposed design of tight-fitting pants and short shirts, saying, 'Everyone must wear the *shalwar kameez*. At least that hides the men's behinds properly, as the Shariah requires.'[20]

Although Mullah Omar had remained behind in Kandahar, as the Taliban movement's spiritual leader he continually bombarded the ministers in Kabul with decrees and radio announcements on what had to be done in Kabul and the rest of Afghanistan. He never moved to the capital, though; some say this was because he was afraid of being killed.

From the newspaper articles and interviews, I see evidence that Mullah Omar and his team of untrained mullahs tried to start rebuilding a city that was in shambles. There was hardly any electricity, for example, and Mullah Omar was desperate to get it up and running again. Some generators were connected up, with prominent announcements in the Taliban newspaper every time this happened as it was seen as a sign of progress.

Around this time, calls started appearing in newspapers, not just in Afghanistan but also in Germany, Canada, and the U.S., for educated Afghan refugees to return home and put their skills to use in rebuilding the country. The renowned Afghan physician Wardak, who was living in India, got a phone call asking him to return to Afghanistan as soon as possible. He was initially deployed in a military hospital in Kandahar because the Taliban felt he was badly needed there.[21]

Wardak told me he would never forget the first time he met Omar. The Taliban leader was sitting in a dark corner on the cold ground. 'Is that you?' Wardak asked. 'After all, I'd never seen him before. I didn't know what he looked like – no one did. He wanted to test my ability as a doctor,' Wardak told me. Mullah Omar and Wardak discussed a complaint Omar's mother was suffering from and Wardak made suggestions. Wardak was brought back a week or two later and Omar hired him.

The Taliban also called on the assistance of the incredibly rich traders in the truck mafia who had been crucial in the movement's early days.[22] 'They must do their duty again,' said Mullah Omar.[23] The Taliban newspapers carried enthusiastic reports on the investments that these men had made in the installation of 10,000 new Siemens phone lines.[24] The traders' trucks were also deployed in large numbers for transporting food and fuel to Kabul.[25] Many Kabul residents soon noticed that both food and fuel had become cheaper under the Taliban regime now that illegal toll collectors on the roads around Kabul had been driven out – as they had before in the south. Kabul Airport was also reopened after having been out of operation for a year due to the civil war.[26]

Even so, Mullah Omar's dream of an ideal Islamic state had to wait. He segregated the women (promising them improvements once the country had been restructured and rebuilt, which would not happen), but paved roads, functional factories, and electricity for all inhabitants were still a long way off. Efforts to impose the Taliban state in Kabul were making slow progress. Omar's priority was the fight for control of the last five provinces, which was taking up much of the available budget. For all Omar's visions of a better Kabul, an American ambassador who visited the capital at that time told me the city felt more like Stalingrad. 'It was very ambitious of the Taliban to think they could make these improvements when they weren't able to govern the city.'[27]

———— ♦ ————

As in 1994, Mullah Omar attached great importance to his jihadists setting an example, but now they would be doing so to all Afghans. They were supposed to exemplify the Islamic virtues at all times, whether or not they were fighting. That hadn't become any easier as the war continued. Omar was very worried by the plundering and rapes that had become the order of the day during the civil war. Especially after the capture of Kabul, many soldiers had defected to the Taliban from Hekmatyar's militias, for example. They did not take the Islamic values so seriously. That was why Mullah Omar insisted on strict observance – even in the metropolis of Kabul – of the rules that he had learnt in the *hujra*. He believed those rules would keep the troops in line and protect the weak in society, especially women.

Responsibility for enforcing these stringent rules was assigned to the Ministry for the Promotion of Virtue and Prevention of Vice, just as President Rabbani had envisioned back in 1992 and as the Taliban had been doing elsewhere since 1994. In provinces such as Kandahar and Uruzgan, the rules fitted seamlessly with local traditions. Mullah Omar expected more trouble in what he considered to be the heathen city of Kabul. He warned his religious police to be extra alert.

All temptations that might lead Kabul's inhabitants astray were to be banned. The Taliban soldiers from the remote villages had never seen photos or statues back home, for example (my translator from Kandahar, who is not a Taliban, still puts a small statuette of an elephant out of sight in the cupboard whenever he has to pray). Now the villagers imbued with these notions were being ordered to take control of Kabul and bring its morals up to their standards. Omar's troops marched through the streets with knives, cutting up any posters depicting people or animals, whether they were advertising washing powder or announcing a meeting with a Sufi leader.

The Taliban also took aggressive action against television, a medium many of the young Vice and Virtue officials from the villages had no first-hand experience of. They hauled TV sets out of people's homes and smashed them to pieces, without really knowing what it was they were destroying. Photography was banned too, with the exception of passport photos. Hiring musicians to liven up a wedding was no longer allowed (although this rule was regularly broken). Cars were stopped and the tapes pulled out of their cassette players and destroyed. Piles of abandoned cassette tapes lined the roads into Kabul. Betting was forbidden, and with it the dog- and cock-fights that had been popular in the park in the center of Kabul. The 'national sport' of *buzkashi* was banned with immediate effect. Even a peaceful game like chess was no longer allowed.

Not all forms of entertainment disappeared. Poetry evenings were still held across the country, with participants competing for trophies. Mullah Omar himself often joined in such events.[28] Musical instruments may have been forbidden but there was still singing, just as in the *hujras*. The *thali* that Omar used to drum on as a boy was still permitted.

Sports like soccer (which was very popular) were not abolished but the players now had to wear long trousers. Spectators were no longer allowed to clap or cheer if a team scored either. In short, it was unacceptable for a crowd to get overexcited. A lot of volleyball was played; Mullah Omar himself often enjoyed a game in the garden of the governor's compound, and any successful shot by the leader would undoubtedly not have been greeted by total silence.[29]

Rules on conduct and clothing came into force for both women and men. According to Mullah Omar's decrees, women had to cover themselves up entirely and were not allowed out on the streets without a male chaperone. The idea was that this would protect them from other men. This chaperone – known as a *maghrem* – could be a woman's husband, son, or father. Often a woman would be accompanied by her young son. Even with a male chaperone, women were not allowed in shops, which was a big change for the women of Kabul.

Men had to have a beard that was at least six weeks old, in imitation of the Prophet Muhammad. They also had to wear a *shalwar kameez* just as he had done. Western clothes, also known as 'Beatles outfits' (T-shirt, pants, sweater, and jacket), were not acceptable, although boys could be seen in Kabul wearing these clothes. Only two groups were exempt from these clothing rules: the traffic police and the pilots of Ariana Airlines, Afghanistan's national aviation company, as they wore uniforms.[30]

Omar's regime required men to pray five times a day, which infuriated many people. Some men would hide in the back of their shops until prayer time had passed. Eventually, the Taliban started to set up roadblocks in an attempt to trap men who were roaming the streets.

Kabul's inhabitants tried all kinds of tricks to circumvent the Taliban's rules. They were soon buying small satellite dishes so they could continue watching TV secretly. Photography also proved difficult to ban, since taking passport photos was still permitted.[31] Afghan photographers put a great deal of effort into these photos. Taliban fighters would have their photo taken wearing a black turban and with a plastic flower in their Kalashnikov, standing in front of a poster showing a clichéd Swiss landscape.[32] Affluent women (also outside of Kabul) liked to have their photo taken in their own homes, sometimes by foreign photographers.[33]

The American diplomat Bradford Hanson saw how the rules were enforced in both Kandahar and Kabul, and was struck by the differences between the two cities. The Taliban's rules did not have much impact on daily life in Kandahar because people were already used to most of these restrictions, so there was less resistance. The Taliban also trusted the people of Kandahar more than the residents of Kabul. According to Hanson, in the capital the Taliban acted more like an occupying force. You barely saw any women on the streets, whereas women could be seen everywhere in Kandahar, sometimes even unaccompanied by a man.[34]

———— ◆ ————

Women undoubtedly suffered the most from all these measures. As long as the state of emergency remained in force, women had to stay indoors as much as possible, because Kabul was full of conservative soldiers from the provinces who had never seen a woman other than their mother or sisters and were quite unused to women appearing in public. Both the troops and the women had to be protected from the uncomfortable situations this could cause.

That was all part of Mullah Omar's worldview, which had its roots in Deh Rawod and Haji Ibrahim, where women played no role in public life, despite the Islamic rules that formally gave them more freedom.

I still never see any women about when I drive through these areas. It is unheard of for a woman to have a job there. Men decide all aspects of a woman's life in this patriarchal society: she has no money of her own and has no right to inherit. The women go along with whatever their menfolk decide – they have no choice.[35] Yet the Islamic Hanafi jurisprudence (which the Taliban adhere to) states, for example, that women should receive their bride-price themselves, not the men, and that women can inherit, although this hardly happened at all under the Taliban rule.[36]

I was fortunate enough to get to know Bibi, the wife of the businessman Issa from Haji Ibrahim, through my conversations with him and his son Ahmad. She had known Mullah Omar's wife, sister, and mother in Haji Ibrahim. These women visited Bibi in her home in Kandahar after Omar came to power. Their lives were very different from hers. Mullah Omar was a real village mullah living in his own little world, whereas Issa and his wife had moved on from that long ago. Bibi still well remembered the conversations she had had with those women.

Mullah Omar's female relatives were overawed by what for them was the big city of Kandahar. It was a real adventure. It was just twenty minutes away in the taxi but it felt like another world to them. During their visit, they looked around in amazement. Did Bibi really have an entire house, with multiple rooms and multiple stories? At mealtimes they were given cutlery, a new experience for them. In fact they didn't use the cutlery; instead, they would take a piece of *naan* and use it to scoop up the rice in the traditional fashion. When they had finished the bread, they just ate with their hands.

The women were very impressed with Bibi's iron. They wanted to know how she got it hot. They had heard of electricity but had no idea how it worked. Bibi recalled how they had stared at the lightbulb glowing in the middle of the room. When Bibi asked her to turn off the light, Mullah Omar's wife flapped her veil at the bulb as if it were a candle.

It was a huge contrast with their lives in Haji Ibrahim. They told Bibi proudly how they kept guard over their little mud-brick home. It turned out that Mullah Omar's wife was a sniper, and had once shot a snake dead with a Kalashnikov after it got into the house.

When Omar's sister was picked up the next day by her husband, she had to lie down on the back seat so that no one would catch a glimpse of her eyes under her burka. When I asked whether the sister had a problem with this, Bibi shook her head. On the contrary, she was proud that her husband wanted to keep his wife hidden from sight.

Later, I heard how complicated it was for Mullah Omar if one of the three women needed to visit the doctor – who was often a man. Once, Dr. Wardak saw a jeep in the parking lot of the military hospital in Kandahar with a rather pathetic-looking burka-clad heap on the back seat. Then his phone rang. It was Mullah Omar. 'That's my mother,' he said. 'You can't look at her but you need to help her.' Ill as she was, Omar forbade perhaps the one man who could cure her to touch his mother. Dr. Wardak claims he obeyed these orders. He spoke to Mullah Omar's mother and prescribed drugs based on that conversation, after which the jeep left.

Mullah Omar's intention with the new rules of conduct for women was to ensure that the women of Kabul ran just as little risk of coming into contact with male strangers as the women in Haji Ibrahim. He thought women were in great danger in the chaotic capital, especially during the state of emergency. But in Kabul, where a decade earlier women had even been able to walk around in miniskirts, many women still had jobs, not just in education and health care but in other sectors too. This was an abomination to Mullah Omar. What horrified him was not only the fact that women were working but also the possibility that a Taliban fighter who needed treatment might encounter men and women working together in the operating theater. So Mullah Omar tried to change this by issuing decrees from Kandahar. Within twenty-four hours, the decision was taken to ban women in Kabul from working with immediate effect for the duration of the state of emergency.

Mullah Omar urged speedy action, but in most cases the measure did not lead to instant change. Some offices kept their female staff on for a while. Women made up a substantial proportion of the health-care workforce in particular, but Omar wanted these women fired as well. This eventually happened in 1997. Taliban fighters went around to the hospitals and drove out the female patients, nurses, cleaners, and doctors, sometimes by force.

This also happened in Kabul's largest hospital by far, known as the 'four-hundred-bed hospital'. Built with money from Pakistan, this hospital offered a standard of care on a par with the best in Asia. The plan was that women would now be treated in a new, central women's hospital. The new place already had beds and mattresses but lacked staff and drugs. A former minister in Rabbani's government who had recently defected to the Taliban sounded the alarm. 'You don't know what you're doing!' he said to Mullah Omar. 'If you only have men working in the hospitals, who's supposed to give the women first aid or help them when they are giving birth? In such a big city, you need female doctors and nurses to look after the women.'[37] But Mullah Omar still had his doubts; he was concerned about the effect of female personnel on the state of mind of his fighters. In the end, a compromise solution was found. Female doctors and nurses were allowed to return to their jobs in the four-hundred-bed hospital but they had to work separately from the men if at all possible. And there was to be no publicity at all surrounding their return, as that might demoralize his soldiers, who believed they were fighting for an Islamic state in which women remained out of sight.[38]

This was the kind of solution that the Taliban would tolerate repeatedly in the years that followed. Mullah Omar was able to consent to this because, unlike the tribal culture in the south where he and many of his fighters had grown up, Islam does not forbid women to work in a profession of their choosing (not only education and health care).[39] Mullah Omar saw the segregation of men and women, as was common in Saudi Arabia, as the practical solution for what he considered to be the unnatural relations between the sexes in Kabul, though he would never implement these rules properly.[40]

Separate rooms in hospitals, offices, and schools was a possible solution.[41] But according to the Taliban it was not always easy to put the theory into practice. The funds were lacking to build the facilities for the segregation of the sexes, as the fight against former president Rabbani's men always took priority. It also took a lot of courage for the Taliban to allow women to work or girls to study, even separately from men. Many conservative leaders from the south didn't know how to relate to women in the workplace. Their presence was tolerated at best, and women always faced the threat of maltreatment or some other form of harassment. This policy of segregation made huge demands on the layout of government buildings and company premises, and on the infrastructure. The Taliban had hoped to introduce separate bus lines for women so that they could travel to work or school without any problems.[42] But this plan was destined never to be implemented as the Taliban did not reserve any money for it. Shuttle buses were used as an interim solution to fetch these women and take them home. The buses had curtains everywhere, covering the windows and shielding the women from the bus driver so that he couldn't see them.

This segregation policy also applied in schools in the capital and elsewhere in Afghanistan. The education system had suffered hugely during the jihad against the Soviet Union and the subsequent civil war. Around two thousand schools had been destroyed during the jihad and thousands of teachers killed. The civil war also did untold damage to the education system. A Swedish study shows what a devastating effect the war had on education. There were 1,844 schools in 1991 but only 864 in 1995. After the many years of fighting, only 39 per cent of the schools had their own building; the rest had to hire premises or teach children in someone's home. This was partly because the Americans had withdrawn their financial support. After the jihad ended, all aid from Western countries to Afghanistan was reduced, including funding for girls' education. In 1995, UNESCO reported that 95 per cent of the population was unable to read or write.[43]

While girls under twelve had attended the *hujra* together with boys before the jihad and civil war, now the official rule was that they could only continue their studies after the age of twelve if they did so in a class without boys. In practice, the Taliban barely made any investments in education to facilitate this segregation. In Kabul, female teachers were sent home, which meant girls were unable to get schooling. Promises were made that girls would be able to go to school again once the Islamic state had been established throughout Afghanistan. All this meant only a small fraction of Afghan children had access to the segregated public education system under the Taliban regime.

Meanwhile, girls' schools were set up by courageous women all over Afghanistan, and tolerated by the Taliban. In Kabul, which had even fewer segregated classrooms for pupils than the rest of the country, various forms of home schooling popped up. Small groups of children were taught in a family's home, either by hired teachers or by the parents. Sometimes girls and boys were taught separately, but not always. Despite all these initiatives, only between 10 and 25 per cent of children went to school, most attending the poorly functioning public schools, although there were a few better schools available, funded by a Swedish aid organization.[44]

For many women and girls, the situation under the Taliban regime remained desperate. Shortly after Kabul was captured a video clip surfaced that showed a woman in a burka being severely beaten by a Taliban soldier because her ankles were still visible. There were other reports of brutal maltreatment on the streets by the religious policemen (often young men from remote villages) charged with enforcing the Taliban's strict code.[45] The issue was often a failure to comply with the clothing rules, with punishments for even the most minor 'offenses'. But neither were the police prepared to overlook other infringements. Men and women found talking to one another, people discovered setting off fireworks, in possession of photos, or listening to music: you could be beaten up for any of these infractions. It is therefore hardly surprising that by this point the inhabitants of Kabul had a great fear of the morality police. In 1998, a human rights organization interviewed 160 women. Around 70 per cent of them said they had been detained for an hour or so at some point for not wearing their burka properly, and that this had involved physical abuse.[46]

Mullah Omar and the other Taliban leaders were very concerned about the intimidating behavior of the religious police in Kabul.[47] The violence on the streets was having a negative effect on Omar's reputation. Sometimes the Taliban tried to deny the abuses by ascribing them to provocation by former president Rabbani's men. Mullah Omar regularly published decrees in which he condemned certain incidents involving his religious police, with a detailed description of the incident in question. He would threaten the men involved with harsh punishments.[48]

Honorable men/Taliban fighters,

Peace and Allah's blessing be to you.

Do not be heartless and do not misuse public money. For example, the Taliban arrested two people for theft in Qeshla-e-Jadeed. Both men were beaten to death by them. The High Court ordered the payment of two billion Afghani from public funds as a blood debt (de-yet). This is just one example. Similar incidents have occurred in which people were beaten with cables.

The High Court has decided that such punishments require permission from a religious leader (imam) or a commander (*Amir*). Without that permission, anyone who misbehaves in such a way will be subjected to the same punishment. I will not tolerate these kinds of beatings. I do not have the authority to change the Shariah [which forbids unjustified beatings, B.D.]. Therefore be warned!

Peace be with you,

Servant of Islam,
Commander of the faithful.

Mullah Mohammad Omar (Mujahid)[49]

Behind the scenes, Omar also reprimanded Mullah Turabi, the minister responsible for the religious police (this important tribal figure was still a prominent personality in the Taliban insurgency, in spite of his questionable reputation). But despite arguments between the two mullahs that escalated into screaming matches, Mullah Omar eventually backed down and Turabi was not fired. Abdul, the man in charge of Kandahar Airport, was present at one of these screaming matches. Mullah Omar called Turabi every name under the sun and refused to let him into his office. Turabi had to stand in the doorway.

Mullah Omar was worried about the religious policemen's behavior not only because it was bad for his image. Mawlawi Shahabuddin Delawar, one of the most senior judges in Kabul at the time of the Taliban, who I'd met during my investigations in Doha, told me Mullah Omar was genuinely disappointed in how the morality police were acting.[50] 'He actually wanted to use the Shariah to improve the rule of law in society compared with the situation under the tribal Pashtunwali.' While the Pashtunwali could be very arbitrary, the Shariah stipulated that you had to have witnesses, for example, to prove adultery. This was a significant constraint on an individual's power compared with the traditional procedures.

While Islam had spread to Afghanistan very early on, the Pashtunwali rules remained dominant. Mullah Omar believed he had been given the divine task of putting an end to tribal law for good. His Islam was egalitarian: everyone was protected by the law and no one was above the law. He often referred to the story told of the Prophet Muhammad, who had said that he would not make an exception even for his daughter Fatima: if she was found guilty of theft, she too would have to lose her hand.

Mullah Omar issued decrees in which he tried to forbid tribal practices. Murders could no longer be compensated by donating two daughters to the victim's family. Widows could no longer be married off. This was what had happened to Omar's mother, giving him a stepfather with whom he got along badly. Often, Mullah Omar spoke of Muslims' duty to care properly for orphans. But these more 'modern' Shariah rules were only introduced on a piecemeal basis. The Islamic rulebook of Afghanistan (the Hanafi rules) allows women to work, including in senior positions in the government, for example, but Mullah Omar let the Pashtunwali prevail here, and he never appointed a woman in his government, let alone as a minister.

It should also be noted that Mullah Omar was certainly not opposed in principle to harsh corporal punishments such as beating, amputation, or stoning. His anger at how the religious police were behaving was mainly directed at the lack of evidence and the arbitrary nature of the punishments. If someone's guilt had been established through the proper course of justice, he had no problem with applying the tough punishments that he had been taught were part of the Shariah.

It is unclear how often extreme punishments such as stoning were applied in practice under the Taliban regime. There is little evidence for the common assumption that executions and stonings were being held every Friday in large stadiums in cities such as Kabul and Kandahar, and that local people were forced to attend.[51] Mutawakil said that in the Taliban time the severe Shariah punishments such as executions were mainly intended as a deterrent and were hardly ever carried out in the end. In the Islamic state that Omar had in mind, only the courts could impose the death penalty for adultery, for example, and they rarely did so since proving it required a great deal of evidence. On three occasions after a court had passed the death sentence, Mullah Omar wrote to the victims asking whether they would be willing to forgive the perpetrator. It was the victims themselves who demanded that the punishment should be carried out in these cases, said Mutawakil.

Alex Strick van Linschoten, a researcher at King's College, London, who speaks and reads Pashto, examined all the available Taliban media from the 1990s to determine how many executions and stonings had actually taken place. He published the results a couple of years ago: 'I might have missed two or three executions in the countryside but they definitely were not taking place at a rate of one a week, and not even one every six months.' According to his tally, the Taliban had carried out six stonings between 1996 and 2001.[52]

———— ◆ ————

Mullah Omar was a rather invisible leader right from the start – both to his supporters and to the people of Afghanistan. He was nearly always to be found in his 'broom cupboard' in the governor's house in Kandahar, where he occasionally received local guests in the early days. He was almost never spotted outside Kandahar. Nobody had a photograph of him and there was no question of him appearing on television – a medium he considered to be forbidden by Islam.

Omar's anonymity sometimes led to bizarre situations in Kandahar. For example, once he was driving alone back to his home in Haji Ibrahim long after the curfew had started when he was stopped by the police. The police officer didn't recognize Mullah Omar and made him spend the night in jail because that was the rule. One of his ministers had to come and pick him up the next day.[53]

The mystery surrounding his person was even more of a problem in and around Kabul, which he probably only visited once or twice in his life. The fact they had never seen him made the residents there very receptive to rumors. These ranged from descriptions of Omar as a monstrous beast with a tail to assertions that he didn't really exist at all – he was an invention of Pakistan, Saudi Arabia, or the U.S.[54] Stories also circulated – and these sound more plausible to me – that Mullah Omar was afraid to leave Kandahar as he feared losing control of the city and falling prey to the leaders who had joined former president Rabbani.

Mullah Omar had initially wanted nothing to do with radio. He had barely listened to it in his younger days as there was always the risk of inadvertently hearing some music. Only when he started driving back and forth between Haji Ibrahim and Kandahar with his colleague Mutasim did he start listening to the transistor radio in Mutasim's car. They would listen to the B.B.C. Pashto service together, which broadcast a lot of news about Afghanistan and Pakistan.

That was where Mullah Omar first heard items about himself and the Taliban. He soon became gripped by curiosity and started asking Mutasim to update him every few hours at the office with a report on what news he had heard about Omar on the radio. Later, Mutasim was even ordered to bring his radio into the office, on condition that it should be turned off as soon as any music started. In the end, Mullah Omar became so addicted to Mutasim's radio that Mutasim had to hand it over.

It is not entirely clear when Mullah Omar realized that he could use the radio as a medium for spreading his message. At any rate, the Taliban took control of Radio Kabul almost immediately when they captured the capital. The radio station was renamed the Voice of Shariat. All music programs were replaced by endless recitations of verses from the

Quran. From early on there was also a popular talk show where listeners could send in questions about their dreams for the prominent mullah, Deobandi. Although this was in principle a phone-in show, because there were so few telephones people mainly submitted their questions in letters sent to Deobandi's studio in Kandahar. Each week, this mullah explained how best to live your life as a good Muslim, namely, by keeping to the rules advocated by the Taliban.

The Taliban troops also took possession of the national television studios in Kabul, but of course they never used them for broadcasting. I was told later by a current Taliban leader in Doha that they carried out weekly checks to make sure everything in the studios was still functioning, as they were considering restarting broadcasts once the state of emergency was lifted.[55]

Mullah Nizami soon became another prominent figure on the Voice of Shariat, alongside Mullah Deobandi. Before the arrival of the Taliban, he had enjoyed national fame as a radio star during the jihad against the Soviet Union, when Radio Kabul was still called The Voice of the Mujahideen. When I met him in Kabul in 2012, he told me that he had initially broadcast his programs from Kabul but that Mullah Omar soon made him move to Kandahar. He would visit the Taliban leader every day in the governor's building.

'He sat there in the smallest room I'd ever seen, but it *was* in the emirate's palace,' said Nizami. 'I thought he was a real angel. He had put an end to the civil war but he remained so humble.'

Nizami continued, 'From that day on, I would sit with Mullah Omar every morning making notes on what I would say on the radio that afternoon. He often thanked me for being prepared to work with him. 'It's high time we let ourselves be heard so that we can disprove the rumors spread by our enemies,' he told me. Mullah Omar saw the Taliban as neutral peacekeeping forces who wanted to put a stop to the conflict between the belligerent parties. He wanted to disarm them and then introduce the Shariah throughout the country.'

It wasn't only Nizami's voice spreading Mullah Omar's message over the airwaves; Omar also regularly spoke on the radio himself. He would call in to Nizami's studio on a crackling walkie-talkie or satellite phone, which made him difficult to understand at times. 'The Saint on the satellite telephone,' the British journalist Michael Griffin called him, describing Mullah Omar's radio performances in his book *Reaping the Whirlwind*.[56] 'Behave well,' Mullah Omar would often say, adding, 'Young men who don't keep to these rules about beards will be thrown out of the army.'[57] And so the people of Kabul could get to know him a little after all.

6

Looking for International Recognition
(1996)

As the Taliban saw it, the capture of Kabul meant that the Afghans themselves had regained control of Afghanistan for the first time in a long while. And they thought it should stay that way. Foreign powers had been meddling in the country's affairs since the late 1970s. After the invasion by the Soviet Union in 1979, not just the Soviets but also Pakistan and the U.S. had tried to steer the situation in Afghanistan to suit their own agenda. That had cost the lives of hundreds of thousands of people and led to the complete disintegration of society in both the cities and the countryside. The Taliban saw foreign interference as a curse. It was important for everyone to realize that the Taliban had emerged 'from within' the country. 'The hands of outsiders have been cut off from our country,' wrote the *Shariat Weekly*, the Taliban's English-language mouthpiece. 'Our movement's successful capture of Kabul is proof that Afghans want to manage their own affairs again. This is a national movement, driven by Islam.'[1]

This emphasis on national independence was directed not so much at the two Cold War superpowers, Russia (the former U.S.S.R.) and the U.S., as at Pakistan. Ever since the end of the Second World War, Afghanistan had had a complicated relationship with its neighbor. Pakistan saw Afghanistan as a potential springboard for Indian aggression and therefore constantly sought to influence domestic politics in Afghanistan.

Its influence reached a peak when the U.S. started using Pakistan as the channel for its military aid to the Afghan jihadists fighting the Soviet Union. Furnished with large quantities of weapons and cash, Pakistan could decide at will which groups to support. At first, it bet on Gulbuddin Hekmatyar's party at a time when the leader was still a powerful player. Pakistani soldiers who had fought against India in Kashmir trained in Hekmatyar's camps.

With the rise and success of the Taliban in 1994, Pakistan widened the scope of its support. Both the Pakistani government and various Islamic groups increasingly sought contact with Mullah Omar's Taliban. Also, there is the mysterious I.S.I. I have tried to nuance the 'Pakistan created the Taliban' narrative, but the facts concerning the help provided by these once so powerful I.S.I. agents are murky and very much hidden from sight (or perhaps they did not meddle much; this is unclear).

It is, however, clear that after promoting Pakistani influence during the jihad, the U.S. embassy was focused on monitoring potential Pakistani influence. Dozens of cables covered the topic, mentioning anecdotal evidence like the I.S.I. trucks, 'sealed off' but with identifiable number plates, that crossed the border at Torkham.[2] One Taliban source claimed that the I.S.I. was behind the truck mafia who, as we saw earlier, were in close contact with the Taliban.[3] The C.I.A. also wrote that a method they had used during the jihad was being used again: the I.S.I. deployed trucks belonging to private companies to drive supplies into Afghanistan.[4]

Then there is the narrative of the Pakistani government elite in Islamabad. Their encounters with the Taliban did not always go as Pakistan had hoped. In general the Taliban leaders were pleased with the offer of support, but they were not at all interested in the political quid pro quo that Pakistan wanted. The influential Pakistani officer Colonel Imam experienced this firsthand. He was often in Afghanistan, since he was still responsible for the consulate in Herat. He behaved like a king: Australian researcher David Mansfield saw this firsthand on numerous occasions when they both flew in from Islamabad on U.N. flights. But this attitude towards civilians didn't necessarily work with the senior Taliban, it seemed. Colonel Imam claimed to have had many meetings with the Taliban leader (which is probably an exaggeration, since I did not find many people who could recall these meetings); Mullah Omar always listened in silence and seemed understanding, but 'would never change his decisions. [...] He only implemented his own orders.'[5]

This was also a conclusion in one of the many cables from the U.S. embassy in Islamabad.[6] In 1996 the embassy wrote how Pakistani officials from the Foreign Affairs ministry 'consistently complained' to them about the 'willfulness of the Taliban'. 'None of the Taliban, as far as we can make out, is very controllable,' one of the American diplomats wrote. The Pakistani president Benazir Bhutto said that she had given the I.S.I. carte blanche to assist the Taliban financially, but Mullah Omar had ignored the service's military and political advice. 'They were incredibly stubborn,' the I.S.I. told her.[7]

The Pakistani ambassador Iftikhar Murshed, whom I spoke to during my research in Islamabad, also recalled how frustrating meetings with Mullah Omar could be. He had visited the Taliban leader in 1996. 'It was actually almost embarrassing how indifferent Mullah Omar appeared towards me,' said Murshed, an observation he makes in his book too.[8] 'I was with him for an hour and a half, during which he spoke for five minutes at most.' Omar was primarily interested in military matters, and much less in politics. 'When I started talking about peace negotiations with President Rabbani, who was still in Kabul at that point, he fell silent. 'I'll talk to my *shura*' – that was all I could get out of him.'

I heard of a similar experience in Karachi when I spoke with former Pakistani minister Moinuddin Haider, who had had a number of meetings with Mullah Omar, partly at the request of the U.S. 'We always had an enjoyable time. Mullah Omar was a good man who I liked a lot. But as soon as we got onto political matters, he'd clam right up. The Americans thought I'd get more out of him as a Pakistani than they would, but that was a complete illusion.'

Pervez Musharraf, another former president of Pakistan, wrote in his memoirs that relations with the Taliban leader were never easy; in fact, they were 'quite uncomfortable'.[9] This was despite 'the strong ethnic and family links with the Taliban', wrote Musharraf, referring to the Pashtun, who lived on both the Afghan and Pakistani sides of the border.

Given all this, the claims of some Pakistanis that they should be seen as the founding fathers of the Taliban movement must be treated with skepticism. One source of such a claim was Samiul Haq, the head of the Haqqania madrassa in Pakistan where Mullah Omar had in fact never studied (as I discussed in Chapter 1). The Pakistani Islamic leader Fazal Rahman also enjoyed boasting about his relations with Mullah Omar, as I heard from a source close to Omar. The media frequently referred to Fazal as the father of the Quran students. But when Fazal Rahman visited Mullah Omar in Kandahar in order to explain rather loftily how he should tackle the fighting, Mullah Omar replied, 'What exactly are you doing here? You people support Benazir Bhutto, a female leader with a daughter who's studying in London. You need to focus on getting an Islamic state in Pakistan first.'[10]

Lieutenant-General Hamid Gul, the head of the I.S.I. in the 1980s and another alleged godfather of the Taliban, said when interviewed in his office in Rawalpindi that this sobriquet was somewhat exaggerated.[11] 'When the Taliban emerged on the scene, I did a lot of interviews in the

Pakistani media to express my support. It seems that some journalists and the author Ahmed Rashid assumed then that I had also helped them, that I was supposed to have created the Taliban. But that is complete nonsense and it's led to many unfortunate misunderstandings. I would like to have met Mullah Omar but have never managed to, probably because I had supported Gulbuddin Hekmatyar. Mullah Omar refused to see me.'

There was also a lot of support for the Taliban among ordinary Muslims in Pakistan. During the jihad, collections had been organized in many Islamic countries to raise money for the fight against the Soviet Union. After all, a good Muslim had a duty not just to pay taxes but also to donate money to religious causes such as mosques or Islamic aid organizations. Many Pakistani believers who had given generously to the Afghans during the jihad against the Soviets saw the Taliban as a chance to revive the ideal of an Islamic state, which had lapsed during the civil war between the Afghan warlords. People were magnanimous with their donations, helped by the fact that it was fairly easy to dodge the taxes payable to the corrupt Pakistani government and give your cash to a 'good' Islamic organization.

Mullah Omar's employee Abdul Rahman recalled that many people who wanted to donate money had trouble with what they saw as the Taliban's 'strange, outdated' rules, such as the mandatory thick beards. 'When I told Mullah Omar this, he shook his head.' He knew about these Pakistani requests. Omar replied, 'On Judgment Day, Allah will say, "I gave you the power to let people return to the pure Islam. Why did you allow those deviations [men without beards, B.D.]?" And who will answer then? If you can answer, fine, but I'll have to as well. I'm really not that interested in beards or hair length. But I have to answer to Allah. I'm not out to get as much money as possible. I just need to enforce the Shariah.'

The big man behind the Taliban donations was the Pakistani mufti Rashid Ahmad of the Binori madrassa in Karachi. His Al Rashid Trust, with forty branches in Afghanistan and Pakistan, collected money not just for Afghanistan but also for other Islamic groups, for example, in Chechnya.[12] A mullah who acted as an agent for this aid organization in Afghanistan said that there was close consultation with Mullah Omar on how to spend the money. It was used for all manner of things: mosques for travelers along the main roads between Kandahar and Kabul, bakeries in the capital, sewing machines for war widows, segregated clinics with male and female doctors, thousands of sheep and goats to celebrate the end of Ramadan, and a computer center in Kandahar.[13] This Al Rashid agent also described Mullah Omar as stubborn. 'He wouldn't listen when I gave him advice on his leadership style. I was allowed to donate money, and that was it.'[14] When I spoke with the aid worker in Islamabad, he told me Mullah Omar kept a close watch on all these donations. 'He was definitely somewhat mistrustful of our organization. Some Afghans thought we wanted to steal marble from their quarries and sell it to foreigners.'

The aid organization Al Rashid was put on the U.N.'s terrorist list soon after the 9/11 attacks because of its connections with Al Qaeda, Osama bin Laden or the Taliban. The Pakistani government froze its bank accounts at the request of the U.S.[15] Al Rashid filed lawsuits and some Pakistani banks continued to support the organization.

———— ◆ ————

The notion that the Taliban were actually a continuation of the jihad against the Soviet Union encouraged solidarity that was more than just financial. Tens of thousands of Afghan and Pakistani youths had received military training in the border area between the two countries during the struggle against the Soviets – in collaboration with the I.S.I. and the C.I.A. Many of them had spent the civil war that followed the jihad without work in refugee camps in Pakistan. After 1994, many joined the

Taliban, some permanently and others temporarily, in some cases just for the school vacation.

Although the Taliban's Afghan opponents such as Rabbani and Hekmatyar called this exodus an example of Pakistani interference in Afghanistan's affairs, the Pakistani border guards said they could (or would) do little about movements between the two countries in this impenetrable border region. In 2000, the Pakistani Minister for the Interior Moinuddin Haider asked Mullah Omar to make less use of the fighters from Pakistan so as to avoid giving the impression that Pakistan was meddling in Afghanistan. To which Mullah Omar replied, 'I don't invite them. Lots of your fighters support us and come here voluntarily. They want to help us.'

———————◆———————

Mullah Omar's approach to Pakistan – accepting aid but not interference – applied to other countries too. For example, in 1996 he sent a Taliban delegation to Germany to ask for development aid and recognition of his regime. Germany had made substantial investments in Afghanistan in the days of King Zahir Shah, for example, in a cotton mill just outside Kandahar, which had fallen into disrepair after the civil war.[16] The Taliban hoped that the Germans would come to their aid again and help rebuild this factory, and the country as a whole.[171]

Mullah Omar took the same attitude towards the U.S. He knew America as an old ally from the days of the jihad against the Soviet Union. As far as he was concerned, they had spent years fighting the Communists together. The C.I.A. had given large quantities of weapons to combatants like his group in Haji Ibrahim, including the famous Stinger rockets that had brought down many a Soviet plane. Some jihadists from those days had even been invited to the White House as 'freedom fighters' by President Reagan.

Mullah Omar thought that the Taliban's efforts at that time to create an Islamic state in Afghanistan were precisely what the Americans wanted. He expected compliments from the Americans. After all, in 1996 he had achieved what the Americans had also been aiming for with their support of the jihad.[18]

Shortly after the capture of Kabul, it seemed as if Mullah Omar's hopes of American support were not in vain. Initially, diplomats working for President Bill Clinton responded positively to the Taliban's success. They recognized that the movement had control of Kabul and large parts of the country. According to America's diplomats in Islamabad, 'the United States has a long history with the Afghans' and they said they would view the Taliban as 'the new authority in Kabul'.[19] 'We hope you will soon propose an envoy who can represent your government in Washington,' ran the message.[20] The Americans reported that they were considering opening a U.S. embassy in Kabul soon, 'once the security situation allows'.[21]

The Americans praised the Taliban's ideas 'on paper' to give the different nationalities and ethnic groups in Afghanistan equal rights.[22] According to their communication records, it should not make any difference whether someone was a Hazara, a Tajik, or a Pashtun. 'That is what we think too,' was the message from the U.S. embassy in Islamabad. The Americans supported the Taliban's plan to seek ways to rise above tribal conflicts. Based on his beliefs as a Muslim, Mullah Omar wanted to free Afghan society not only from the tribal fighting among the Pashtun but also from the divisions along ethnic lines that had become entrenched in Afghanistan during the civil war.[23] But despite his intentions, it became clear soon enough that Mullah Omar would not be able to put these ideas into practice.

A spokesperson for the State Department in Washington said at a press conference that there was 'nothing reprehensible' about the Taliban's Islamic laws. At the U.N., the U.S. Assistant Secretary of State Robin Raphel said that despite international 'doubts', the Taliban should be recognized as an 'indigenous' movement that had demonstrated it would hold onto power.[24]

———•◆•———

For Mullah Omar, the most significant form of international recognition was not political recognition by any particular country but a seat in the U.N. General Assembly.[25] That seat was still held by President Rabbani's regime. The U.N.'s recognition of the Taliban as the lawful government of Afghanistan would be the ultimate reward for Mullah Omar's work.

Each year, the U.N. evaluates whether all the member countries are still in compliance with the membership requirements. To this end, the governments have to submit their credentials. For most countries this is a formality. To qualify for membership, the government must be in control of that state's entire territory with the consent of its people, and it must accept the obligations enshrined in the United Nations Charter. Women's rights are an important element.

In his attempts to gain membership of the U.N. for the Taliban despite the issue of women's rights, Mullah Omar often pointed to Saudi Arabia, which had been a member ever since the U.N. was founded in 1945. Saudi Arabia was an Islamic state with Shariah law and harsh corporal punishments. It was mandatory for women to wear the Saudi version of the burka, and the country also enforced the segregation of men and women, just as Mullah Omar wanted for Afghanistan.

The Afghan Foreign Minister Wakil Ahmad Mutawakil was tasked with drawing up the country's credentials. He was the son of a famous local poet whom Mullah Omar much admired. Like many of the Taliban's leaders, he had been educated in the *hujras* in the south of Afghanistan, and he had been involved in the movement from the very beginning.

Mutawakil had very little international experience and did not speak a word of English. But the document was eventually drawn up with the help of U.N. officials.[26] Mutawakil discussed the position of the deposed president Rabbani in an annex to the credentials, stating that Rabbani was no longer 'authorized' to speak on behalf of Afghanistan, which would make his place in the U.N. General Assembly illegal.

The U.N. Special Envoy to Afghanistan and Pakistan, the German Norbert Holl, visited Kabul in 1996 to discuss the possibility of admission to the Assembly. His opinion was that it would be difficult to grant the seat to the Taliban, mainly because of their strict enforcement of the Shariah. At the same time, Holl reported that progress had been made on women's rights. 'But this is all taking place in a gray zone rather than the formal, legitimate route,' said Holl.[27]

Mullah Omar did not let this get in his way. Mutawakil and the other Taliban leaders already had someone in mind who could speak on their behalf at the U.N.: the thirty-five-year-old Hamid Karzai. He was a scion of an influential Popalzai family from Kandahar that had long supported Zahir Shah but had expressed sympathy for the Taliban relatively early on, in 1994. In the end, Karzai was not chosen. Mullah Omar did not trust him because of his previous support for King Zahir Shah.[28] He was afraid the Karzai family wanted to reinstate the king with the help of the Americans.[29] Karzai eventually became the president of Afghanistan in 2001 after the Taliban had been driven out. When I interviewed him around then, he was not at all interested in discussing his nomination as the Taliban's U.N. candidate in 1996, since by that time he had become a supporter of the Americans' War on Terror.

Ultimately it was the madrassa student Abdul Hakim Mujahed, whom Mullah Omar knew and trusted, who was chosen to be sent to the U.N. in New York. Mujahed had grown up in a refugee camp in Pakistan, had fought in the jihad against the Soviets and had then joined the Taliban. He also spoke English.

But Abdul Hakim Mujahed soon learned that he would have to postpone his trip. In November 1996 the U.N. announced that a 'complex situation' had arisen concerning the membership, as not one but two requests had come from Kabul for the seat in the General Assembly.

In addition to Mutawakil's letter, the U.N. had received a letter from President Rabbani that he had sent two weeks before the fall of Kabul. The General Assembly therefore resolved in a majority vote not to take a decision on Afghanistan. As a result, the situation remained unchanged, with President Rabbani's representative holding the seat.[30]

This outcome was a bitter pill for Mullah Omar. It fueled his suspicions about the impartiality of the U.N.[31] Those suspicions had arisen when U.N. envoy Norbert Holl had first visited Afghanistan. He had started by paying a visit to President Rabbani, who was still in Kabul at that point.[32] When Holl subsequently indicated that he also wished to visit Mullah Omar in Kandahar, the Taliban leader – who had yet to take Kabul – reacted emotionally and turned down the request.[33] He could not understand why the U.N. had given priority to President Rabbani.

When Holl's successor, the Tunisian Mahmoud Mestiri, contacted Mullah Omar after the disappointing resolution concerning the U.N. seat, the Taliban leader was keen to discuss the question of international recognition for the movement with him. But Mestiri had another issue in mind: he wanted to chide Mullah Omar for the 1995 hijack of a Russian plane, which had been stuck at Kandahar Airport for a year now.[34] Mullah Omar informed Mestiri that he was not welcome if that was what he wanted to talk about.

The context for the Taliban leader's obstinacy was the reason why his movement had brought the plane down in the first place. After their humiliating defeat in the jihad, the Russians had made renewed attempts to gain a foothold in their neighbor country, which was still strategically important for them, and had set their sights on the Tajik president Rabbani.[35]

In 1995, Russian cargo planes started landing with some regularity at Kabul Airport, carrying secret shipments of weapons for Rabbani and his military commander Massoud. The plane hijacked by the Taliban turned out to contain a shipment from the notorious arms dealer Viktor Bout. In an attempt to arrange the speedy release of his crew, Bout implicitly admitted that the plane had been carrying arms for Rabbani and Massoud.[36] He even came to see Mullah Omar but the mullah firmly showed him the door.[37] The crew was still being held captive.

Under pressure from his staff, Mullah Omar eventually consented to talk to Mestiri but the meeting did nothing to improve relations between the U.N. and the Taliban. Abdul Rahman was there, and said it went something like this: Mestiri placed some photos of blonde women in tears in front of Mullah Omar, who was sitting on the floor. These were pictures of the wives of the crew of the hijacked plane. Mestiri reminded the Taliban leader that the pilots had wives and families too, and so he should release them.

Hardly any response came from Mullah Omar. He mumbled that there should be an end to the supply of arms to Rabbani. Then he pushed Mestiri's photos to one side and fetched a pile of papers with the names of the many missing Afghans. Angrily, Omar said he was still searching for a hundred thousand Afghans whose whereabouts the Russians knew.[38] He was referring to the victims of the persecution by the Communist president Taraki in 1978. This incident had left deep scars in Afghan society. The thousands of male victims had left widows behind who were unable to remarry because they could not bury their husband's body and, as a result of the tribal rules, were living in dire poverty with their children.[39]

Abdul Rahman said that Mullah Omar became increasingly irate. 'You come up with eight women,' he said to Mestiri. 'I've got thousands and thousands. Are your women worth more than the Afghan women?' He stood up and left the room. As it happened, the pilots were able to make a miraculous escape with the hijacked plane shortly afterwards. One year after the hijacking, during one of the regular check-ups of the plane – carried out by the pilots themselves – they seized the opportunity to escape. It seemed they had been planning this for some time.[40] The Taliban security guard who was on board the plane at the time was apparently taken unwillingly with the pilots. Rumor has it that it was his first flight, and he was so afraid that he banged the plane window with the back of his Kalashnikov, in the hope that he could get off. The plane landed in Dubai, where he was briefly detained.

———————•———————

In 1997, the Taliban submitted another request to take over Afghanistan's seat in the U.N. General Assembly. But not long afterwards the movement experienced a dramatic turnaround in the battlefield. What had appeared to be a victory in northwestern Afghanistan had since degenerated into an appalling defeat. It involved the city of Mazar-e-Sharif, which was controlled by General Dostum, an ally of the deposed president Rabbani.

After Mullah Omar and Dostum weren't able to come to a deal themselves (the Taliban also invited Dostum to become part of the regime, but Dostum didn't trust the proposal), the Taliban had reached an arrangement with Dostum's second-in-command, General Malik (a Hazara from that area), namely, that Malik would be given a degree of autonomy in Mazar-e-Sharif as long as he enforced the Taliban's rules. At first everything seemed to go according to plan, and at the end of May 1997 the Taliban easily gained control of the city. The capture of Mazar-e-Sharif was significant for the Taliban because, immediately afterwards, Pakistan, Saudi Arabia, and the United Arab Emirates recognized the Taliban as the lawful government of Afghanistan, which they had still hesitated to do after the capture of Kabul.

However, the Taliban's joy did not last long. Two days after the city's capture, another deal fell through. General Malik and the Taliban parted company, and Malik attacked the Taliban after all. Soon the Hazara leader gathered his people and a mass slaughter of Taliban troops started. Some Taliban were executed summarily, others were buried alive in wells or thrown into containers that were then sealed. The death toll rose fast. There are no reliable counts: some speak of 1,500 victims, others of 3,000.

Mullah Omar was shocked by this defeat, the biggest and bloodiest in the history of the Taliban up to that point. He tried several times to bring in the International Committee of the Red Cross to help find the men who had been killed. But General Malik would not give aid workers permission to enter the area. It was not until November 1997 that the Red Cross published a press release calling on the Hazara leader to give access to the graves and jails in the area. Mullah Omar was indignant that the incident had not caused an international furor – with so many fatalities, he had expected a stronger response. 'How often in the world do you see so many people killed?' he had asked his assistant.[41]

When I studied the newspapers later, I found little had been written about the mass slaughter. I mainly came across ominous reports on how the Taliban were gaining 'control' of Afghanistan and disapproval of Pakistan's diplomatic recognition of the Taliban.[42] The French press agency A.F.P. only mentioned the death toll several days after General Malik's attack, stating that the 'Afghan opposition have made huge gains' in which 3,000 Taliban fighters had been 'killed or executed'.[43] No reports appeared in the months that followed. According to Human Rights Watch – which did not report on this incident for a year either – the international community had certain preconceptions regarding the Taliban. This meant there was little interest in writing about the Taliban from a neutral perspective.[44]

It would take until November before General Dostum returned to the area and had twenty mass graves opened to show the U.N. what General Malik had done in his absence. This was followed by a statement from the U.N. Secretary-General Kofi Annan saying the slaughter at Mazar-e-Sharif should be investigated.[45] Around the same time, the U.S. Secretary of State Madeleine Albright paid a visit to a large Afghan refugee camp, where she sharply criticized what she saw as the Taliban's serious violations of human rights – without mentioning the events in Mazar-e-Sharif.[46]

———————•◦•———————

Mullah Omar's movement saw its reputation deteriorate in Europe and the U.S. in 1997. At the end of September 1997, Emma Bonino, an Italian Member of the European Parliament (M.E.P.), visited a women's clinic in central Afghanistan accompanied by a C.N.N. film crew. When she let the patients be filmed – knowing this was against the rules – things got out of hand. Bonino was arrested at once by the Taliban's religious police and held in custody. One of her staff was beaten with the butt of a Kalashnikov. The images were seen all over the world and everyone expressed their horror at the Taliban. U.N. staff in Kabul were far from pleased with her 'P.R. plan', as they called it. The incident significantly soured relations between the U.N. and the Taliban.[47] A Taliban minister had to negotiate hard with the religious police to get Bonino released.[48] In an official comment, the Taliban said they considered the M.E.P.'s actions outrageous. 'Would she have behaved like this in Saudi Arabia?'[49]

Shortly afterwards, things went wrong during a visit by Satu Suikkari, a senior representative of the U.N. refugee organization United Nations High Commissioner for Refugees (U.N.H.C.R). Many refugees were returning to Afghanistan as large parts of the country had become safer under the Taliban. When the Taliban asked the U.N.H.C.R. for advice on how to deal with this, the organization sent the female Finnish expert Suikkari to Afghanistan.

After much discussion, Suikkari reached an agreement with the Taliban that she would take part in the meeting hidden from view behind a curtain. But when she began to speak from behind her curtain, three of her U.N.H.C.R. male colleagues walked out in protest. The Taliban members present were so indignant at this that they called a halt to the meeting and the three men were deported immediately. The incident shows once again how fragile the relationship was between the Taliban and the international community.

———————◆———————

In the meantime, the Taliban's second request to be allowed to take over the country's seat at the U.N. in New York had also come to nothing. Once again, the U.N. decided not to honor the request and Rabbani's delegate was permitted to represent Afghanistan for another year. That same year, the Taliban's application to take over the Afghan seat in the Organization of Islamic Cooperation (O.I.C.) in Jeddah in Saudi Arabia was also refused. President Rabbani was no longer permitted to send a representative to the O.I.C. either, so the seat remained unfilled.[50]

After the second rejection by the U.N., Mullah Omar ordered the two Taliban diplomats who had been provisionally assigned to this position to pack their bags anyway and fly to the U.S. in order to lobby the U.N. Abdul Hakim Mujahed and his assistant Shaheen rented an apartment at their own expense in the New York neighborhood of Flushing, only a couple of miles from the gleaming U.N. headquarters overlooking East River. During my investigations, I was able to talk to both of them about their experiences in New York. I interviewed Mujahed in his office at the Afghan Peace Council in Kabul and Shaheen in Doha, where he was a member of the Taliban's political commission. 'I remember I was very impressed with the skyscrapers. There was so much energy and creativity in them. Wouldn't it be wonderful to have buildings like that in Kabul? I wondered whether I would ever live to see that.'

When the two men arrived in New York, they were full of optimism about their mission to persuade the world of the Taliban's good intentions. 'We were definitely no Hezbollah or Hamas, anti-Western terrorists who wanted to harm the U.S.,' said Mujahed. He remembers that they were received cordially at first. 'We truly believed things would work out.

Many diplomats from Europe and the U.S., and from other continents too, visited our little apartment in Flushing because they were curious.'

However, the positive atmosphere soon turned into mutual distrust, Shaheen said. 'They insisted that we should stick to international norms, especially where women's rights were concerned. Everyone wanted to explain to us what changes had to be made in Afghanistan for us to qualify for recognition – in terms of education, in terms of equality between men and women, and in terms of the legal system. Then I would explain patiently that these things were not that easy after the devastation to the country caused by the jihad and the civil war.'

Of course topics such as the stoning of women were also raised regularly, said Shaheen. 'I would tell them that it didn't happen nearly as often as people seemed to think but I never managed to make that clear to them. "What you guys think you know isn't the real situation, it's an exaggeration," I would say. But I could feel our goal slipping through my fingers. The West was afraid of our Islamic regime.'

Mullah Omar was often on the phone with his envoys in Flushing. Mujahed and his assistant Shaheen bombarded Omar with advice, which mainly involved him needing to steer a middle course. Sometimes they would send him a letter in the hope that this would make a deeper impression than a telephone call. 'We really need to do something about the complaints about the religious police,' Shaheen wrote. 'Beating women in the streets of Kabul violates our own rules too. It would help our credibility in New York if we could stop that.'

They also asked Mullah Omar to stop focusing exclusively on the armed struggle against Rabbani and to start thinking about how to increase employment in various sectors in Afghanistan. Both diplomats suggested setting up more direct contacts between the Taliban and U.N. diplomats to foster 'more mutual understanding'. They felt the Taliban should concentrate on getting more support among the Afghan people by bringing together tribal and religious leaders, academics, and other experts in *shuras* that could advise the movement. 'We need to listen to the hearts of the Afghan people,' said Shaheen.

They did not get much of a response from their leaders, according to a disappointed Shaheen. 'The argument was usually that it was too soon for the changes we were proposing. Mullah Omar was adamant that he wanted to take control of all of Afghanistan first before he started implementing changes. He thought such changes could affect his soldiers' morale and that would only make the war last even longer.'

———————◆———————

When the Taliban managed to capture Mazar-e-Sharif after all, one year after the major defeat in 1997, the soldiers who entered the city took revenge for the slaughter of their own people. While Omar abhorred vendetta killings, many others did not abide by his rules. Human Rights Watch concluded that many civilians were killed. The soldiers' victims were largely Hazaras. In 1997, the reverse had happened: Hazaras had killed many Taliban fighters and now the Taliban were seeking vengeance.

The U.N. diplomat Lakhdar Brahimi said in one of our interviews that the lack of justice behind the first slaughter in 1997 gave the Taliban the feeling that they would be able to wreak revenge in 1998 without any consequences. After all, many of them believed the rest of the world was clearly not watching, said Brahimi. But unlike in 1997, this time international organizations such as Human Rights Watch and Amnesty International, and the media reported at length on the massacre.

The U.N. was also quick to arrive this time, in part because the Taliban had taken ten Iranian diplomats hostage during the fighting for Mazar-e-Sharif. Iran was so enraged at the capture of its diplomats that it immediately threatened war.[51] Lakhdar Brahimi flew to Afghanistan at once to hold talks. By the time he arrived there were already 60,000

Iranian soldiers on the border with Afghanistan, poised to invade Iran's neighbor at any moment. Brahimi got a cool reception from Mullah Omar in Kandahar. The mullah took him straightaway to a cemetery where thousands of Taliban soldiers killed in the fighting a year earlier were buried. However, Brahimi was able to persuade Mullah Omar to release the ten Iranians.

———•———

Over the past few years I have met Brahimi a few times in the center of Paris, where we both teach at the same university, Sciences Po. As a senior diplomat who had previously been Algeria's Minister of Foreign Affairs, he was used to disappointments. After his post in Afghanistan, he worked for the U.N. in Iraq and Syria, two more countries where bringing about peace is no simple matter.

Brahimi remembered Mullah Omar as a young, somewhat shy man with a surprisingly soft and almost timid voice, especially when talking to strangers. He called him 'detached' from the world, surrounded by people who thought the same as he did and who were also very mistrustful. When he visited him in 1998, Brahimi found Mullah Omar to be a good speaker, and a good listener too. 'I realized at once that this Taliban member was not the worst person on Earth. In retrospect, I believe the international community had made a big mistake in isolating the movement, especially once they had conquered most of the country. It was a big mistake to condemn the Taliban summarily for their interpretation of the Islamic faith.'

He continued, 'We make mistakes like this far too often in international diplomacy.' Instead of investigating the movement and investing in a good relationship, the Taliban were immediately impugned as terrorist pariahs. 'But the Mullah Omar I met in 1998 and 1999 was definitely not a terrorist,' said Brahimi. 'He didn't have the mindset of a terrorist either. No, he was a patriot and deeply religious.'

Brahimi says that in retrospect he personally should have done more to plead the Taliban's case at the U.N. in New York. 'But there was no way of getting through to them. Everyone already had an opinion about the Taliban and that included a lot of preconceptions. Perhaps the most important of these was the supposed relationship between the Taliban and Osama bin Laden.'

7

An Awkward Guest
(1998)

IN the dead of night in May 1996, an unmarked plane landed at an airport in Jalalabad in eastern Afghanistan. It was carrying Osama bin Laden.[1] He was the son of a Saudi family that had made a fortune in construction. Banished from his home country, now he was returning to Afghanistan, the country where he had joined the jihad against the Soviet Union in the 1980s like so many other young men in the Arab world.

Bin Laden had spent the past few years in Sudan, offering his services to the Sudanese president Omar al-Bashir, who wanted to establish an Islamic state in his own country. But Sudan expelled Bin Laden at the insistence of the U.S. and Saudi Arabia because those services allegedly mainly consisted of organizing terrorist activities. Almost no other country was willing to take Bin Laden because of the pressure from the Americans and Saudis. The only place he could go was turbulent Afghanistan, which no longer had a functioning government. As they flew over Saudi Arabia in the plane taking them from Sudan to Afghanistan, Bin Laden's son Omar bin Laden saw his father sweating with fear. It seemed Osama was afraid they would shoot him down with rockets.[2]

Who was Osama bin Laden back then? I only heard about him after 9/11 and I always assumed he must have been masterminding various terrorist attacks all his life, including when he was living in Sudan. It is known that from 1991 onwards, Bin Laden invested millions of dollars in various construction projects in Sudan that were legal in themselves. But according to Western embassies in Sudan, Bin Laden had brought an army of jihadists over to Sudan from Afghanistan, ostensibly for these projects but in reality to prepare them in training camps for the jihad against America and its allies.[3]

It was clear that as a veteran of the Afghan jihad against the Soviet Union, Bin Laden still had some involvement in the fate of the Arab combatants who had remained behind in Afghanistan after that war ended. Many of them were no longer welcome in their home countries, such as Saudi Arabia and Egypt, where they were seen as potential opponents of the regimes.

In 1991, when he was still in Saudi Arabia, Bin Laden had allegedly proposed uniting these unemployed jihadists in a new army that could defend Saudi Arabia against a belligerent Iraq in the Gulf War. Iraq had already captured Kuwait and some feared it could invade Saudi Arabia at any moment. The Saudi government eventually decided to call in the help of the U.S. military with more than 500,000 troops, which infuriated many Saudis, including Osama bin Laden.[4]

Bin Laden also financed four guesthouses in Pakistan for the former fighters, some of whom continued to give military training while others worked for local N.G.O.s or local newspapers.[5] He also sent money regularly to the jihadist training camp of Khalden in Khost Province in eastern Afghanistan. This camp had been set up by the C.I.A. early on in the struggle against the Soviets. Arab militants carried on training here even after the jihad.[6]

In the final U.S. Congress report on the 9/11 attacks, Bin Laden, who had initially been a non-violent critic of the Saudi regime, was depicted as a leading financer of terrorism from the start of the 1990s.[7] In Sudan, Osama bin Laden purportedly set up 'a large and complex set of intertwined business and terrorist enterprises' and supplied 'weapons, explosives, and technical equipment for terrorist purposes'. The investigative commission concluded that he had already been the Al Qaeda linchpin during this period.[8] This is also evident from internal State Department documents from the start of the 1990s. As the *Washington Post* revealed, at that point he was seen as 'one of the key financial backers of extremist Islamic activities in the world'.[9]

But this seems less certain than the American government and media claim, and other researchers refute this conclusion and see it as exaggerated. According to Alex Strick van Linschoten and Felix Kuehn, there *was* no single large terrorist organization in the 1990s; it was more a conglomerate of groups of former combatants from the Afghan jihad operating independently.[10] The journalist Jason Burke also says an Al Qaeda organization with centralized leadership did not exist back then. Locally operating jihadists often took action autonomously and then dubbed it an initiative by Al Qaeda or gave it some other label. To assume this was a centrally controlled operation was far too facile.[11]

While open to question, the assumption that Bin Laden was already at the head of a large, international, centrally run terrorist organization in the early 1990s and giving orders for acts of terrorism led to his name invariably being linked to attacks by radical Muslims in the years that followed. That happened when the first attack on the Twin Towers took place in 1993, when explosives were detonated in a truck parked in the garage under the northern tower of the World Trade Center, badly damaging the first seven stories. Six people died and over a thousand were injured.[12]

Bin Laden was also alleged by some to have been involved that same year in the infamous Battle of Mogadishu in Somalia, in which an American Black Hawk helicopter was shot down.[13] The West states that Al Qaeda operatives were involved, but it turned out that Bin Laden was not.[14] And in 1995 he was supposed to have masterminded an attack on a National Guard training center in Saudi Arabia in which seven people died, including five Americans.[15] Although it was unclear who was behind this attack, Saudi Arabia still put the blame on Bin Laden and his ex-jihadists. Four young men who had nothing to do with the incident were sentenced to death in front of the television cameras. According to the confession they were forced to give on television by the authorities, they had fought in the jihad in Afghanistan and supported Bin Laden.[16]

One year later, it happened again. This time, Bin Laden was supposed to have been behind an attack on the Khobar Towers complex in Saudi Arabia where the Saudi oil company Aramco had its headquarters. Nineteen Americans died in this attack. However, it is unclear whether Bin Laden was actually involved in this incident and, if so, how. According to Bruce Riedel, the Saudis already knew that Iran had been behind this attack as well.[17] Bin Laden was also held responsible for an attack on the Egyptian president, Mubarak, in 1995, which was actually claimed by an Egyptian group operating from Sudan.

In short, various attacks were carried out by various groups in the course of the 1990s without conclusive evidence of Bin Laden's involvement in any of them.

———— ◆ ————

After a great deal of pressure from the Americans and the Saudis, Sudan eventually agreed to expel Bin Laden in 1996. Sudan first wanted to put him on trial for his involvement in various acts of terrorism before deporting him. The Sudanese had wanted to see evidence of what Osama bin Laden was supposed to have done, but the pressure was ratcheted up to such an extent that in the end they made him leave the country anyway. Neither the U.S. nor Saudi Arabia wanted to take Bin Laden. The Americans were afraid they would not be able to get a conviction under the U.S. judicial system and he would be acquitted. Years later, the *Washington Post* quoted the Deputy National Security Adviser Sandy Berger as saying, 'The F.B.I. did not believe we had enough evidence to indict Bin Laden at that time, and therefore opposed bringing him to the United States.'[18]

The *Washington Post* quoted some American diplomats who hoped what they saw as Saudi Arabia's 'more resolute' judicial system would resolve the Osama bin Laden problem for them. That hope evaporated when Saudi Arabia made it clear to the U.S. that it too was not prepared to take him in. The Americans were not sure why that was. Saudi Arabia may have wanted to avoid any trouble from what was by now a well-known opposition figure. Or perhaps its pride had been hurt when Sudan proved willing to extradite Bin Laden to the Americans after previously rejecting the Saudis' requests.

When the Americans learned that Bin Laden would be going to Afghanistan, the first reaction was relief. According to U.S. diplomats, it did not matter much where he went as long as he was no longer operating in Sudan. There were no U.S. troops deployed in Afghanistan – in contrast to Somalia, for instance – who could be a target for Bin Laden's terrorist attacks.[19] Even so, the C.I.A. stepped up its efforts. In April 1996, President Clinton signed the Anti-Terrorism Act, which allowed the U.S. to block the assets of terrorist organizations. Its first application was to block Bin Laden's access to his fortune of an estimated $250,300 million.[20]

———— ◆ ————

When Osama bin Laden landed in Jalalabad in 1996, there was no Mullah Omar standing at the foot of the aircraft stairs to welcome him.[21] The notion that Mullah Omar and Osama bin Laden had worked together from the start became entrenched after 9/11, in part thanks to Ahmad Rashid's widely read book. It is also often assumed that Omar had invited Bin Laden to come to Afghanistan, but that was not the case.[22]

Bin Laden's oldest son Omar was fifteen in 1996. In 2010, he wrote the book *Growing Up Bin Laden* about his adventures with the father who went on to become so notorious. I interviewed Omar bin Laden (who is the spitting image of his father) a couple of times in Doha. We talked about the years in Afghanistan with his father. He did not remember getting a particularly warm reception in the provincial city in the east.

His father's entourage was met in 1996 by a delegation of local Afghan warlords affiliated with Gulbuddin Hekmatyar, the man whose army had managed to keep the Taliban out of eastern Afghanistan up to that point. But as Omar well remembers, a local governor immediately let it be known that Omar's father was not welcome in his district. A number of people in the delegation that met the entourage were even murdered shortly afterwards. 'At first we were put up in a really nice summerhouse that used to belong to the Afghan king Zahir Shah. But after those murders my father didn't feel safe, so we moved to some cave dwellings dozens of miles away in a mountain called Tora Bora,' Omar said.

Osama bin Laden felt uneasy there too, according to his son, and he planned an escape route across the Pakistani border. Yet he did not trust the Pakistani government either, which he felt was under too much pressure from the Americans and was liable to suddenly decide to arrest him. That was why in the end Bin Laden preferred to remain in anarchic Afghanistan where the central government was so weak.

Omar bin Laden said the idea (shared by many people in the West) that his father was wealthy was exaggerated. For example, Sudan had frozen Bin Laden's assets at America's request, and he could no longer get hold of these millions (his son Omar said he was now trying to get the money back from the Sudanese government). Nor did he have access any more to the money in his Saudi Arabian bank accounts. Saudi Arabia later blocked the accounts of Bin Laden's private donors as well.[23]

Omar described their life in Afghanistan as trying times for the Bin Ladens. That was especially the case for Osama's four wives, who had never known anything other than a life of luxury with spacious villas and days spent horseback riding and painting. Suddenly they were having to sit on the freezing-cold floor, living in Afghanistan's inhospitable eastern region surrounded by an apparently untrustworthy and hostile community.

———◆———

Few people in southern Afghanistan had heard of Osama bin Laden (Bin Laden fought in eastern Afghanistan during the jihad). Mullah Omar probably first found out about the Saudi guest residing in the east of the country in the summer of 1996, when the Saudi ambassador to Pakistan, Abdul Aziz al Mutabbaqani, paid him a visit.[24] The ambassador insisted that Mullah Omar was not to become involved with Bin Laden as he was suspected by Saudi Arabia and the U.S. of terrorist acts.

This irritated the Taliban leader, who replied that the ambassador was talking to the wrong man. At that point, eastern Afghanistan was still in the hands of the Taliban's enemies, the alliance of President Rabbani and Vice President Gulbuddin Hekmatyar. Mullah Omar wanted to know why the ambassador hadn't gone to see them.

When the ambassador persisted with his message, Mullah Omar asked him what evidence there was for these suspicions. With sufficient evidence, the U.S. and Saudi Arabia could take Bin Laden to court in Kabul, and if he were found guilty, the Taliban would hand him over at once, Mullah Omar said, taking his own government very seriously.

It is interesting that Mullah Omar's approach in this meeting was to demand evidence and talk of a possible trial for Osama bin Laden – the same approach taken by Sudan. This position was different from the

Pashtunwali rules on hospitality, which state that even visiting criminals should be treated as guests. His request for proof of the accusations leveled at Bin Laden referred to the Shariah, the Islamic legal system that he believed should bring an end to the arbitrary approach based on tribal customs.

Mullah Omar shared Bin Laden's surprise that a country like Saudi Arabia, the guardian of the holy cities of Mecca and Medina, would raise suspicions about a fellow Muslim (who like him had fought the Soviets) without any proof. The ambassador was unable to answer Mullah Omar's request, nor was he able to furnish any evidence.

———— ◆ ————

In fall 1996, Mullah Omar's Taliban took over eastern Afghanistan. Bin Laden's son Omar said his father, who had not felt welcome in Jalalabad anyway, was filled with dread at this seizure of power. His hosts – fierce opponents of Mullah Omar – had frightened Bin Laden by calling the Taliban barbaric and Communists.

'I saw the fear in my father's eyes,' said Omar bin Laden. 'He had no idea who the Taliban were, or that Mullah Omar was their leader. For a while he even thought they were allies of America because they were so keen on getting international recognition. When the Taliban advanced into eastern Afghanistan, he was afraid they would seize the Arab jihadists in Afghanistan. My father feared we would be shot dead on the spot.'

The Taliban's progress eastwards was relatively free of violence; many local leaders negotiated a surrender.[25] Mullah Omar's troops dealt rigorously with the numerous military camps set up by his main enemy, Gulbuddin Hekmatyar.[26] These camps were full of foreign jihadists who had once been valiant fighters in the struggle against the Soviets and had never left. The Americans and Saudis were of the opinion that these fighters should now be considered terrorists. Mullah Omar's main aim, however, was to gain control over these camps in order to undermine

Hekmatyar's power. The Taliban closed a number of the camps and the foreign jihadists were sent back to their home country, or else they went into hiding in Kabul, where President Rabbani was still in control (this was a few months before he was driven out).

Pakistanis who returned home from the Hekmatyar camps were arrested immediately and detained in Pakistan at the request of the Americans. However, the I.S.I., in conjunction with the Taliban, deliberately allowed some combatants to remain in the camps so that they could train for the conflict in Kashmir.[27] The Taliban believed that some jihadists who were sent back to Egypt were shot dead on arrival at the airport, without a trial. Jihadists returning to Saudi Arabia could not expect a warm welcome either. They were arrested at once and held in custody – getting the same treatment as many other returning Arab jihadists before them.

The harsh treatment of the foreign jihadists in their home countries gave Mullah Omar doubts. The Taliban realized that these were men who had fought side by side with them in the 1980s against the Soviet Union and for an Islamic state, the same objective the Taliban were now pursuing.[28] This made the return of these fighters a more complex issue.

In the end, Mullah Omar did not close all the camps, partly at the request of Pakistan. Fourteen camps for foreign fighters were kept open: five near Kabul, seven in eastern Afghanistan, one in Kandahar, and one in Herat. The Khalden camp, which received significant funding from Osama bin Laden, was one of those that stayed open.

After the shutdown of some camps in eastern Afghanistan, Osama bin Laden briefly considered leaving the country with his family. According to his son Omar, he did not feel welcome. The Taliban approach to Bin Laden was not straightforward. In 1996, the prominent Taliban leader Mullah Khaksar (who is now part of the Taliban's Doha team) apparently met Bin Laden in a guesthouse belonging to Mullah Rabbani; he told an American journalist this after 9/11. At the meeting, he asked Bin Laden on a personal note to depart. 'It's time for you all to leave the country,' the mullah is supposed to have said.[29] Mullah Khaksar is quoted as having said that Afghanistan didn't need Osama bin Laden's help to resolve its internal differences (Bin Laden had helped some parties in the civil war before the rise of the Taliban in the hope of brokering a peace deal). This meeting caused friction between Bin Laden and the mullah; later on, Bin Laden even accused this mullah of being mentally ill.

Rather than leaving Afghanistan, Bin Laden moved to Kandahar shortly afterwards to live in Mullah Omar's home city.[30] It is not clear why he went there. Had Mullah Omar ordered him to come so that it would be easier for him to keep an eye on Bin Laden, as his former foreign minister Mutawakil claimed?[31] Or did Bin Laden move south because he had become afraid for his safety in the east now that some of his supporters had been murdered?[32] Or was Ahmad Rashid right: did Omar and Osama bin Laden want to strike up a friendship?[33]

Bin Laden's move to Kandahar was delayed for several months, during which he stayed in Kabul. Mullah Rabbani, the Taliban's second in command, kept a close watch on him. Bin Laden and his entourage were not given permission to use cars in Kabul, for instance.[34] The mullah distrusted Bin Laden because of his constant criticisms of Saudi Arabia, a country with which Rabbani happened to be on very good terms.[35]

Osama bin Laden made much more use of the media during his time in Afghanistan than when he had lived in Sudan. His statements became more radical too. For example, in August 1996 he wrote the 'Declaration of War Against the Americans' and in 1997 he invited the British journalist Robert Fisk to Jalalabad with the aim of using him to spread his propaganda. Fisk had already visited Osama bin Laden in Sudan in 1993 and had written an article describing Bin Laden as an 'anti-Soviet warrior' who was now 'putting his army on the road to peace'.[36]

The tone of his new article was different. Bin Laden criticized Saudi Arabia mercilessly; he was furious with the country. Although he very likely had nothing to do with the Khobar Towers attack, now he suddenly claimed it, possibly because he hoped this would bring him more support among the divided jihad groups. Bin Laden said he hoped more such attacks would take place in Saudi Arabia.[37]

When Osama bin Laden finally arrived in Kandahar, he and his entourage were housed in abandoned military barracks on the outskirts of the city, on the edge of the Red Desert. When I visited Tarnak Farms, as the place was called, in 2013, no one was living there. Most of the barracks had been damaged in aerial bombing in 2001. Craters up to six feet deep were still visible in places. A curtain was hung up in the door to Bin Laden's barracks. Inside, I found a small mirror and toothbrush among the rubble. A rope was attached to a post in the corner of the compound where Bin Laden and his family used to keep their horses.

I have obtained information about what was probably one of the first meetings between Osama bin Laden and Mullah Omar, soon after Bin Laden arrived at Tarnak Farms.[38] Although much has been written since 9/11 about the close alliance between Mullah Omar and Osama bin Laden, the Taliban leader did not have a particularly friendly message for the Saudi man. Omar told Bin Laden he needed to stop his propaganda for an international jihad against Saudi Arabia and America. The Taliban disputed Bin Laden's authority to issue fatwas against his enemies; they said he was wrongfully acting as a religious leader in doing so. Moreover, Mullah Omar did not have much sympathy for Bin Laden's plans for a global jihad. After 9/11, people in the U.S. government, among others, often assumed the Taliban had embraced Bin Laden's plans and supported his international jihad. But that was not the case at all. Mullah Omar felt Bin Laden was exploiting Afghanistan.

Mullah Omar made it clear to the Saudi that the Taliban had an exclusively national agenda. Their Islamic state would be restricted to Afghanistan. Moreover, his regime actually wanted to be on friendly terms with other countries. Mullah Omar ordered Bin Laden to refrain from talking to the international media in the future.[39] The Taliban leader was no friend of the foreign media anyway, as they essentially gave his archenemy Rabbani a voice. He also reminded Bin Laden that he was

now in a country where images of people were forbidden – in accordance
with the stipulations in the Quran. That was clearly a reference to a recent
appearance by the Arab guest on C.N.N.[40]

Later, Bin Laden said of this meeting that he was 'frustrated' by all
the restrictions Mullah Omar had imposed on him. Bin Laden had even
asked Omar for permission to talk to the media about the Taliban's
goodness and the importance of their struggle, and how Muslims all over
the world should support them in that struggle. But Mullah Omar would
not allow that either.

Bin Laden hastily promised that to make amends he would build
roads and factories, in other words contribute to the reconstruction of
Afghanistan as he had done previously in Sudan. According to Mutawakil,
Bin Laden made himself popular at first with these promises, but Mullah
Omar soon began to have doubts about the true level of his commitment.
Omar was not sure how much money the Arab still had.[41] One of Mullah
Omar's colleagues joked that it would probably be more lucrative to hand
Bin Laden over to the Saudis as they had promised a large bounty for his
extradition.[42] The Taliban fighters thought anyway that the Americans
were only magnifying Bin Laden's importance by taking his propaganda
so seriously. They thought the foreigners should pay more attention to
the Taliban's constructive plans rather than listening to the provocations
of a lone firebrand.[43]

The big differences between Mullah Omar and Osama bin Laden
make it highly implausible they had a close friendship. Especially after
9/11, international media reports spoke of the close bond said to exist
between the two men – partly on the authority of anonymous sources in
the American secret service. They were apparently such good friends that
they used to meet up regularly, for example, to go fishing together. There
were even stories that Mullah Omar had married one of Bin Laden's
daughters and vice versa, that Bin Laden was married to one of Omar's
daughters.[44]

Osama bin Laden's son Omar has no memories of this supposed close friendship.[45] 'Relations were not good. Mullah Omar didn't really want anything to do with my father but he couldn't ignore him totally, precisely because he was being attacked so fiercely abroad.' The story about marrying one another's daughters was met with laughter in Kabul and Kandahar. Mullah Omar's four wives all came from the vicinity of Deh Rawod. Osama bin Laden had many wives – more than four at any rate – but none came from Afghanistan.

———————•———————

In early 1998, American distrust of Osama bin Laden grew while the relationship between the two Islamic leaders in Afghanistan deteriorated. Bin Laden had not achieved much in the twelve months following his first meeting with Mullah Omar, and his calls for more attacks in Saudi Arabia had met with no response. During 1998, Bin Laden intensified his efforts to publicize his message. Increasingly, he sent audiotapes of sermons to mosques and sympathetic media outlets in the hope of persuading Muslims all over the world to join his international jihad and commit attacks.

On February 23, 1998, Bin Laden published his notorious statement 'Global Islamic Front for Jihad against the Jews and Crusaders',[46] in which he advocated a jihad against the Americans.[47] According to him, they had supported the corrupt Saudi regime in the run-up to the Gulf War in 1991. As a result, their military had been in the country ever since as an occupying force, just like the Russians in Afghanistan.

The statement ended with what is known as a *hukm*, a call to all Muslims that they had a duty to kill Americans, whether civilians or military, all over the world. Bin Laden's call met with a mixed response, both in his own circle and in the wider Arab world.[48] The U.S. security services had long seen Bin Laden as a major threat and, as far as they were concerned, this *hukm* was confirmation that he now meant business.[49]

Despite Bin Laden's reference to Afghanistan, none of the five signatories to the statement were Afghan.[50] In addition to Bin Laden and his Egyptian jihad friend Ayman al-Zawahiri, the statement was signed by someone called Taha from Iraq, who later retracted his support as he had not realized what he was being used for. The statement was also signed by a Mir Hamzah, a Pakistani Islamic 'secretary' about whom little is known. The final signatory was Fazlur Rahman, Amir of the Jihad Movement in Bangladesh. It is not clear if this was the same Fazal Rahman as the leader of Harkat-ul-Jihad al-Islami, a Pakistani political party, who regularly used to visit Mullah Omar.[51]

The Taliban were not particularly afraid of Bin Laden's supposed power; many of them thought he was just bluffing. They saw him as a propagandist who was trying to rile the West with his media-hyped calls for action.[52] Mutasim told me they did not even think Bin Laden capable of organizing a major attack. He did not appear to have much money, judging by his modest circumstances in Kandahar, and many of his assets had been frozen.

Even so, many Taliban leaders were worried about the response from 'the world'. In their view, the outside world took him far too seriously. Mullah Omar sighed to one of his visitors that he was being driven 'crazy' by all the diplomats wanting to talk to him about 'that Osama'. He thought they were making Bin Laden far too important by paying him all this attention. Yielding to the pressure by extraditing Bin Laden was still not an option for Mullah Omar. He didn't want to lose face. He was afraid that enemies, such as President Rabbani, would tear into him and label him a fake Muslim if he were to hand over such a big prize to the U.S. 'It would be our downfall as a regime if we blindly handed him over,' said Mutawakil during a meeting at the American embassy in Islamabad.[53]

Mullah Omar saw how Bin Laden continued unabated with his inflammatory statements in the media about Saudi Arabia and the U.S. Even organizations that had previously adopted a more moderate approach, such as the European Union and the U.N., were now infected by the fear of Bin Laden and increasingly opposed to the Taliban as a result. It was as if the Taliban's foreign policy was being held hostage by their Arab guest.

Despite the growing unease, Bin Laden scheduled a press event in May 1998, not in Kandahar where the Taliban were based but in Khost Province, in the Arab insurgents' camp of Khalden, which he had funded for so many years. The camp mainly housed Arabs from various countries; there were hardly any Afghans there. Surrounded by these Arabs, he repeated his threats to the U.S. as the cameras of the international media rolled.[54]

The Pakistani B.B.C. journalist Rahimullah Yousafzai, who was on good terms with Mullah Omar, later told me the Taliban leader had been furious at this performance. 'How can he keep doing such things without my permission?' he had shouted on his satellite phone to Yousafzai. 'There can only be one leader in Afghanistan. Is it me or is it Bin Laden?'

Yousafzai understood Omar's anger all too well; he said to me: Mullah Omar clearly did not have Bin Laden under control. According to Yousafzai, the lower ranks in Omar's movement were increasingly wondering who their real leader was.[55] A letter written to Osama bin Laden shortly after the latter's media appearance in Khalden could be evidence of his anger. This letter was found later in the home of one of Bin Laden's supporters. It included the following passage, apparently from Mullah Omar:

> I don't think anyone truly believes in the Good anymore. Everyone has trained their own supporters, and all they care about are their own status, their own reputation, and their own position. People have forgotten how to follow orders and respect their leader.[56]

On August 7, 1998, two suicide bombings were carried out almost
simultaneously in the American embassies in Dar es Salaam (in Tanzania)
and Nairobi (the capital of Kenya). More than 220 people were killed.
The claims that were published afterwards were confusing, to say the
least. The attacks were initially claimed by an unknown group called
the Islamic Army for the Liberation of the Holy Places.[57] On August 18,
more than ten days later, the Global Islamic Front, a movement that some
believed Osama bin Laden belonged to, denied all involvement while at
the same time issuing a warning of more attacks.[58]

In the following week, the Federal Bureau of Investigation (F.B.I.)
discovered what they saw as the most significant proof that Bin Laden
was indeed implicated in the attacks: one of the men involved, whom
the F.B.I. had been able to get hold of alive, had received training in the
Khalden camp that Bin Laden was financing. He had also phoned a
number in Yemen that had previously been called by Osama bin Laden.[59]

The Americans were soon in contact again. Secretary of State
Madeleine Albright made an urgent call to Mullah Omar asking him to
hand Bin Laden over. 'If the Taliban want us to recognize their regime,
they must not harbor individuals who we consider to be terrorists.'

In the night of August 19 to 20, a number of training camps in Khost
Province were hit by sixty cruise missiles fired from an American aircraft
carrier in the Indian Ocean. The targets included a Pakistani camp and
one belonging to the independent ex-jihadist leader Jalaluddin Haqqani.
The U.S. also fired at a supposed camp in the Sudanese capital Khartoum,
though it turned out to be a pharmaceutical factory rather than a terrorist
camp as the Americans claimed.[60]

Twenty-one people were killed in Khost. Bin Laden was not among
the victims, even though he had visited one of the camps that were
bombed earlier that same day.[61] According to his son, he had left for a
hideout two hours before the attack after receiving 'a secret phone call'.[62]

The Taliban were completely unprepared for the sixty missiles raining
down on Khost Province. Mullah Omar had not yet woken up. The B.B.C.

Pashto journalist Daud Junbish told me he had phoned Omar from Moscow, where he was working as a correspondent at the time. When he asked Omar whether he already knew about the missiles being fired at his country, the mullah first led out a loud sigh. 'Does America want to destroy us?' he said. According to Junbish, this was followed by a fierce tirade that showed how angry Mullah Omar was. He was not interested in America's reasons for this attack. Even though they had not been able to furnish him with any proof of Bin Laden's guilt, they had gone ahead and hammered the Taliban anyway.[63]

According to Latif, who was working for Mullah Omar at that time, the mullah now lost all faith in the Americans. Omar said things like: 'It's the fault of the American intelligence services. They keep on accusing Osama even though they can't find any evidence that points to Bin Laden's involvement.' He went on to say, 'If the whole world carries on opposing us despite our assurances and keeps asking for Bin Laden, then we won't hand him over; instead, we'll defend him to our last drop of blood.'[64]

Mullah Omar continued to fume in the local press in the days following the Khost bombing. He said these attacks were aimed not at Bin Laden but at the Islamic state. In his opinion, this showed deep contempt for the Afghan people. 'America itself is a terrorist state. There isn't much difference between the attacks in Tanzania and Kenya and these attacks on Afghanistan.'[65] The enraged mullah also accused President Clinton of using the bombings to divert attention from the scandal of his affair with the White House intern Monica Lewinsky, which was dominating the news in the U.S. Many other people thought the same, not just in Afghanistan and Pakistan but also in America itself.[66]

Two days after the attacks on Khost, a scheduled phone call with the U.S. (planned before the incident) went ahead despite the publicly shared anger. It was conducted between Mullah Omar and the American diplomat Michael Malinowski. According to my information, it was the first and last call Mullah Omar would have with representatives of the U.S. government.

To make sure that the person on the other end of the line really was Mullah Omar, the Americans had asked the Voice of America journalist Spozhmai Maiwandi, who was originally from Afghanistan, to listen in and verify whether that was the Taliban leader's voice. After she had confirmed to Malinowski that this was indeed Mullah Omar speaking, Omar asked in turn for confirmation that the person talking to him really was Malinowski.[67]

'Our conversation was initially pretty awkward, but other than that it went smoothly. Neither of us was angry,' Malinowski recalled. 'I remember I made a lame joke early on that made Mullah Omar laugh. I said, 'Osama bin Laden may be a guest, but he's standing on the neighbors' roof and shooting at you.' That made Mullah Omar laugh, which broke the ice.' So this is a real human being I'm dealing with, thought Malinowski.[68]

According to Malinowski, Mullah Omar started the conversation – in his typical dry tone – by saying he was open to a dialogue with the Americans.[69] This was followed by a long list of wishes and recommendations – what Malinowski called Omar's 'hobbyhorses'. Despite all the tensions after the attack, Omar still wanted an American embassy in Kabul and he asked for economic aid for the reconstruction of Afghanistan. He advised the Americans to get rid of President Clinton as that would improve their reputation in the Islamic world. Malinowski told me this was a reference to the sex scandal with Monica Lewinsky. The rockets that the U.S. had fired at Afghanistan two days earlier had not done the country's reputation any good either, according to Mullah Omar. He argued it would only increase Islamic solidarity and hostility towards the U.S. and actually make terrorist attacks against Americans *more* likely. Finally, Malinowski said the Taliban leader concluded he could not hand Osama bin Laden over as no proof could be given to back up the accusations of terrorist activities.

Malinowski replied to Mullah Omar that there was 'substantial and solid' evidence against Bin Laden and, based on that evidence, the U.S. 'wanted to protect its children as a father'. According to Malinowski, 'Mullah Omar needed to realize what Bin Laden was up to in Afghanistan. The missiles we fired on his camps in Khost were not aimed at Afghanistan and the Taliban; they were the U.S. acting in self-defense.' Malinowski said economic aid was not an option while Afghanistan was still so unstable and while Bin Laden was operating from within the country. There could be no question of a U.S. embassy in Kabul either, said the diplomat. Mullah Omar would just have to deal with the American embassy in Islamabad, in Pakistan.

When I asked Malinowski what he had done with Omar's specific request for more evidence against Bin Laden, he replied that he 'had collated some things'. 'We didn't really get the information we wanted from our secret services. But I thought the evidence was clear enough. Well, on the other hand how do you prove something like that? It wasn't like there were photos showing Bin Laden's involvement.'[70]

———————◆———————

The case against Bin Laden came before the court in Kabul on October 28, 1998. The judge, Nur Thaqib, had asked all the countries involved to hand over their evidence against Bin Laden to the court, after which he would be tried by the Taliban judge. Many countries did not respond to this call. Some simply assumed the Taliban were not interested in a fair trial and just wanted to delay things. Other countries did not want to become involved in the court case, as it would be tantamount to recognizing the Taliban regime. 'So everyone was caught up in a conundrum: How to get rid of Bin Laden through legal channels without recognizing those legal channels as legitimate. It would prove to be a puzzle that no one could solve,' concluded an Afghan consultant to the State Department who visited Kabul at the time.[71]

There were differences of opinion in the American embassy in Islamabad on how to respond to the Taliban's request for more evidence on Osama bin Laden's involvement. Some diplomats didn't take the Taliban particularly seriously and ignored the request.[72] The U.S. Justice Department used legalistic arguments: they did not want to share anything beyond the charge itself, as they believed the Taliban were in league with Osama bin Laden; they were therefore reluctant to give the movement more information. Alan Eastham, the deputy chief of mission for the U.S. in Pakistan, told me in an interview that he would have liked to 'test' the Taliban by giving them more evidence. But it is not clear whether the Justice Department actually had more evidence.

In the end, the Taliban were provided with the charge and a film. In Mutawakil's words, the U.S. handed over 'some papers and a video'.[73] A few Taliban members watched the film, but they saw nothing new and nothing that added to the case, said Mutawakil.[74] Osama bin Laden was eventually convicted for giving press conferences against the wishes of the Taliban and for his political statements. The charge that Bin Laden was the head of a terrorist network was ruled not proven by the Taliban.

That same month, Mullah Omar was honored with another visit by an impressive international delegation: Turki bin Faisal al-Saud, the head of the Mukhabarat, the Saudi intelligence service, and General Naseem Rana, the head of the I.S.I. At that point, Saudi Arabia and Pakistan were the only countries other than the United Arab Emirates that had recognized the Taliban regime. Both these countries had an embassy in Kabul.[75]

Mullah Omar had hoped the men had come to talk about the tensions surrounding Mazar-e-Sharif, the city he had just recaptured from Rabbani and Massoud's troops. He was also still embroiled in a serious conflict with Afghanistan's neighbor Iran, which had tens of thousands of soldiers gathered at the border. Support from Pakistan and Saudi Arabia would be more than welcome.[76] When the two men told Omar that they had come to discuss Osama bin Laden again, Mullah Omar became irritated.[77]

To his surprise, Turki said he and his Pakistani colleague had come to fetch Osama bin Laden, as Omar had apparently given him permission to do three months ago. Turki said a large plane was waiting at Kandahar Airport to take Bin Laden, his family, and all their possessions. Others who witnessed this encounter said Mullah Omar had to leave the room in order to calm down.[78] When he returned, he snapped at his guests that he had never promised to hand Bin Laden over. According to the Saudi intelligence chief, he started shouting at them.[79]

After this meeting, all diplomatic relations were broken off between Saudi Arabia and Afghanistan. Even requests from Afghans who applied for a visa for the hajj in Mecca were rejected. Now Pakistan was the only country to still have an embassy in Kabul.

People from Mullah Omar's circle at the time have never been able to agree on whether he had actually promised to give Bin Laden up to the Saudis or not.[80] Some are convinced that the two secret service chiefs were bluffing in order to intimidate the Taliban leader. Others do not rule out the possibility that Omar did make a promise, but they think he decided to renege on it after the attacks on Khost.[81] Latif told me that the Khost incident broke something in Omar. 'It was as if Mullah Omar never really got over it. The sixty cruise missiles essentially drove him into Bin Laden's arms.'

———◆———

It seems that Latif was right. The American cruise missiles on Khost had had the unintended effect of improving Osama bin Laden's reputation among the jihadists: he became a cult figure. The American embassy in Islamabad had a 'Most Wanted' poster made of him. Although this didn't result in his capture, it did make him incredibly popular in Pakistan. Abdel Bari Atwan, the editor-in-chief of *Al-Quds Al-Arabi*, an Arabic newspaper published in London, agreed: 'The American rocket attack bolstered Bin Laden's image.' Atwan said Bin Laden was 'the underdog who was being attacked by all-powerful America. That gave him huge authority in the eyes of people who were frustrated by the subordinate position of the Arab and Islamic communities on the international stage.'[82]

In a new, notorious series of interviews, including with Al Jazeera, Bin Laden called on jihadists to seize chemical and nuclear weapons. He said they were 'obliged by their religion' to use these weapons against the Americans. The Taliban gave the go-ahead for these interviews on condition that Osama bin Laden would say positive things about them and that he would deny his involvement with the attacks on the embassies in Africa. Bin Laden was only too happy to keep to these instructions. He had always denied any involvement with the attacks, possibly in part because he had been afraid of extradition. Now he gave a flat denial of everything. B.B.C. journalist Rahimullah Yousafzai, who was present at one of the interviews, said there were two Taliban leaders from the Foreign Ministry sitting in on Bin Laden's interview, probably to check that he did not say anything that had been prohibited.[83]

Osama's positive message about the Taliban was completely overshadowed by the new threats he levelled at the U.S. Inevitably, the Taliban were held partly responsible for Bin Laden's statements.[84] When American diplomats reacted furiously, Mullah Omar said that Bin Laden 'had been put under pressure by the journalists' who, he argued, had persisted with their questions.[85] One of Omar's envoys said on a visit to the American embassy that the interviews had been a disaster and the Taliban had made 'a mistake'.[86] The interviews helped the U.S. get more support in the U.N. for sanctions against Taliban-controlled Afghanistan.

As a result, for Mullah Omar, Bin Laden soon became 'a bone that sticks in your throat so that you can't swallow it or spit it out either', as the mullah is supposed to have said in a conversation with the I.S.I.[87] Bin Laden was becoming more and more of an obstacle to Mullah Omar's plans for Afghanistan, but the mullah still refused to concede that the Americans were right about Bin Laden and hand him over. This increasingly became a source of dissension within the Taliban. Some believed Bin Laden: the attacks ascribed to him could have been organized by young men elsewhere in the world. Some warned Mullah Omar not to give in to the pressure from America as this would harm the Taliban's reputation in the region.[88] Other prominent Taliban members, however, wanted to be rid of Bin Laden and pushed for him to be extradited.[89]

A portent of the increasing threat of international economic sanctions against Afghanistan was the collapse of the negotiations that had been going on for years with the Union Oil Company of California (UNOCAL) for a gas pipe across the country. This American company was the last oil company to still be talking to the Taliban.[90] It was a bitter pill for Mullah Omar to swallow as he had always given the negotiations his personal support, not just because of the economic benefits but also in recognition of the diplomatic prestige of having such a pipeline.[91] However, the oil company was under a great deal of pressure. American feminists organized large demonstrations to protest the 'appalling gender apartheid' of the Taliban regime. The U.S. Secretary of State Madeleine Albright also repeatedly declared that the U.S. would not have anything to do with the Taliban as long as they continued to oppress women.[92]

Meanwhile, Mujahed and Shaheen, the two Taliban representatives in New York, conducted a hopeless campaign from their little apartment in Flushing. While they did gain access to people like the U.S. Assistant Secretary of State Karl Inderfurth ('a nice man,' remembers Mujahed), they accomplished very little. In line with his leader's statements, Mujahed would always stress that the Taliban were a *national* movement. 'We're not an international organization and we don't have plans for territorial expansion. The Afghans have never committed acts of terrorism.' Or he would point to the Taliban regime's similarities to Saudi Arabia. 'The United States is on friendly terms with that country, so why not with the Taliban too?'

Mujahed asked Inderfurth whether the Americans could perhaps tone down their criticism of the opium industry, the human rights situation, and gender inequality in Afghanistan. 'If you continue to adopt such a rigid position, that will make it very difficult for Mullah Omar to persuade the Afghan people to take a benign view of the Americans.' But to Mujahed's dismay, Inderfurth did nothing with his requests, Mujahed told me.

———————◆———————

Omar bin Laden says that in the summer of 1999, he saw a long procession of jeeps turning up at the place where Bin Laden was staying just outside of Kandahar where the vast expanse of the Red Desert starts. Omar bin Laden had never seen Mullah Omar before that day, but he knew immediately that the tall man in the black turban was the leader. 'He was even taller than my father,' said Bin Laden's son.

Mullah Omar had given advance notice of his visit, and Bin Laden had gone to great trouble to arrange a special lunch that bordered on a feast. But Bin Laden's son soon realized that Mullah Omar was not in the mood for delicacies. The Taliban leader barely greeted Osama and sat down far away from him. Mullah Omar even asked for a chair, which was unusual for him. Omar would regularly sit on the ground, but now he probably wanted to give an impression of power.

Omar bin Laden said Mullah Omar's message to his father was crystal clear: 'It's not working – you have to leave.' Mullah Omar talked about his concerns for the state of his country and about the threats Afghanistan was receiving from abroad. 'They're already angry about the drugs and women's rights. I can't have the mess of your extradition on top of that.' According to Bin Laden's son, Mullah Omar acknowledged that under Islamic law he did not have the right to hand Bin Laden over without convincing evidence against him, but he still hoped Bin Laden would leave of his own accord. Osama bin Laden replied that he had spent many years of his life in Afghanistan, he had fought for the Afghans in the jihad against the Soviet Union, and now he had returned in order to build a village for his family and friends.

'Where are we supposed to go?' he asked Mullah Omar insistently. But the mullah was unmoved; the time had come to leave, he said. Bin Laden referred to his stay in Sudan, a country that also had been under tremendous pressure from the U.S. to expel Bin Laden (although Osama bin Laden was not so well known back then, B.D.) and had eventually complied by letting him leave in complete secret. When Bin Laden reminded the Taliban leader that Sudan had let him stay five years and he had only been in Afghanistan for three and a half years, Mullah Omar stood up and left. Osama's son recalled that Mullah Omar refused to shake Bin Laden's hand.

———— ◆ ————

In September 1999, the U.N. Security Council had frozen all Taliban assets held outside of Afghanistan. On October 15, 1999, the Council unanimously adopted Resolution 1267. It contained a long list of accusations leveled at the Taliban regime, including the production and trading of drugs, human rights abuses, the oppression of women, and aggression against Iran.[93] The demand that drew most attention was the call to hand over Osama bin Laden, preferably to the U.S. directly and otherwise to a third country that would then itself extradite him to the U.S. Failure to comply with this demand within thirty days would be met with far-reaching economic sanctions. At the same time, the U.S. promised a reward of $5 million for any tips leading to the arrest and conviction of Bin Laden.[94] If the Taliban refused to hand over Bin Laden, Afghanistan would be cut off from the rest of the world. Commercial flights to and from Afghanistan would be banned, and all assets and funds belonging to the Taliban and donations to the regime would be frozen.

Against the wishes of a growing group of prominent Taliban, Mullah Omar decided not to yield to the Security Council's demands (a decision that was not entirely unexpected). The Taliban leader mentioned various reasons for refusing. The Americans had not recognized his country and were consequently not formally in a position to demand anyone's extradition. Nor did he want to provoke anger among other Islamic countries – which donated money to his cause, unlike the Americans – by turning Osama bin Laden out of his country. He was also convinced that the U.S. and other countries wanted more than just the extradition of Osama bin Laden.[95] He suspected that even if he did hand Bin Laden over, he would then be required to allow women out in public without a burka, to put an end to the segregation of the sexes in health care, to ban corporal punishment, and so on. In short, the Taliban would no longer be able to use the Shariah as the divine guide. So Mullah Omar rejected the demand and let it be known that he hoped Bin Laden would not feel he was being hunted down by the U.N. resolution.[96]

After 9/11, more evidence gradually emerged that Mullah Omar had indeed tried behind the scenes to rid himself of Osama bin Laden, but there was always the question of where he could be sent. The Taliban wanted to set up a council of Saudi and Afghan Islamic experts in the hope that this would enable them to hand Osama back to Saudi Arabia without loss of face but it was unclear if Saudi Arabia would accept the return of Bin Laden, who might attract a lot of attention in Riyadh. According to Mutawakil, this course of action became impossible after the incident between Mullah Omar and Turki, because Saudi Arabia was not able to swallow its pride.[97]

Mutawakil had also discussed less-diplomatic solutions with the Americans. According to one U.S. C.I.A. officer, he gave permission for them to eliminate Bin Laden with a rocket attack or a sniper.[98] The Americans did make attempts to bribe tribal leaders who might be willing to polish off Bin Laden, but their contacts with these tribal leaders were not good enough to persuade anyone to actually shoot him dead.[99] The U.S. did not send any of its own commandos 'as the Americans did not have any bases close to Afghanistan' from which they could operate. Nor did the Americans go ahead with a rocket attack as the C.I.A. did not see legal options for this, something that profoundly frustrated Robert Grenier, the agency's chief responsible for Pakistan.[100]

Another C.I.A. plan was to kidnap Bin Laden with the help of Afghan infiltrators. He would then be smuggled onto a plane and flown to Egypt, where he would probably be tortured and possibly die from his injuries. A practice run of the kidnapping was carried out in El Paso, Texas, but the F.B.I.'s head of Counterterrorism eventually put a stop to this plan. 'I don't want to kill the man, I want justice,' he told the C.I.A., so the plan was abandoned.[101]

The Taliban had previously offered to put Osama bin Laden on trial before an Islamic court in another Islamic country with experts in Islamic law. The idea was that this would be an independent trial in which America could submit its own evidence, but the Americans were not willing to do this. They no longer believed that the Taliban had serious intentions.[102] Robert Grenier even thought the proposed trial was a diversionary tactic.[103]

The American embassy also knew of the Taliban's plan to have Bin Laden 'monitored' by the Organization of Islamic Cooperation or the U.N., but diplomats spoke of a 'solution' in their letter to Washington, which implies that this plan too was not taken seriously by the U.S.[104]

Mullah Omar also phoned the Pakistani journalist Rahimullah Yousafzai in Peshawar, whom he had consulted on several occasions in the past, to ask whether Bin Laden could perhaps be sent to Chechnya, which had been declared an Islamic republic in 1997. Yousafzai did not recommend this option as he thought the journey across land to Chechnya would be dangerous for Bin Laden.

Omar also made some rather clumsy attempts to deceive the U.N.
and U.S. For example, at one point he announced via the *Voice of Shariat*
that Osama bin Laden was missing and the Taliban were no longer in
contact with him. Then came an announcement that Bin Laden was
seriously ill and did not have long to live, which would make extradition
pointless.[105]

———————◆———————

The international sanctions came into effect in November 1999. The
sanctions had the effect of almost completely isolating Afghanistan, both
financially and in terms of accessibility. All commercial flights to Kabul
and other Afghan airports were banned. Afghanistan had been suffering
for some time from a blistering drought, which had parched the land
despite Mullah Omar's calls to combat it with prayer sessions. Many
people saw the drought as a punishment by Allah because not enough
Afghans truly believed in their Islamic state.[106]

Instead of handing Osama bin Laden over, Mullah Omar attempted
to appease the U.N. with another offer. Long before the sanctions
were introduced, he had asked the U.N.'s Special Envoy to Afghanistan
Lakhdar Brahimi whether the international community would recognize
his regime if he put a stop to the cultivation of poppies in his country.[107]
At that point, Afghanistan was one of the biggest producers of poppies
in the world, with the plants being used to produce opium, morphine,
and heroin. These were essentially the country's most important exports.

As the Taliban extended their control over Afghanistan, they had
destroyed many a poppy field, for the production and use of drugs
contravened the Shariah. But the scale of such destruction remained
modest as many poppy farmers had little alternative if they were to make
a living.[108] In 1997, the U.N. Office on Drugs and Crime (U.N.O.D.C.)
had started an equally modest program giving Afghan farmers money if
they stopped growing poppies.[109]

Brahimi gave a rather hesitant response to Mullah Omar's proposal. It was not his responsibility, but he promised he would raise the issue with the U.N.[110] Mullah Omar did not hear much more from him after this, so rather than wait for Brahimi's answer, he decided in early 2000 to reduce poppy production by two-thirds. Omar thought a blanket ban would be going too far as the farmers had so few alternatives. In March 2000, Mullah Omar wrote in a regulation: 'Now we will see how the global community reacts. If other countries offer economic aid to replace the opium, there is a chance the campaign against the poppy industry can be successful.'[111]

The measure soon had a marked effect.[112] Global opium poppy production fell by 34 per cent. Bernard Frahi, the head of the U.N.O.D.C. in Pakistan and Afghanistan, was full of praise for the Taliban leader, saying, 'This is the first time that a country has decided to eliminate in one go – not gradually – these crops on its territory.'[113]

Unfortunately, the sanctions brought the modest U.N.O.D.C. aid program to a virtual standstill. The organization warned that this could endanger Omar's attempt to combat the cultivation of opium poppies.[114] 'If we want this to work, we need to systematically tackle the poverty. To do that, we need funds and donors but most countries now want nothing more to do with the Taliban,' reported the U.N.O.D.C. They were soon proved right. Many of the former poppy farmers got into financial difficulties. They were preyed upon by the warlords and drug barons whom the Taliban had usurped years before but who seized this new chance. Before long, the farmers were returning to their old crop.[115]

———— ◆ ————

The worsening relations with the U.N. and the U.S. turned the Taliban into an increasingly inward-looking, mistrustful movement. In the early years, Mullah Omar could be approached by anyone. His sober office was open to everyone with a complaint or problem, and they could be sure of a hearing. Now Omar had a new office outside Kandahar. The city itself was no longer safe for him after the American attacks on Khost in 1998 and an attack on his old office in Kandahar in 1999, in which he lost two half-brothers and only narrowly escaped with his own life.

Omar's new office was a concrete fortress with thirty-inch-thick walls and a ten-foot-thick roof protecting him like a rectangular concrete helmet. In addition to this place, he also had a small mosque built. It was unusually colorful for an Afghan mosque. The minarets were purple, pink, and yellow, the walls bright blue and mint green, while the windows had purple floral decorations on a pink background. It was a little like the mosque in his village in Deh Rawod, which was also very colorful, whereas most Afghan village mosques were little more than mud-brick huts, often without even a minaret. Only confidants and employees working closely with Omar met with him in the fortress office in Kandahar. There were no more spontaneous visits. Nothing was left to chance and most people were kept away from him.

While the economic situation in Afghanistan worsened, Mullah Omar's office produced a steady stream of regulations that many found irrelevant. One decree banned people from bowing when greeting someone, which is a common custom in large parts of Asia. Instead, the Islamic greeting *Salam alaykum* ('peace be upon you') became mandatory. Restrictions for women were tightened further still. After 2000, the only jobs they were allowed to do were in health care, and they were banned from driving.

Because of the sanctions, the Taliban also imposed stricter rules on the aid organizations in the country. They made it harder for aid workers to obtain visas or travel around Afghanistan, and even arrested them in their offices.[116] The editorial staff of the international media met with similar obstacles as Mullah Omar thought they were too critical of the Taliban. Even the well-connected B.B.C. journalist Kate Clark, who had lived in Kabul for years, was forced to leave.[117]

——————•◆•——————

October 2000 saw another terrorist attack, which the U.S. and a number of other countries immediately ascribed to Osama bin Laden. In the Gulf of Aden, the U.S. marine vessel U.S.S. Cole was bombed in a suicide attack by two Yemeni in a boat. Seventeen American crew members lost their lives. This attack prompted the Americans to make another attempt to persuade Mullah Omar that Osama bin Laden was involved in the acts of terrorism targeting the U.S. Talks were held in Pakistan's capital city Islamabad, where the intermediary, Pakistani Minister for the Interior Haider, spoke for over seven hours with C.I.A. and F.B.I. agents.

Haider told me that after that briefing, he was quite convinced that 'a group of Arabs who would later be called Al Qaeda' was responsible for the attacks in Dar es Salaam, Nairobi, and the Gulf of Aden. 'They were also able to convince me of the links between those Arabs, Afghanistan, and Osama bin Laden,' said Haider. When I countered that I had heard from other Pakistani government members that they found the evidence weak and the story of a collaboration with Bin Laden unconvincing, he replied – like Michael Milanowski previously – that you obviously could not expect photographic evidence demonstrating Bin Laden's involvement. 'It was a bit like with Al Capone. Try proving he was involved.'[118]

When the Americans asked Haider to convey the evidence they had briefed him on to Mullah Omar, the minister became irked, replying, 'You Americans are always telling us Afghanistan has done this, or Afghanistan has done that. But why are you talking to us if it's our neighbor who is in the wrong?' He refused to comply with the Americans' request. In the end, the information was passed on to Mullah Omar via the Taliban ambassador in Islamabad, but the mullah did not find the evidence very persuasive.

————————◆————————

At the end of February 2001, Mullah Omar announced that he planned
to destroy two iconic statues of Buddha in the province of Bamyan.
Their destruction came as a surprise to both members of the Taliban
and Westerners.[119] The unique statues were 174 and 115 feet tall, had
been carved from a cliffside about 1,500 years ago and were a UNESCO
World Heritage Site. Mullah Omar's announcement met with shock and
outrage among the Taliban themselves and around the world, but he was
unperturbed. It was as if he was no longer interested in what the U.S. or
other U.N. countries thought of the Taliban. 'I'm not concerned about
our relations with the world,' he told a local journalist. 'My task is to
implement the rules of Islam, no more or less than that.'[120]

In recent years, local commanders had been arguing that the statues
did not belong in an Islamic state. One commander tried to shoot at them,
as had been done several times in the civil war in the 1990s (destroying
part of the Buddhas' faces).[121] But Mullah Omar had previously wanted
nothing to do with these objections. Although the Taliban regime forbade
the worship of images – and the huge Buddhas were classic examples of
idolatry – Omar had opposed taking action as he said the statues were
part of Afghanistan's cultural heritage and should in fact be protected. In
July 1999, the Taliban Minister of Culture spoke about the respect due
to pre-Islamic antiquities and saw a risk of retaliation against mosques
in Buddhist countries if they destroyed the Buddhas. He made it clear
that, although there were no Buddhist believers in Afghanistan, 'Bamyan
would not be destroyed but, on the contrary, protected.'[122] In 2000, the
group publicly declared that Afghanistan's pre-Islamic heritage would be
protected under Taliban rule.[123]

'That was good news for us after eighteen years of war,' said
Robert Kluijver, who was working at the time for the Society for the
Preservation of Afghan Cultural Heritage (SPACH). Kluijver, who

speaks Dari, was living in Kabul at the time. According to him, almost all of Afghanistan's cultural assets had been destroyed or looted during the jihad against the Soviet Union and the civil war. Earthenware pots, countless Buddha statues, copper medallions, and other museum objects had been shot to smithereens or had ended up with illegal traders in Pakistan, who sold them to Parisian auction houses and London antique markets.

While many of these objects were reported missing, very few were returned from Paris or London after the civil war. When the National Museum in Kabul closed, Kluijver and his staff quickly took the artefacts that were still left after the civil war to the Ministry of the Interior. Kluijver said the Taliban's conquest of Kabul brought a lot of benefits for the nation's cultural heritage. 'The period when the Taliban were in charge was actually the best time for us,' he told me. 'They did much better in terms of cultural protection than everyone had expected. It was a huge improvement on the civil war.'

Mullah Omar dealt rigorously with theft and robbery. When the Taliban reopened the museum in Kabul in 2000, its displays included pre-Islamic artefacts such as Buddhas. Such objects were part of the country's history and, it was argued, should therefore be protected. According to Kluijver, the Taliban were still hoping such a policy would help it achieve international recognition. It was a major disappointment for the Taliban leaders that this recognition never came. 'I was in Kabul, and they mistakenly thought I was UNESCO. "Will you open an office, will you open an office here?" they begged. They were so eager for aid and recognition from the world.'

It was only a couple of months after this rejection that Mullah Omar announced his intention to destroy the large Buddhas. Many wonder what changed his mind. The American archeologist and writer Nancy Dupree, who had lived in Afghanistan for a long time, told me 'it was the Arabs'. The Western narrative also embraced the idea that Osama bin Laden had made Mullah Omar change his mind. I haven't been able to corroborate this, though I have learned in my investigations for this book that Mullah Omar did not have regular contact with Osama bin Laden. In general, Mullah Omar didn't accept much advice from outsiders, especially regarding political decisions. I know the Taliban invited an Al Jazeera journalist to film the destruction, and he was later sent to Guantanamo Bay because he was (falsely) suspected of working for Al Qaeda.

According to the U.N. employee Michael Semple, who visited the province of Bamyan at that time, the rhetoric against 'these idols' had started already in January 2001 and 'everybody knew it was coming'.[124] Earlier, towards the end of 2000, the Taliban government asked the U.N. for help for a drainage system to protect the Buddha statues (but this U.N. unit had no budget). However, things changed in the beginning of 2001. A worried Semple says he wanted to 'trick' the Taliban and build a brick wall in front of the towering Buddhas. He hoped 'the Kandahari brothers', as he called the Taliban, would forget about Afghanistan's heritage. At around the same time, museum pieces were smashed in Kabul, but it wasn't clear whether this had anything to do with Taliban policy or was simply looting.[125]

In general, the situation in Bamyan was extremely sensitive at the start of 2001. The Taliban faced ongoing resistance from the men of the United Front (Rabbani and Massoud) and did not have full control of the province. In January 2001, the Taliban advanced to take the district of Yakaolang. They met with fierce resistance from the Hazara group Hizb-I Wahdat (part of the United Front; in 1996 Hizb-I Wahdat was one of the first groups that surrendered to the Taliban) and lost thirty Taliban, according to Human Rights Watch. At that time the local Hizb-I Wahdat had acquired reinforcements with hundreds of troops. The Taliban won the battle and started searching every house in the district out of revenge – which was in fact forbidden by their own rules. They lined up men, some say at least a hundred, beat them and killed them in the square. According to Human Rights Watch, three hundred people were killed in total; according to Semple, it was less.[126] Human Rights Watch also states that the local Taliban commander Mullah Abdul Sattar said that the fighting had to stop, and that Mullah Omar had ordered a general amnesty. 'He instructed the elders to go and meet with the Hizb-I Wahdat commander Khalili and tell him not to fight any more, or there would be more killing.'[127] The Hazara leader Khalili refused the surrender, and the area was soon full of dead bodies and the evidence of massacres, mostly men rounded up from their homes and killed. For the Taliban, everybody had become an enemy, and they acted as gods, killing everybody they wanted to kill, in the space of just four days. The Taliban also banned 'these biased' journalists from visiting Yakaolang. According to Mullah Omar's statements, they were only relying on 'rumors and gossip'. The Taliban kept Yakaolang for two weeks only, after which they lost it again and the fighting resumed.[128] In February 2001, the Taliban reported that 120 of their people were killed in a massacre, something that was denied by their enemies.[129]

Soon the center of Bamyan was garrisoned by the Taliban. They were a mixed bag: local mujahideen, Tajiks (from Bamyan) and Hazaras who sided with the Taliban, plus Taliban troops from Kandahar and Helmand. The resistance continued in the vicinity, and supply lines were re-opened. The Hazara leader Khalili was back in the field. It is against this background of brutal killings and an ongoing local war that Mullah Omar decided to destroy the iconic statues.

According to Kluijver, it was not Al Qaeda who influenced Mullah Omar. 'The U.S. and U.N. sanctions were a factor, as was the refusal to grant the Taliban a seat in the General Assembly. I saw how this weighed more heavily on the Taliban with every passing month,' said Kluijver. Francesc Vendrell, who succeeded Lakhdar Brahimi as the U.N.'s Special Envoy, agrees. 'It is quite possible that the sanctions and increasing isolation of the Taliban encouraged the orthodox forces and this is why that decision was taken.'[130] Latif, who worked closely with Mullah Omar until 2000, was somewhat more explicit. He said the destruction of the Buddhas was 'Omar giving the finger to the West.'[131]

Attempts by the U.N. and Pakistan to persuade the Taliban leader to change his mind were to no avail. Once again, Mullah Omar did not listen. He told the Taliban newspaper *Shariat Weekly*: 'The foreigners care more about those statues than about the Afghan people.' Michael Semple tried independently to involve the local commanders and convince them to postpone the decision, but this too didn't go anywhere.

The B.B.C. journalist Daoud Junbish could not believe his ears when he heard about Omar's plans. He phoned Foreign Minister Mutawakil and begged him to spare the statues. Mutawakil assured him that the plan would not go ahead, as even he could not believe Mullah Omar was serious about this.[132] Mansour, the Minister of Aviation, refused to fly one of their few working fighter jets stationed in Kandahar to destroy the Buddhas from the air (the initial plan).[133]

On March 9, 2001, explosives were hung from the Buddha statues and detonated. The news appeared first on Al Jazeera. Their report showed a ball of fire followed by pieces of the old carved rock flying through the air.

———— ◆ ————

A couple of months after the destruction of the Buddhas, Mullah Omar did secretly make one final attempt to reach an agreement with the Americans about his awkward Arab guest. It was around this time, in July 2001, that Mutawakil warned the Americans in their embassy in Pakistan and the U.N. of an unknown attack planned by the Arabs, a tip-off by Uzbek fighters.[134] To examine the accusations against Osama bin Laden, Mullah Omar proposed organizing an Islamic tribunal in Doha. The U.S. would be able to present its evidence there. The Taliban would make sure the suspect turned up.

Such a tribunal had previously been seen as an option by the American embassy in Islamabad when they had discussed the possibilities for a trial.[135] But by 2001, Washington had other ideas. The U.S. Secretary of State Colin Powell rejected Omar's offer, referring to the U.N. resolution, which he said stated that Bin Laden had to be tried in the U.S.[136] According to Ambassador Alan Eastham, the mood in the American embassy in Islamabad was one of despondency and huge mistrust of the Taliban; they had long since given up taking proposals like this seriously.

8

Mullah Omar Knew Nothing
(2001)

WHEN two planes bored into the twin towers of the World Trade Center in New York – the first hitting the North Tower and the second striking the South Tower sixteen minutes later – on the morning of September 11, 2001, it was already evening in Kandahar. The city was under curfew. A few fruit and vegetable carts still stood along the sides of the streets. If you had flown over the city at that point, you would have seen the line of dots formed by the oil lamps attached to those carts, before the traders put them out and left the city almost pitch black.

That evening, Mullah Omar was in his heavily guarded office on the outskirts of the city as usual. Almost immediately after the first tower collapsed, he received a phone call from his Foreign Minister Mutawakil. Mutawakil said Mullah Omar was initially rather unemotional and didn't want to issue an official response as yet. 'Let's wait a bit. We need to know more first,' he told his minister.

When the second tower collapsed, Mutawakil called Omar again. The minister realized instantly what repercussions this attack would have; he was expecting the U.S. to hold Osama bin Laden responsible, and Mullah Omar's Taliban along with him. 'Regardless of whether this was actually the case,' said Mutawakil, who asked Omar once again how the Taliban should respond.

At about 9:30 in the evening, the Foreign Minister gave a statement at a packed press conference in Kabul. Wearing a white turban and sunglasses, he condemned the attacks and expressed grief for the victims in the U.S. on behalf of Mullah Omar. 'We were the first country to condemn the attacks,' he told me later.[1] There was a sad undertone to his voice when he told me this: Could things have gone differently?

During the press conference, Mutawakil discussed the possible involvement of Osama bin Laden. According to him, a lone operator, as the Taliban continued to see Bin Laden, could not possibly have organized something so major. 'This form of terrorism is too big for one person,' he told the international press, as Mullah Omar had instructed him to do.

Mutawakil was somewhat surprised at his boss's laconic attitude. Omar was apparently assuming that the Americans would take their time to collect and produce evidence on Bin Laden's involvement. Like Mutawakil, the Taliban's ambassador in Islamabad, Abdul Salam Zaeef, also warned Mullah Omar of the possibility of retaliation by the U.S. 'The Americans think you are very close to Bin Laden and you are therefore partly responsible for what happened in the U.S.,' he said.[2] But Mullah Omar did not agree. Zaeef told me that the Taliban leader estimated the likelihood of Afghanistan being attacked at a mere 10 per cent at most.

Omar compared the attacks in the U.S. with the bombings in Africa in 1998. In the latter case, the U.S. had retaliated without any proof of Bin Laden's involvement, according to Mullah Omar. So, he argued, if the U.S. was now immediately pointing the finger at Afghanistan, it would mean they hadn't learned anything. Zaeef and Mutawakil, who was also present, fell silent. They were amazed at what they saw as Omar's naiveté. Wasn't it rather late to be asking for evidence, given that the U.S. was already on the warpath?

On September 15, Robert Grenier, the C.I.A. chief responsible for Pakistan, met with a delegation from the Taliban in Quetta with Mullah Omar's consent.[3] Omar wanted the Taliban delegation to find a way out of the impasse, but would not allow them to make any commitments. The delegation was led by Mullah Osmani. Grenier believed that unlike Omar, Osmani wanted to be rid of Bin Laden but did not know how to arrange it.

According to Grenier, Mullah Osmani admitted that Bin Laden was a problem for both sides and they should therefore work on a solution together.[4] This gave Grenier hope, so he proposed that Mullah Omar issue a statement saying he had seen evidence from America that Bin Laden was the mastermind behind the attacks. Furthermore, Omar was to cooperate with Bin Laden's extradition or immediate execution, to be performed by the Americans, either alone or with the aid of the Taliban.

Grenier said the talks went on for hours without any solution being found for Osama bin Laden. Osmani oscillated between calm responses and eruptions of anger, screaming that if America attacked Afghanistan, the Taliban would crush the Americans as they had the Soviets before them. Osmani eventually agreed to put the proposal to Mullah Omar, but he added that he did not think it would lead to anything.

Meanwhile, Mullah Omar seemed distinctly unimpressed by the threats coming from America. It was almost as if he was ignoring the uproar around 9/11 and was going about his daily life regardless. Despite warnings that the Americans could be making all kinds of plans to target him personally, he continued his weekly visits to pray at the graves of his favorite Sufi leaders.

At a large gathering in Kabul, the Taliban leader won the support of over three hundred mullahs from across the country who were there to discuss the possible extradition of Bin Laden. But they demanded more evidence of his involvement in the attacks in the U.S. and proposed asking the U.N. to conduct a 'sound and thorough' investigation. These mullahs shared Mullah Omar's viewpoint that while Bin Laden should be asked again to leave, he should not be driven out. The mullahs made it clear that if the U.S. were to attack Afghanistan, they would respond with a jihad.[5]

A few days later, Mullah Omar let it be known once again that he was not afraid of an American attack on his country. This was the first time that Mullah Omar had spoken to the international media since the four attacks in the U.S. He was interviewed by Spozhmai Maiwandi for the Voice of America radio station broadcasting to Asia. Maiwandi had previously been involved in the phone call between Mullah Omar and the American diplomat Malinowski. After intervention by the U.S. Department of State, the journalist received a reprimand from her editor-in-chief for giving the enemy a platform. In the end, only a few quotes by Mullah Omar were broadcast.[6]

Mullah Omar said he was convinced the Americans would never catch him. 'I have heard two promises. The first is a promise from Allah that we will find shelter and protection throughout our country. The second is a promise from President Bush that there is no place on Earth where I will be able to hide. We will see which promise turns out to be true.'

———— ♦ ————

Pressure from Afghanistan's neighbor Pakistan also could not persuade Mullah Omar to change his mind about handing over Bin Laden. At the request of the U.S., a large Pakistani delegation left for Kandahar at the end of September. The group included several leading muftis who were thought to be on good terms with the Taliban.

Their reception by the Taliban leader was almost hostile. Mullah Omar had recently learned that earlier that month, the man heading the delegation, the I.S.I. boss General Mahmoud, had yielded to American threats regarding Pakistan's alleged support for the Taliban. Joe Biden, then a senator, had told General Mahmoud, who happened to be in Washington on a visit on 9/11, that if they did not stop their support for the Taliban immediately, the Americans would kill Omar. The head of the I.S.I. had apparently replied that Mullah Omar was 'a man with humanitarian instincts and not a man of violence', but Biden was not listening.[7]

So when the same general urged Mullah Omar to expel Bin Laden, the mullah did not mince his words. Omar complained that Pakistan and the I.S.I. were only thinking of themselves. 'You gave in to pressure from the Americans and you let the U.S. into your country. Soon you'll be coming back with your tails between your legs, asking for our help in driving out the Americans.'[8]

On October 2, Grenier had a follow-up meeting with Mullah Osmani. Grenier later said that he admitted in that meeting that the Americans had abandoned Afghanistan to its fate after the victory over the Soviet Union. But if the Taliban were now to extradite Osama bin Laden and his Arab supporters, the country would be able to count on vast amounts of aid. 'We want to hunt down the terrorists but we also realize that they will be back unless we have a stable Afghan government. If the Taliban want to form that stable government, that is acceptable to us.' When Mullah Osmani again said that he would pass on the proposal to Mullah Omar, Grenier suggested that he would be better off organizing a coup against the Taliban leader and then implementing the proposal himself. Osmani promised to call Grenier back but the American never heard from him again.[9]

———————•◆•———————

The fact that they did not hand over Bin Laden was further confirmation for the Americans that the Taliban had been involved in 9/11 and therefore that they and their leader Mullah Omar should pay the price for the attacks. After 9/11, the notion took hold that the Taliban and

Al Qaeda were in cahoots and that Mullah Omar had helped with the preparations for the attacks – under pressure from the allegedly incredibly wealthy Bin Laden. In his widely read book *Bush at War*, the American author Bob Woodward indirectly quoted C.I.A. boss George Tenet, who had told President Bush only hours after the attacks that they had to deny Al Qaeda sanctuary, that they had to tell the Taliban that they were done with them, and that the Taliban and Al Qaeda were really the same.[10]

As I think this book shows, I have not found any convincing proof for the assumption that Mullah Omar and the Taliban were directly involved in the events of September 11, 2001. I realize that it must have been difficult for some U.S. policymakers to grasp that the refusal to expel Bin Laden did not necessarily imply support for Bin Laden or adherence to a similar ideology; not all Islamic groups are the same, despite their common religion. The distrust between the two groups is more apparent to me. By now, as I write this, there is an increasing amount of evidence available, including within the U.S. government, pointing to the differences between the Taliban and Al Qaeda. The Taliban had a different ideology, different religious beliefs, different goals, and no interest in attacking the U.S., to the point that Al Qaeda didn't feel comfortable sharing details with them. I will never forget an anecdote I had heard (I am no longer able to trace the source but the story is too telling not to mention). Bin Laden was afraid that his plans would be leaked to the Taliban, who were after all not exactly favorably disposed towards him. That was why hardly any of the Arabs in Afghanistan had known of the plan either. Apparently, on one occasion Bin Laden told the few Arabs who had been informed that they were not even allowed to dream about the coming attacks. If they did, Mullah Omar would be able to read their dreams and the plan would be unmasked.

Robert Grenier also thinks it very unlikely that Mullah Omar knew anything about 9/11 beforehand:

As far as Mullah Omar and 9/11 are concerned, I don't believe he had been told of the plans in advance, although I can't prove this. Given the lack of convincing evidence that he knew of the plans, I can only assume he had not been informed. Bin Laden and his Arabs didn't trust the Afghans, and Bin Laden and Omar had a complex relationship defined by deep mistrust. So I find it difficult to believe that Bin Laden would have entrusted Omar with such a secret, given that he probably assumed anything he told Omar would be passed on to the other senior Taliban. And any leak about an impending attack on the U.S. could have serious consequences for Al Qaeda's plans. I have not seen any evidence at all to the contrary.

———◆———

In Washington in the days following 9/11, there was little interest in the nuances of the relationship between Al Qaeda and the Taliban, says Grenier. The U.S. was 'under attack', as the shocked American media put it. The Americans had not suffered an attack on home territory since the Japanese bombed Pearl Harbor in 1941. Pearl Harbor had resulted in the deaths of around 2,400 soldiers; now the number of fatalities was higher, and they were mostly civilians.

Within a matter of days, the Congress had voted to give President Bush unprecedented powers to lead what had soon been dubbed the War on Terror. George Tenet, the then head of the C.I.A., explained how the U.S. would frame this. He saw the war in sixty countries, he said. 'We have a sixty-country problem.' Bush replied, 'Let's pick them off one at a time.'[11] The U.S. government assigned countries to this War on Terror in less than twenty-four hours, without providing a specific list. According to the U.S. government, the Taliban in Afghanistan, Saddam Hussein in Iraq, and the Gaddafi family in Libya were the worst culprits in aiding and abetting international terrorism.[12] It was a declaration of war in barely sixty words:

The president is authorized to use all necessary and appropriate force against those nations, organizations, or persons he determines planned, authorized, committed, or aided the terrorist attacks that occurred on September 11, 2001, or harbored such organizations or persons, in order to prevent any future acts of international terrorism against the United States by such nations, organizations or persons.[13]

The nations, organizations or persons who were deemed to have any kind of connection to terrorism could not expect to be dealt with mercifully. The legal protection that is customary in democratic states would be dispensed with for the sake of the War on Terror. The powers accorded to President Bush meant that the investigative agencies were given free rein to hunt down terrorist suspects as they saw fit, in the U.S. and elsewhere.

Only one member of the Congress, the Democrat Barbara Lee, expressed reservations about the carte blanche that the U.S. president and his agencies were being given in the War on Terror. She felt people were being guided too much by their raw emotions and not enough by an examination of the facts. But no one paid heed to Lee's objections. On the contrary, she was inundated by letters and phone calls calling her un-American and a traitor, and she even received death threats.[14]

9

The Unwanted Capitulation
(2001)

IN the night of October 6, 2001, a Predator 3034 hovered over Mullah Omar's office in Kandahar. It was a new kind of unmanned aircraft, equipped with cameras and a Hellfire rocket.[1] This was the first time that the U.S. had deployed a drone as a weapon. It was 9:30 in the evening. The sky was cloudless and full of stars. Mullah Omar and his colleagues inside the building were unaware of any danger.

Thousands of miles away, in the C.I.A. headquarters in Langley just outside Washington, senior C.I.A. officers watched the camera images sent by the drone as it approached the Taliban leader's office building. A bomb hitting the office itself would cause too many civilian casualties, so they waited patiently for him to emerge.

When three Land Cruisers eventually drove off the premises carrying more armed men than could really fit in, the officers in Langley felt sure one of the vehicles must be carrying Mullah Omar. But the Hellfire was not launched because two generals could not agree on the timing of the attack. The three Land Cruisers drove along a busy street with many civilians walking along, and then disappeared into another complex.

Two large grey fighter planes with heavy-duty bombs on board, big enough to blow off the roof of the building, were not given permission to release their weapons yet either. The outline of a small mosque could be seen on the screen in Langley and the C.I.A. did not want to risk hitting it. But they did fire the Hellfire at a truck close to the complex in the hope that the explosion would make Mullah Omar and his companions flee the building. If they did, the plan was for the fighter planes to finish the job off.

But with all the dust and clouds of smoke generated by the exploding truck, the C.I.A. was unable to spot Mullah Omar on the screens in Langley. President Bush, who was watching as well, realized that it was all going wrong and gave the order to bomb the entire complex anyway. But it was already too late. Mullah Omar had escaped and remained unharmed.

The war that President Bush had declared on the Taliban – Operation Enduring Freedom – started for real the next day. Initially, it mainly involved air raids with cruise missiles and heavy bombardments of the Taliban's military bases, airfields, and government buildings, primarily in and around big cities like Kabul and Kandahar. These attacks were launched from American aircraft carriers or air bases in neighboring countries like Uzbekistan.

The bombings in eastern Afghanistan employed daisy cutters – weapons that were given this name in Vietnam because they could flatten an area of forest and turn it into a helicopter landing pad. Now they were used in Afghanistan to bombard this mountainous region where large numbers of Al Qaeda's Arab fighters, possibly including Osama bin Laden, were thought to be hiding out.

At first, only a few American soldiers were deployed on Afghan soil. After the first bombings, some Special Forces units and C.I.A. commandos were dropped by helicopter in northern Afghanistan. The idea was that they should make contact with the soldiers of the Northern Alliance, the fierce opponents of the Taliban, whose leaders included the former president Rabbani, driven out by the Taliban, and the notoriously cruel Uzbek general Abdul Rashid Dostum, who had fought on the side of the Soviet Union and the Communist president Najibullah until 1992. A U.N. official once told me about four colleagues who had had their passports stolen back then. When they confronted Dostum about this and told him they suspected his troops of the theft, Dostum shot several of his soldiers dead on the spot.

The leader Ismail Khan, who had previously been imprisoned by the Taliban but had managed to escape, was also persuaded to provide 'boots on the ground' for America's fight against the Taliban. Suitcases full of C.I.A. dollars were often used to persuade potential allies who were hesitating.

Along with the bombs and rockets, thousands of pamphlets were also dropped on Afghanistan. The Americans hoped this would persuade the local people to choose freedom. The pamphlets showed Bin Laden with Mullah Omar as a dog on a leash. They also listed the radio frequencies of stations broadcasting to Afghanistan, frequencies that had been deliberately chosen to disrupt the reception of the Taliban channel the Voice of Shariat.

A couple of days into the bombing, a Taliban commander repeated the Taliban idea of delivering up Bin Laden. *The New York Times* reported this. 'We would be ready to hand him over to a third country,' said Maulvi Abdul Kabir, the second-in-command to the Taliban's supreme leader, Mullah Muhammad Omar. 'It can be negotiated provided the U.S. gives us evidence and the Taliban are assured that the country is neutral and will not be influenced by the United States. But Mr. Bush, who at a news conference last week said he would be willing to "reconsider" military operations if Mr. Bin Laden was handed over, gave no such signal today.'[2]

One month later, the Americans launched the first major ground offensive in Operation Enduring Freedom. The target was Mazar-e-Sharif in northwest Afghanistan. This city had been the scene of fierce fighting between the Taliban and other factions in 1997 and 1998, with merciless acts of revenge on Taliban combatants (in 1997) and Hazara fighters (in 1998). Now General Dostum's militias headed for the city – some in tanks, some on horseback – accompanied by American commandos who could also call on the support of their air force if necessary.

The battle did not last long. Before the fighting really got going on the ground, the American fire power from the air had already caused carnage among the Taliban and a group of Arab Al Qaeda combatants who were defending the city. Hundreds of fighters were killed. Others surrendered to General Dostum. Yet another group retreated to Kunduz, a city in northern Kunduz Province, where they joined Taliban soldiers who were gathering there after having been driven out of other parts of the north.

The battle was essentially over by the time a thousand young Pakistani madrassa students turned up in Mazar-e-Sharif. The C.I.A. had ordered Pakistan to hold these fighters back behind its borders, but that proved impossible. The Pakistani mullah Sufi Mohammed, among others, had called upon the youths to defend the Islamic state of the Taliban against the Americans. Now the students refused to surrender, having taken shelter in a school. After the Americans had bombed the building, Dostum's militias fired on the survivors as they fled the school. About eight hundred were killed.

In that same week, the Taliban lost Herat, the western city which they had captured in 1995 after fierce fighting with the leader Ismail Khan. In a complicated plot that even involved Iranian commandos, the city was infiltrated and the local people were urged to rise up against the Taliban. This they did, and Ismail Khan was able to regain control of the city with very little fighting. Large numbers of Taliban soldiers surrendered.

One day later, on November 14, Kabul fell. After a day of persistent rocket attacks and heavy bombing, thousands of Taliban soldiers and their leaders took flight, heading south to Kandahar. At first, the Americans tried to prevent the militias of the former president Rabbani from taking control of the capital, fearing a repeat of the events of 1992, after the fall of the Communist president Najibullah, when Kabul descended into chaos as rival warlords fought one another and wreaked havoc. The Taliban's rapid retreat caused some surprise. There had been no time yet to reach an agreement on how power was to be shared should Omar's movement be driven out. The American offensive in Afghanistan was relying largely on the same warlords who had brought so much turmoil to the country after the previous intervention by foreign powers.

After the Taliban had left, Kabul was soon reoccupied by Rabbani's troops. Rabbani rushed to the presidential palace that he had been forced to leave in 1996. The U.S. tolerated him for the time being after he agreed to the proposal for a U.N. conference to be arranged speedily to discuss Afghanistan's future. Special envoy Lakhdar Brahimi was to preside over the conference, which was scheduled to take place in Bonn, Germany, in a few weeks' time.

Although people rejoiced in the streets of Kabul at the departure of the Taliban, fear also reigned in those first few weeks as residents wondered how the struggle for power between the various 'pretenders to the throne' would develop.

———————— ♦ ————————

With the fall of Kabul, the Taliban had lost control of the northern half of Afghanistan in just a short space of time. Only in Kunduz, on the border with Tajikistan, were there still several thousand Taliban soldiers gathered together with a large group of young Pakistani volunteers sent by Mullah Sufi Mohammed and a group of Arab fighters. But they were gradually being encircled by Dostum's militias, with support from American commandos.

The city was subjected to heavy bombing from the air for eleven days, aimed at breaking the men's resistance. Incidentally, most of that resistance came from the Pakistani volunteers and other foreign fighters. As had already become clear in Mazar-e-Sharif and Kabul, the Taliban themselves had little stomach for fighting to the bitter end. Flight was not an option in Kunduz, so they tried to negotiate a surrender, but, as journalist Seymour Hersh wrote, this was adamantly and successfully opposed by the Bush administration.[3]

Because the Taliban were afraid of the revenge Dostum's militias might take, they attempted to contact the Americans and the U.N., but they got no response. However, some say an air bridge was formed for the Pakistani fighters at the insistence of the Pakistani president Musharraf; the Pakistanis, like the Arabs, were usually shot dead ruthlessly by Dostum's militias if they tried to give themselves up. Apparently, Musharraf persuaded the Americans to arrange the evacuation of these fighters by arguing that there would otherwise be considerable criticism in Pakistan of his support for America's offensive in Afghanistan.[4] The organization of the air bridge did not go smoothly, and it was thought that key Al Qaeda fighters might have managed to slip in among the thousands of Pakistanis who were evacuated. American and European TV channels were soon calling the Pakistani evacuation the Airlift of Evil.

The Taliban eventually surrendered to General Dostum's militias on November 23. Their fear of the revenge he would wreak turned out to be justified. After the surrender, hundreds of Taliban were shot dead while handcuffed. Hundreds more died en route to Dostum's Qala-i-Jangi prison. When riots broke out in the prison as well, American fighter jets bombed the building, causing hundreds more casualties.

After the prison uprising, thousands of prisoners were taken to the nearby Sheberghan jail, packed into containers that were then locked shut. Thousands of Taliban soldiers died a gruesome death in those containers. Whether or not the American commandos knew about this is unclear.

In 2002, the U.S. government tried to forestall an investigation into these events by human rights organizations. General Dostum went on to become vice president of Afghanistan in 2014 under President Ghani. In 2017, he moved to Turkey following allegations that he had raped a political rival.

What had been feared but had largely failed to materialize in Kabul did happen in northern Afghanistan. After the fall of Kunduz, Tadjik and Uzbek militias drove the Pashtun out of their towns and villages, regardless of whether or not they had any links to the Taliban. According to reports by the U.N., over half a million Pashtun from northern Afghanistan fled south in the final months of 2001.

———————◆———————

The major setbacks in the defense of his regime seemed to have little effect on Mullah Omar. He continued to urge his Taliban soldiers on in radio broadcasts, as if there had never been any defeats or surrenders. He did not just address his own men either. In a variation on President Bush's statement that 'you are either with us or you are with the terrorists', the Taliban leader said:

> The Islamic world also needs to make a choice now. It is appalling that the Americans think they are so powerful that they can start an illegal war against us. We are not terrorists, nor do we shelter terrorists. The Americans just want to see things that way. They have attacked us without giving any evidence for their accusations. We offered shelter to an innocent and homeless Muslim who had nowhere else to go. But they were simply looking for a pretext to attack an Islamic country. Because that is our real sin as far as the Americans are concerned: the fact that we introduced the Shariah in Afghanistan. Will your faith allow the United States' barbaric treatment of Muslims? Will your faith allow you to stand by and support the Americans? Everyone knows

that the Soviet Union and the British suffered defeat in our country.
That will be the fate of the Americans too. We will not be welcoming
them with roses. They will be taught a far harder lesson than the Soviets
were taught.[5]

However, Omar's combative attitude in his publicity statements did not
reflect the reality on the ground. His words sounded aggressive but that
sentiment was no longer shared by most of his commanders (including
some who had been with him since the start), especially after the fall of
Kunduz on November 23. Even in southern Afghanistan, hundreds of
soldiers were ready to give up. They were convinced any attempt to resist
the Americans was doomed to failure and were therefore prepared to
relinquish their weapons and negotiate an amnesty, in the time-honored
Afghan tradition when faced with inevitable defeat.

Mullah Omar warned his men, 'Make sure you continue to fight back
and don't listen to the propaganda of the mercenaries who are helping
the Americans. They delivered our country into the hands of foreigners
in the past. Anyone who deserts his position will die like a headless
chicken in an open sewer.' But however vehemently the Taliban leader
urged his soldiers to fight on, his words no longer had any effect.

———————— ◆ ————————

At the end of November, the Americans and their Afghan allies advanced
on Kandahar, all the while bombing the city ceaselessly. Many people
wondered whether Mullah Omar was even still alive; countless rumors
circulated that he had fled.

Hamid Karzai was now active in the area north of Kandahar. He was
the scion of an important family among the Popalzai, a Pashtun tribe,
and had once been considered a possible Taliban ambassador to the U.N.
Years before the events of 2001, Karzai had started mobilizing Pashtun
leaders, including some Taliban sympathizers, with the aim of seizing

power. Mullah Omar had driven Karzai out of Uruzgan only a few weeks earlier but he had been rescued by American commandos and was back in the area thanks to their help. Now Karzai was holding intensive talks again with Pashtun leaders in southern Afghanistan. His name was also mentioned in Kabul in connection with the U.N. conference due to start in Germany.

Mullah Omar braced himself one last time to counter his commanders' growing doubts about the wisdom of continuing to fight. Speaking via a satellite phone, in an interview with the B.B.C. Pashto radio station that he arranged personally, he once again called on the Taliban to fight and said it was disgraceful that people should choose to collaborate with the Americans. 'The men who are now selling themselves to the American invaders have made great mistakes in the past. We shall never accept government by these guilty men. We prefer death to collaboration with such a regime.'

Shortly after the fall of Kabul on November 13, Mullah Omar had ordered his key commander and deputy Mullah Berader to attack Karzai in Uruzgan again. The attack was a disaster. Hundreds of Taliban soldiers became cannon fodder for the American fighter jets that came to Karzai's aid. This hopeless debacle convinced the Taliban military, who were concerned about Mullah Omar's intransigence, that they needed to take action. Like the Taliban, Karzai was a Pashtun who respected the same age-old tribal traditions for resolving armed conflicts. Those traditions revolved around demonstrating who was the strongest – using violence if necessary. Once that had become clear and the loser had acknowledged the winner, it was time for various forms of amnesty that would allow the losing group to 'take part' again, but in accordance with the new balance of power.

In their advance on Kabul, the Taliban had also often allowed defeated warlords to maintain their local position of power in return for a promise to observe the Shariah. The way the Northern Alliance and the Americans had treated the Taliban in Mazar-e-Sharif and Kunduz was completely at odds with these traditions. In this context, surrender to Karzai seemed an increasingly attractive option, all the more so because it increasingly looked as if he, rather than Rabbani, would be put in charge in Kabul. 'Everyone will have a role to play,' was Karzai's motto. 'I don't mean the Arabs, but all Afghans are my brothers.'[6]

Even Mullah Omar's deputy Mullah Berader was having doubts. Back before the attack on Karzai in Uruzgan, Abdul Salam had heard him say they would pay a very high price for fighting on. There had been too many defeats, too many casualties and too many civilian victims: he believed the time had come to stop.[7] (Mullah Berader eventually accepted an amnesty and returned home to live in Deh Rawod for at least one year until the U.S. bombed his house.)

More and more Taliban soldiers had sought contact with Karzai without their leader's knowledge. They included Mullah Obaidullah, the Taliban's Minister of Defense, Mullah Zaeef, and Mullah Jillal, who had held talks with the C.I.A. about the extradition of Bin Laden before the American attacks.[8] Karzai told them that every Taliban fighter who laid down his weapons would be free to return home. When asked specifically by Mullah Zaeef, Karzai confirmed that this applied to Mullah Omar too. When I researched Karzai's rise to power in 2001, I had not heard about the surrender, which was hardly covered in the media at the time. But Karzai's men mentioned it, and later on I found more interviewees confirming this move that could have potentially ended the war.

Karzai's men were not the only party advancing on Kandahar with the aim of taking control of the Taliban's center of power. To the south of the city, the Americans had found another longstanding player who was willing to do the job for them, namely, the former governor of Kandahar Gul Agha Sherzai. He had been one of those responsible for the chaos that reigned in Kandahar in 1994, the main reason why Mullah Omar set up his movement in the first place.

Gul Agha Sherzai had spent the Taliban years in Pakistan. Now he was on his way to Kandahar with the unconditional support of U.S. Special

Forces and a number of C.I.A. commandos in the hope of reaching the city before Karzai. The Americans had given him carte blanche to deal with anyone who got in his way as he saw fit. In early December, Sherzai captured Kandahar Airport in an attack that resulted in hundreds of deaths among Taliban and Arab soldiers attempting to flee to Pakistan. Even a delegation of Taliban soldiers who wanted to discuss a surrender with Sherzai was shot at instantly.[9]

———— ◆ ————

It was December 4, 2001. Mullah Omar slowly sank down onto the cold concrete floor in the basement of a spacious two-story villa that was under construction in the heart of Kandahar. He was wrapped in a thick brown woolen shawl to protect him from the chill of winter. There was no natural light in the twenty-by-twelve-foot basement room. The long, narrow windows high up in the wall were covered by cushions to make sure no one could see in. A gas lamp placed in front of Mullah Omar cast large shadows on the wall. Someone had chucked down a sheet of blue canvas to cover the cold floor.

The Taliban commanders descended the stairs one by one. 'I was afraid. We didn't know what was going to happen,' said Mullah Abdul Salam, a small, stocky man who was at the meeting and whom I interviewed years later in his luxury villa in Kabul. Like the others present, he had served as Mullah Omar's commander for a number of years. He was a member of Omar's *andiwal*, the group of confidants who gave the Taliban leader advice.

The *andiwal* had been brought to the basement by one of Mullah Omar's most trusted bodyguards, a man he had gotten to know back in Deh Rawod. Mullah Abdul Salam had come all the way from Zabul Province and had to change cars several times to elude any spies looking for Mullah Omar.

The commanders had to hand in their weapons before they were allowed to join Mullah Omar in the basement. Was there anything left of their friendship, Mullah Abdul Salam wondered in alarm. Even frisking a longstanding fellow fighter constituted an insult, and asking you to relinquish your weapons was almost like asking you to hand over your child. The men protested loudly, but did leave their Kalashnikovs with the guard. Only Mullah Berader, Mullah Omar's oldest and most trusted friend, was allowed to keep his weapon.

———— ◆ ————

Mullah Omar sat on the ground, huddled under the thick shawl. In his lap was a smaller, lighter version of the Kalashnikov. The commanders were struck by the changes in Mullah Omar's appearance. He was no longer wearing the distinctive black turban that had always singled out the tall Taliban leader. It appeared he no longer wanted to be recognized, as he now had on a gray *lungee*, the turban worn by ordinary Afghans. He looked as if he was ready to take flight at any moment.

According to Mullah Abdul Salam, it was a long while before anyone in the basement spoke. Then Mullah Omar asked, 'What do you want to do?' But they remained silent. 'We were probably all worried what would happen if we gave an honest answer,' assumed Mullah Abdul Salam. 'If we said we wanted to stop the fighting, perhaps he would just shoot us all dead.' Mullah Omar repeated his question. His voice sounded normal, low and fairly quiet. 'That reassured me, and I then made so bold as to point to his weapon and ask whether it was loaded and whether he would shoot us if we gave the wrong answer. Everyone laughed.'

Once again, the Taliban leader asked, 'What do you want to do?' The commanders answered him one by one. They did not want to carry on fighting. There was no discussion, no dissension. All were agreed they should stop the fighting.

The commanders explained the situation. Many, many soldiers had surrendered in Mazar-e-Sharif, Herat, Kabul, and Kunduz. Others had returned home or fled. Their opponents were stronger thanks to the support of the Americans, and they could not hold out much longer. They knew others would soon be in power and that this would involve merging the old with the new. In Bonn, Karzai was already being discussed as a possibility. Their opinion was that Omar should go and talk to him about what he should do.

Mullah Omar looked at each of them in turn with his one good eye. He did not become angry and his submachinegun stayed in his lap. He remained calm as if he had been expecting this for a long time. 'I am listening to you,' he told his commanders. 'Do what is best for our country.' In the presence of Mullah Abdul Salam and the other commanders, he then handed over power to Mullah Obaidullah, who had been sitting next to him all that time. 'Do you understand?' he asked his commanders. 'Whatever he decides has my support. Do what he says.' Then he stood up, gesturing to the rest to remain seated.

In his reception room in Kabul, Mullah Abdul Salam reenacted the whole scene for me – the last time he saw Mullah Omar. Omar took long strides towards the stairs, then turned around once more. 'We must not forget one another,' said Abdul Salam, citing the words of his leader. Then Mullah Omar mounted the stairs out of the basement, accompanied by only his bodyguard. Mullah Abdul Salam could no longer remember whether he had then heard the sound of a motorcycle.[10]

10

Hideout Revelations

Aᴏᴏᴏ Mullah Omar had left, the Taliban commanders were very fired up, according to Mullah Abdul Salam. They yelled, laughed, and joked about what had just happened. They discussed how they should give themselves up to Karzai. 'We were so happy that the war would soon be over,' Abdul Salam told me later. No one wanted the Taliban to keep on fighting; everyone wanted to focus on the future and on collaborating with Karzai. Some were even prepared to consider working with the Americans. This was a pragmatic attitude and typical of Afghans, for whom ideology is something for rich people, according to Abdul Salam (who worked for Karzai for years).

One day later, on December 5, 2001, a Taliban delegation headed by Mullah Obaidullah, the man just appointed as Mullah Omar's successor, approached Hamid Karzai.[1] Karzai was in an abandoned mud-brick house on the crest of a hill outside Kandahar. He was surrounded by

American commandos who had been accompanying him over the past month on his triumphant march across southern Afghanistan. It now seemed as if Karzai's campaign was going to be rewarded with the capture of Kandahar. He had gotten there not just by fighting but also by talking to his opponents, urging them to surrender peacefully and form alliances. Karzai thought the same approach should now be taken with the Taliban leaders.

But the American commandos viewed Karzai's overtures with a certain degree of mistrust. When Karzai had first sought contact with Mullah Omar's people, the commandos had reported this at once to their superiors in Washington.[2] They felt it was not right to talk to such a fearsome enemy who was partly responsible for the appalling attacks on the United States. Secretary of Defense Donald Rumsfeld personally instructed the commandos to keep a close watch on Karzai.

By this point Hamid Karzai was no longer plain old Hamid. At the U.N. peace conference in Bonn, it had been decided that Karzai should be the new interim leader of Afghanistan. His task was to bring order to the country after the victory over the Taliban. Now, through the mediation of an old friend in Kandahar, he had been able to arrange for the Taliban leadership to surrender to him in return for amnesty. 'You mustn't shoot the men coming to see me,' Karzai ordered his American escorts, 'even if they are Taliban.'

'The mood on that hill was very upbeat,' recalls Aziz. My good friend Najibullah's father was there that day. 'Everyone, including the Taliban delegation, thought things would get better from then on.' The men arrived bearing large *naan* breads. They were not frisked as Karzai said that was not necessary – because 'we go back a long way'.[3]

The Taliban delegation knew that Karzai had recently written dozens of letters guaranteeing the safety of Taliban soldiers who had defected to his side. Now that Karzai was the most powerful man in the country, the remaining Taliban fighters were even more confident that they too would get the same guarantee of safety.

Mullah Obaidullah had a letter from his predecessor with him. The letter was not about the surrender; Mullah Omar said nothing on that subject in the letter. It merely stated that Omar had handed over power to Obaidullah and that Mullah Obaidullah should be listened to. Mullah Omar had known that Obaidullah wanted to surrender – that was clear from the meeting in the cellar. And now it was Obaidullah's turn to convey the wishes of the Taliban. The new Taliban leader told Karzai that his soldiers did not want to continue fighting, and he promised that they would hand in their weapons. The Taliban would broadcast the news of their surrender on the movement's own radio station.

Karzai himself announced the Taliban's surrender that same day via a number of international newspapers and agencies – the Associated Press, *The Guardian*, and *The New York Times*.[4] All printed more or less the same statement: Karzai said that Mullah Omar and the other Taliban leaders would be allowed to 'go in dignity'. In accordance with the Geneva Convention, Taliban soldiers who had been taken prisoner would be released. The new president expected his allies in northern Afghanistan to do the same. It should be noted that the amnesty only applied to the Taliban's Afghan fighters; Al Qaeda's foreign combatants would be prosecuted for their crimes.

While the newspapers publicized this news, Karzai told me years later that a few hours after his announcement of the surrender, a furious Rumsfeld had phoned him and ordered him to rescind the agreements made with the Taliban in public. For the U.S., the Taliban and Mullah Omar were as much of an enemy as Al Qaeda, said Rumsfeld.[5]

With that phone call, Rumsfeld effectively derailed this local peace initiative between these Pashtun groups. 'I thought, I'll get it back on track later,' Karzai told me in 2014, but that never happened. For years after this incident, Hamid Karzai would continue to reject the Taliban's overtures for a surrender, choosing war instead. Many of the American diplomats involved in Afghanistan had never even heard about this historical attempt at peace. There was also no more mention of it in the American media, which followed the line laid down by the U.S. government.

I remember meeting U.S. Ambassador Zalmay Khalilzad in Europe in 2019, when he had just started the negotiations between the Taliban and the incumbent Afghan government. Twenty years after 9/11, the U.S. government wanted to talk. It was the second time I had seen Khalilzad. In 2010 I met him at a United States Institute of Peace (U.S.I.P.) meeting, and I asked him about the surrender. 'Karzai lied to you; that never happened,' he said. He then added jokingly, 'He must have been under some sort of influence when he told you that.' Now, in 2019, Khalilzad's response was different. With a despairing look and his hands in his hair, he said, 'You know, when I was in Kabul after 9/11, nobody told me about the surrender. Nobody. Not even Karzai. Why not, why not?! Denying that surrender is a historical blunder.'

In 2001, Karzai had barely put up any resistance before agreeing to do Rumsfeld's bidding. Now the new goal was war. There were to be no more talks. Instead, they had to hunt down and arrest Mullah Omar and extradite him to the U.S. for his part in helping Bin Laden with the 9/11 attacks. Karzai also declared that the Taliban would never again be allowed to participate in an Afghan government.[6]

Rumsfeld pretended Karzai's first announcement offering amnesty to Mullah Omar and his soldiers had never been made, even suggesting it had been fabricated by the media. 'Nothing is happening in Afghanistan that is contrary to our interests,' Rumsfeld repeatedly told the press.[7] Karzai's decision was soon forgotten.

Thanks to the Americans, Kandahar eventually fell into the hands not of Karzai but of Gul Agha Sherzai, a notorious drug baron who had lain low during the Taliban years. This man was not interested in amnesty or reconciliation, and with American support, he started hunting down the Taliban.

————◆————

A chaotic time followed for the Taliban leaders now that Mullah Omar had gone and their movement had suffered a comprehensive military defeat. What were they to do? Where should they go? Many decided to drop their weapons and return home to their own districts or provinces. But they realized that troops from America and other countries were setting up bases all over the place. Everyone who looked remotely suspicious in the eyes of these foreign soldiers was seized and detained until they could prove they had never been a terrorist or Taliban fighter.

Others hoped to find shelter in Pakistan, but that wasn't easy either. Under huge pressure from the Americans, the Pakistani president Musharraf had promised President Bush all the support necessary to find the men behind 9/11 and their accomplices. This led to countless arrests in Pakistan on the suspicion of terrorism.[8] Many of these men had been taken away blindfolded in unmarked C.I.A. planes to secret prisons in Kabul, Romania, Poland, Egypt, and Cuba. In Cuba, Guantanamo Bay was set up for dealing with 'unlawful combatants' as a location that was not subject to the international law of armed conflicts. There was widespread maltreatment of the suspects held in these prisons, with sexual humiliation and torture – in particular, waterboarding.

While Mullah Omar was out of sight, Karzai and the Americans in Afghanistan were appointing one former warlord after another as governors and mayors. Men who had previously been driven out by Mullah Omar were now back in their old positions. Although these not-so-new leaders were presented by the Americans as the men who would pave the way for democracy in Afghanistan, they soon showed their own agenda. As before, the warlords were mainly out to gain and retain power locally, and they engaged in fanatical struggles with their neighboring rivals. They discovered that it was easy to get the American soldiers to take action against these rivals simply by suggesting they had links with the Taliban. Because of this false reporting, which was very common (see also my examples in Chapter 1), many people who had nothing to do with the Taliban or terrorism were detained, imprisoned or killed.

The Americans did not see this agenda of the Afghan allies. On the contrary, this practice gave them the impression that far from capitulating, the Taliban were still fully active and were regrouping in order to seize power again in Afghanistan. This false notion of a growing rebellion was reinforced by the acts of revenge that the wrongly accused families and tribes often carried out on their rivals and the Americans.

As a result, from 2002 on, there was a strange mix in Afghanistan of Americans zealously rounding up people they suspected (often wrongly) of being responsible for the attacks in New York or possibly knowing something about the attackers, and local conflicts in which American troops became embroiled because they thought they were tackling the Taliban. And so they became trapped in a vicious circle. A sense of panic grew among American policymakers at the increasing level of violence in Afghanistan that was actually internal in nature but was seen purely in terms of an increase in terrorist threat. The Americans responded by sending more troops, which in turn only helped the local conflicts escalate further.

The question is: when did the Taliban actually regroup? My account of the early years of the conflict after 9/11 in Afghanistan deviates from the mainstream narrative, and not much research has been done on the first 'real' Taliban attacks, as it were. For example, the U.N. civilian casualty reports do not give a good picture since the U.N. – along with the U.S. – frames the attacks in those early years as Taliban acts.

I interviewed the Taliban about when they regrouped, and as far as I could discover, it was only in about 2004 that a number of Taliban military men met up in Pakistan to discuss the developments in Afghanistan. 'Of course we saw the horrific things the Americans were doing in Afghanistan, not just to our own people but to others too,' Mutasim told me during one of our interviews. Mutasim would soon be in charge of the finances of the movement after it mobilized again. 'We wanted to put an end to the corruption of the former warlords, as we had done in 1994. Lots of people were becoming increasingly angry at what the warlords and the Americans were doing to them. These people would then carry out an attack and call themselves Taliban,' said Mutasim. So although a few attacks were carried out in those initial years by people who saw themselves as Taliban sympathizers, Mutasim and other Taliban leaders I interviewed told me that organized operations only started in 2004 or 2005 – and according to some, only in 2006. 'It's basically the case that we mobilized when you arrived in Afghanistan for the first time [2006, B.D.]', Mutasim joked when we ate dinner in Kabul (Mutasim moved back to Kabul after spending time in Istanbul).

2006 was also the year in which they decided to produce a new version of the old code of conduct for the *hujra* students – written during the jihad against the Soviet Union – that each Taliban fighter would be able to keep on him. These were the rules for correct behavior in armed conflict that Mullah Omar had introduced in 1994 at the start of the Taliban's jihad: treat unarmed civilians with respect and decency, show discipline with respect to your commanders, and treat prisoners humanely. From 2006 on, the movement grew rapidly again. 'We really didn't have to do anything to recruit people,' a Taliban financer in Dubai told me. 'Militias sprang up everywhere to defend their communities against the warlords.'

In Dubai, I also spoke to the Afghan who was the Taliban's media spokesman from 2007 to 2010. Operating for the first time under the name Zaibiullah Mujahed, he became responsible for the Taliban's media contacts. He was born in a refugee camp in Pakistan, and had no problem living in Pakistan as long as he remained under the radar. (The Taliban installed a spokesman as one of their first actions in 2004. Two predecessors of 'Mujahed' were arrested by Pakistan.) He understood Pakistan's double agenda: they wanted to endorse U.S. policy, but at the same time there was a lot of support in Pakistan for the Taliban, and so they also had to accommodate that. But as he explained, if he were to get too much exposure, America would pile on the pressure and Islamabad would have him detained (in fact, he was detained in Pakistan in 2019, after he had been operating in Dubai). 'Mujahed' started to play the media on behalf of the Taliban. He copied the tactics of the Western media, which attributed every attack to the Taliban rather than explaining that it could equally have been the action of one of the governor's rivals. The Taliban spokesman claimed numerous attacks, even ones that the movement had not actually carried out. 'Unless they had resulted in too many civilian casualties – we kept quiet then. We didn't want to be held responsible for those.'

The situation was in Mujahed's favor, as the Pentagon and the Western media saw every attack as the work of the Taliban. When asked, for example, whether Mullah Omar was still fully in control of the movement, all he had to do was say 'yes'. In fact, he said later, he had never heard anything again from Mullah Omar and he had no idea where the man was. He was sent messages, often from Mutasim, which he then had to circulate online. Each time, he saw Mullah Omar's signature at the bottom, for example, in the Eid messages issued twice a year on the occasion of Eid al-Adha (Festival of the Sacrifice) and Eid al-Fitr (marking the end of Ramadan). But he was certain Mullah Omar had not written these Eid missives himself. 'I knew there were messengers who used to visit Mullah Omar, but I didn't know how often or when,' he said. Mujahed also said that one of the messengers had been severely criticized for having misrepresented Mullah Omar's original message, according to the Taliban leadership in the Pakistani border city of Quetta.

Remarkably little credible information was to be found about Mullah Omar after his departure from Kandahar at the end of 2001. He and Bin Laden were the key targets for the Americans and their allies in Afghanistan, but it was as if the two men had disappeared off the face of the Earth. Hundreds, if not thousands, of investigative specialists and secret agents were tasked with tracking them down, but as the years passed, it became clear how little progress was being made. After almost a decade of searching, Bin Laden was eventually found and shot dead at a location no one had investigated in all those years.

The American and Afghan investigators were never able to find Mullah Omar. In their search for the Taliban leader, they never really got much further than some general speculation about a flight to Pakistan where he was now allegedly being kept hidden, whether voluntarily or not, by the I.S.I. It was thought that Pakistan wanted to be able to use Omar to exert influence in Afghanistan. This fit with the widely held belief in the West that the I.S.I. had helped the Taliban start up in 1994 and that the movement had functioned as an instrument of the Pakistani secret service ever since. This speculation was why the C.I.A. decided to stay on friendly terms with the I.S.I. after 2001. They also hoped Mullah Omar's supposed Pakistani contacts would bring them closer to Bin Laden.

During the years when I was working on this book, I was invited on a number of occasions by high-ranking U.S. military to talk to them about where Mullah Omar might be hiding. These were uncomfortable meetings with men who had often used violence and torture to get their Afghan sources to talk, apparently not realizing that this would just put them on the wrong track. My talks with the Americans only increased my doubts about the claims that Mullah Omar was with the I.S.I. in Karachi or the border city of Quetta.

Those doubts were also fed by my evolving understanding of Pakistan's role in the emergence of the Taliban. From my research on Mullah Omar's life before 9/11, I had the impression that he had deeply mistrusted the Pakistanis from the start, and that this had not changed during the period when the Taliban was in power. Of course Omar would also have known that hundreds of Taliban fighters had been apprehended in Pakistan after 2001 and handed over to the Americans. Only a few leading Taliban were able to stay hidden in Quetta, adopting a false identity in order to remain under the radar.

While the Americans' abortive attempts to find the Taliban leader were sometimes the subject of mockery among the international community in Kabul – 'That Mullah Omar doesn't even exist,' a drunken American diplomat once confided in me – my hopes of finding some information rose again in early 2014. In June 2013, the N.S.A. employee Edward Snowden had passed on large numbers of U.S. government documents to various international media outlets. By this point, the documents were being managed by the newly founded online magazine *The Intercept*. Perhaps these documents would tell me more about exactly what information the Americans had on Mullah Omar, both on what he had done up to 2001 and where he had been hiding since then. It was an exciting moment for me in the offices of *The Intercept* in New York. I handed the keywords 'Mullah Omar' to an employee, who sent them in an encrypted email to a secret server outside the U.S., where another employee sent the results back to us in another encrypted email.

Those results were very disappointing. The twenty reports that the keyword search had thrown up had about a hundred 'highly classified' and 'top secret' pages on Mullah Omar, at least ninety of which I had already seen on Wikipedia or other public sources. It basically meant that over a decade after the attacks on the Twin Towers, the Americans knew barely anything more about Mullah Omar than what you might find in the press clippings folder of a run-of-the-mill newspaper or news broadcaster. The only new information in those hundred pages was a list of 'call signs', nicknames for various Taliban leaders that the Americans used when communicating amongst themselves. They were sinister, belligerent names such as 'Sword', 'Burning Torch', and 'Dragon'. But Mullah Omar, the supreme leader of this feared group, was simply called 'Blanco'. It felt as if in giving him this call sign, the Americans were admitting that they had no idea who this mysterious mullah was, what exactly he was supposed to have done, or what had happened to him.

I felt a strange kind of emptiness. I had 'grown up' with the threat of Omar the great enemy. Every day, I had read media articles about this dangerous leader. But how much of that was true? Did the journalists check their information? The Americans were often the source of these stories and they portrayed him as a monster but the media were quoting sources who actually knew nothing about him. The generals who said they were hot on his heels had no idea. The American military and NATO ascribed every attack to the Taliban, but they did not know who the movement's leader was, how much power he had, or whether or not he was actually pulling the strings in the organization.

I slumped down in the office chair, feeling rather deflated. Outside, New York raced on as hectic as ever, oblivious to my discovery. Surely this shocking ignorance should be headline news. In New York of all places, I thought, the scene of the biggest terrorist attack in history, people should be told about this. Many trusted the American politicians and policymakers to know best how to avenge the three thousand who had died that day in September. They put their trust in the Western generals in Kabul who told the media that they were 'on it'. Year in, year out, more troops were sent to Afghanistan and the war escalated further.

Politicians and generals continued to promise progress. In 2005, the U.S. general David Barno said that this would undoubtedly be 'a decisive year in Afghanistan'. Barno's successor General John Abizaid said one year later, 'I think 2006 can be a decisive year.' In 2007, the British general David Richards repeated the message, saying, 'This will be the crunch year for the Taliban.' And on it went. In 2008 a Norwegian minister said, 'This is a decisive year for the future of Afghanistan.' In 2009, General Abizaid repeated, 'I think next year will be a decisive year.' The eminent general Stanley McChrystal had the same message in 2010: 'We are knee-deep in the decisive year.'[9]

———— ♦ ————

While nobody in the West seemed to know anything about Mullah Omar, in Taliban circles I found a veil of silence cast over the former leader. If I asked about Mullah Omar's whereabouts, the standard answer was that he was still actively leading the movement, without the speaker giving any hint of how he was operating or where. Nobody was prepared to reveal anything about the nature of Omar's decisions either.

Only the Taliban's former financial man, Mutasim, eventually told me that Mullah Omar was in contact with the Taliban leadership in Quetta through two couriers. Mutasim mentioned the names Abdul Bari and Mullah Azizullah, but said he didn't know exactly where the couriers went. He did suspect that Mullah Omar was still in Afghanistan, however. Back in 2003, there were cassette tapes circulating in Afghanistan with the voice of the former Taliban leader, said Mutasim. However, they didn't provide much of a clue: most of the messages that I heard could easily be traced to recordings made before 2001. The only other piece of information Mutasim had for me concerned Mullah Omar's family. After the fall of the Taliban regime, Mutasim had taken Omar's wife and children to a safe place; Mullah Omar had not seen his immediate family since then in order to avoid any risk of discovery, said Mutasim.

In July 2015, the Afghan authorities (and others) announced that Mullah Omar was dead.[10] He had apparently died two years earlier in a hospital in Karachi where he was being treated for tuberculosis, claimed the Afghan secret service. The announcement caused confusion at first as there had been regular reports of Mullah Omar's death since 2001, which were always seen as false. I was cautious too, when asked by various media to comment on the news, as the Taliban did not initially issue any response to the announcement.[11] A few weeks after the first report of Omar's death, Mullah Mansour, who had now been appointed his successor, confirmed that the former leader had indeed died two years earlier. He also confirmed the cause of death but said that Mullah Omar had died not in Karachi but in Afghanistan, where he had remained after 2001. Mansour explained that the Taliban leadership had kept the 'tragic news' secret for two years because at the time of Omar's death senior Taliban thought they would be able to defeat the Americans in Afghanistan for good in 2014. The state of affairs surrounding Mullah Omar's death revealed once again how little the Americans (and I too) really knew about Omar; indeed, many senior figures in the Taliban were in a similar position.

For a long time, it looked as if I would have to end my book on Mullah Omar with this brief description of his final years. I sent my manuscript to the publisher in the summer of 2018. I agreed with them that while they were editing the book, I would have one last go at finding out more details about Mullah Omar's life after 2001.

The name Abdul Jabbar Omari had regularly come up in the many conversations I had had about the Taliban leader over the years. Many people said he was the man who had assisted Mullah Omar after he disappeared from Kandahar in 2001. After Omar's death, Omari had gone into hiding in Pakistan and later in Zabul, the province where he had been born, but he had been arrested in 2017 and it seemed he had probably been held in the notorious Bagram Prison near Kabul ever since. Perhaps he was the crucial link in Mullah Omar's story. I decided to try my luck once more by travelling to Kabul to see if I could talk to Omari there.

In Dubai, on my way to Afghanistan, I met the man who was working on a biography of Mullah Omar for the Taliban. According to him, Omari was not in Bagram after all; he was being held under house arrest in Kabul by the National Directorate of Security (N.D.S.), the Afghan secret service.

Once in Kabul, I managed to arrange an interview with an N.D.S. general who said he would reveal where Omari was being held. As I sat in his office, our conversation soon took a surprising turn. The general was brief: the secret service was holding Omari, but he would not introduce me because I shouldn't waste my time talking to him since Omari didn't know anything. The N.D.S. general then told me in detail what the secret service had found out about Mullah Omar's final years. This account was completely contrary to what the Americans and Afghan authorities had been saying up to now. The general told me that the N.D.S knew for quite some time that Mullah Omar had never visited Pakistan after 2001, or perhaps only briefly – just across the border from Zabul. But he had spent all those years in Zabul Province. He had lived in a small village where he did not dare venture out onto the street. Mullah Omar continued to lead his movement by sending out cassette tapes. Later on, he used written instructions that were circulated by a messenger. 'You should speak to that messenger, Mullah Azizullah,' the general told me. This was the same name I had heard years earlier from Mutasim.

Of course I would have loved to talk to Mullah Azizullah, but that wasn't a realistic option. The man, who had married the sister of Mullah Omar's second wife, was now a Taliban in Helmand Province, which was often the scene of fierce fighting. All lines purporting to lead to Omari seemed to be dead ends. Intrigued by the N.D.S. general's remarkable information, I decided to travel to Zabul with a stopover in Kandahar. Who knows, perhaps I would discover something once I got there.

In Kandahar, I spoke to various people in order to prepare properly for a possible trip to Zabul. Many of them advised me not to go, saying this province was too risky. But soon enough something came up. I remembered a local journalist from Zabul and called him. 'Oh, Betty Dam, the famous author who wrote the Karzai book! I will come to you immediately!' He was at the Indian consulate and raced to my house with my Karzai book in his hand. I signed it and he told me that he had decided to study Political Science after reading my book. I was very touched, and we chatted about how I do journalism. 'What brings you here?' he asked. I explained my plan to him, choosing my words carefully: I was searching for Mullah Omar's hiding place. The journalist didn't really get why I was so secretive. 'That story is out already in Zabul. Everyone there knows,' he said. I let him speak. He gave me the gist of the story. Mullah Omar had been staying in Zabul at two locations, and he was able to point to evidence. Omari had been arrested by the local Zabul authorities, the journalist had met him, and Omari had told the story to the local authorities when he was flown to the Kabul safe house.

I did have a small local article about this arrest on my laptop, with a picture of Omari. 'Is this him?' I asked, and the journalist nodded. 'He's now in Kabul.' The local journalist put me in contact with Atta Jan, a former administrator in the province. Apparently, he knew more about Omari's arrest and was even supposed to have spoken to the man after he was detained. That turned out to be correct. We found Atta Jan the same evening at a dinner with one of the richest businessmen in Kandahar. We ate a meal fit for a king. 'Wow, she's the person who wrote the Karzai book!' I heard the Afghan guests saying.

Atta Jan took time to talk to me and we adjourned to one of the many empty rooms in the villa. Atta Jan said Mullah Azizullah was a key witness to the secret life Mullah Omar led after 9/11. The same applied to Omari. According to Atta Jan, the N.D.S. secret agents stationed in Zabul had had suspicions for years that Omari knew about Mullah Omar's life after 2001. When Omar's death was reported in 2015, the N.D.S. made Omari a secret offer of witness protection if he talked to them about Mullah Omar.[12] He was offered his choice of luxury accommodation in a city such as Ankara, Doha or Istanbul. As Omari himself had disappeared immediately after Mullah Omar's death, Atta Jan had relayed the secret service's offer to Omari's brother at the request of the Afghan President Ghani. Omari had never responded to this offer, Atta Jan said.

In 2017, Omari suddenly featured in the local press, in an article I have on my laptop (thanks to my good friend Anand Gopal). That article (in Pashtu) states that Mullah Omar's bodyguard had been arrested in the center of Zabul. According to the article, this happened during a random check of cars by the local police. Omari identified himself and requested the deal Atta Jan had offered earlier. Later on I heard Omari was arrested in the local bazaar by the police, who treated him very roughly. This had prompted him to take up the N.D.S. offer after all, and Atta Jan was called in to identify the man. Ever since then, Omari had been living in a heavily guarded villa in a secret location in Kabul.

Atta Jan put me in contact with an important Hotak leader from Zabul who lived near the village where Omari was born. I met the man in Kandahar and to my surprise he had Omari's phone number. When I got back to my place, my Afghan colleague Patmal and I dialed the number – and again to my great amazement, Omari answered. We had only been in Kandahar twenty-four hours, but it seemed everyone knew. The voice at the other end of the line sounded cheerful. When I spoke to him briefly in Pashto, he complimented me on my language skills. I asked him whether I could meet him in Kabul. In a calm voice, he replied that I would be very welcome, but I would need to arrange my visit via the head of the Afghan secret service. In the days following that phone call, I tried to contact Omari numerous times on the same number, but I never got an answer.

I decided not to go to Zabul but to return to Kabul instead. Once there, I did everything I could to get access to Omari. Atta Jan had told me that Mullah Omar's hideouts in Zabul had always been arranged by Samad Ostad, a well-known driving instructor in Qalat. Ostad had been Omari's driver during the days of the Taliban regime, and had been killed recently in Pakistan (I didn't have time to find out why exactly but people say it was because of his job for Mullah Omar). In Kabul, I talked to a man I knew from the early days of my investigations into Mullah Omar, Daud Gulzar, a Hotak leader and the former head of Zabul's Provincial Council. In recent years, Gulzar has lived in an expensive apartment in the capital and worked as an adviser to the Afghan president. I sat in front of him, exasperated. 'Gulzar, I should have listened to you,' I said. It was Gulzar who, in the early days of my research, had told me to start my work on Mullah Omar in Zabul. 'That's his tribe's area. That's where his life starts – in the heart of the Hotak community.' I ignored this because I made a Western assumption: Mullah Omar had not been born in Zabul, so his personal life had not started in Zabul. But now I regret this. Omar did rely on his tribesmen when he needed them. I realize now that when I first spoke to Gulzar about this, Omar was still alive, and people in Zabul had been aware of his whereabouts.

Gulzar told me that Samad Ostad used to visit Gulzar in the reception room of his home in Qalat. 'He didn't have any money, so I would give him rice and flour. Now I know that this food was going to Mullah Omar,' said Gulzar with a laugh.

According to Gulzar, the Afghan secret service had had its eye on this driver at the time, something I had also heard from another tribal leader in Zabul. The secret service suspected that Ostad had some kind of connection with Mullah Omar, according to Gulzar, because they had been told as much by the Americans. But local *shuras* systematically protected the driving instructor. Every time Ostad was ordered to report to the secret service's office, he would call on one of his supporters. They included Daud Gulzar. 'What do you want with this poor wretch?' Gulzar would ask the agents. And then they would leave him in peace for a while. Gulzar was struck by the fact that Ostad wore about twenty of the traditional good-luck *taweez* amulets around his neck. 'But I didn't know he was protecting Mullah Omar,' said Gulzar.

Every interview I did only convinced me further that I needed to talk to Omari if I was to find out more about Mullah Omar's final years. After many days on the phone, I eventually got a chance to talk to the head of the Afghan secret service. I hoped he would give me permission to visit Omari in his safe house.

It turned out he was prepared to see me. At some point, my intermediary had to visit him for dinner, and he invited me with the words: 'You won't get much, but you can try.' The boss kept us waiting a long time. A bomb had just exploded in Kabul and it was not yet clear how many people had been killed. When he received us at eleven in the evening, I sat down, he complimented me on the Karzai book and I told him about the biography I was writing about Mullah Omar. 'Then you need to speak to someone I know, and that's Omari,' he said. I nodded. I wasn't sure whether I was relieved or not. Would he grant me access? I explained how important Omari was for telling the story of the Taliban. This worked – he was prepared to help me. 'But you'll need to come back in two months as I have to go to the U.S. for dental treatment,' he said. The intermediary agreed immediately and there was no other option for me: I would have to skip Christmas 2018 and see the boss of the Afghan intelligence service instead.

Two months later, I had to remind the boss of his promise. It all took much longer than I had expected and I was on the verge of overstaying my visa when he finally agreed to set up a meeting with Omari. I was nervous, of course, and rehearsed what I would say a couple of times. Then I drove off to an intelligence safe house, a big villa in the heart of Kabul. It was a strange setting. First we met a secret-service general, who also sat in on the interview. How much information would Omari be willing to give under these conditions and what would he keep mum about, I wondered. I was able to interview him again later; this time, at my request, in his heavily guarded home and without the general. Looking back, there was little difference between the two interviews. If anything, I felt Omari was more cautious the second time.

Omari started talking after I asked him why he in particular was chosen to take care of Mullah Omar. Omari wasn't a high-profile Taliban at all. And I am not sure if the Taliban leadership had a long-term plan for Mullah Omar either. In the days of the Taliban, Omari had twice been governor in one of the northern provinces, where he had gotten to know Mullah Omar from a distance. So he had only a middle-ranking position in the Taliban government. But Omari had also been a tribal leader in Siori District in Zabul Province, where many members of Mullah Omar's Hotak tribe lived and where Mullah Obaidullah, Mullah Omar's designated successor, planned to let Mullah Omar hide out.

Omari said it had soon become clear after the 9/11 attacks that the Taliban's days were numbered – America wanted revenge. Sometime in early December 2001, Omari got a call from Mullah Obaidullah asking him to come to Kandahar at once. When he got there, he met Mullah Shereen, Mullah Omar's main bodyguard (and the man responsible for kidnapping Najibullah). Shereen asked Omari if he would take Mullah Omar to a safe place. Omari did not have to think twice. 'I told him I would be prepared to hide him under my wife's veil if necessary.'

An hour later, Omari was in a car with Mullah Shereen on their way to Maidan Showk, a busy central square in Kandahar City that I had often passed, where Mullah Omar was waiting with a small group. Omari was not willing to reveal who they were, except to say that they included Mullah Azizullah, who later acted as a messenger. Mullah Omar greeted Omari with the words 'Are you going to take me to safety?' 'Only Allah can provide safety, but I'm certainly going to try,' replied Omari. Omari was sent ahead to northeast Kandahar, to the point where the road to Zabul starts. He waited an hour for Mullah Omar, who turned up in a white Toyota with Mullah Azizullah and a third, unknown man (Omari did not want to give his name). That afternoon, the group drove in a small convoy to Qalat, the capital of Zabul Province.

Omari's reply to my question of whether Pakistan had ever been considered as a place to hide out was quite clear. 'I'm not going there, whatever happens,' Mullah Omar had said. Omari himself wondered why not. Pakistan was home to millions of Afghan immigrants, and Mullah Omar had rich friends there who he could stay with in comfort. But Mullah Omar categorically refused the option of Pakistan and a life of ease in exile. He was very emphatic: 'I don't want that!'

Located 125 miles northeast of Kandahar city, Zabul was an ideal refuge at that time. 'Zabul was the place where the Taliban felt safe,' Abdul Rahman Hotaki, Mullah Omar's secretary in the early days, also remembers (he is from Zabul too). Even though the Taliban government of Zabul had fallen, the provincial capital was controlled by tribesmen loyal to the movement. Hotaki had left the Taliban the year before and had returned to his home, in Zabul's Shinkay District, where he met Taliban leaders on the run. According to Hotaki, they had all tried to surrender, but were disappointed in Karzai's 'lack of power'. Taliban leaders complained to him that Karzai 'didn't keep his promises'.

After 2001, Mullah Omar and Omari lived in two different locations in total, according to Omari. They spent four years in Qalat. Omari was careful about not revealing the exact location of the house (we did in fact find this out, but are not publishing the details for security reasons) because he was afraid the Afghan government might destroy the place out of revenge. He pointed roughly to the house on a map, and I could see that it was walking distance from the governor's compound. They felt safe there. The house was a typical Afghan *kala*: a mudbrick wall around a complex of five small rooms, with a well and oven in the front yard. Omari's family was living in the house, and Mullah Omar stayed in an L-shaped room in the corner of the compound with a small kitchen and toilet close by. Omari's wife was told that an important member of the Taliban was hiding in their home, and that she would be killed if she told anybody.

The local government loyal to the Taliban was soon replaced by an ally of the strongman and governor in Kandahar, Gul Agha Sherzai. Most of the Taliban who had fled there feared them and chose to move on to Pakistan. But not Mullah Omar. He stayed. Omari lived in the house with Mullah Omar, and Abdul Ostad did the driving around, organizing their secret life. In those four years, Mullah Omar never left that house, Omari told me.

Omari said that the U.S. troops had gotten very close on two occasions. The first time, Mullah Omar and his bodyguard Omari were sitting in the garden and when they heard the footsteps approaching, they hid in brushwood. They stayed there until deep in the night, when the troops had left. The second time, Omari was not there. This time the troops entered the compound, Mullah Omar told him, and searched the place, but they skipped Mullah Omar's room because it didn't look as if it had a door. There was a cupboard high up on the wall to the room, behind which a secret door had been cut so that Mullah Omar could get in and out. Omari doesn't know if the troops had been hunting for Mullah Omar, or if it had been a routine patrol.

In 2004, the U.S. set up its first base in the area, the Forward Operating Base Lagman, just a few minutes' walk from Mullah Omar's hiding place. As military engineers started building the base, Mullah

Omar decided it was time to move. With the help of the driver Ostad, he and Jabbar Omari relocated to Siori, a district around twenty miles southeast of Qalat, which had become part of the larger district of Shinkay. Mullah Omar's father's family hails from Siori (something Gulzar had told me early on in my investigations) and both Omari and Ostaz had been born there.

They were not really any safer in Siori as there was a lot of fighting in this area. American and Afghan army convoys were all in action. 'We heard the Taliban attacking the convoys from our home but of course we could not let the fighters know we were in hiding close by.' Here too, American patrols sometimes got dangerously close to their hideout.

Omari was very secretive about the location of the second place when he talked to me. 'If I give away this name, the government will go after everyone who lives there.' However, I had already found out about it through other contacts and so I asked him only to point in silence to the location on the map on my laptop. Omari looked at my screen, I zoomed into the village in question, and at that point he closed the laptop. In silence. Then I showed him the nearby American base on another map. He recognized it and said the place was an hour's walk from that base. This was Camp Wolverine, where 1,000 Americans were stationed up to 2009 and 4,000 between 2009 and 2014, after President Obama sent additional troops to Afghanistan.

When I published these findings about Mullah Omar's hiding place in the American media in 2019, the storm of tweets and media attention that greeted these revelations included a tweet to my account @Bettedam from an unknown Afghan along the lines of 'I am from that village too'. I was curious. Was that really so? I left him a Direct Message, we chatted a bit online and we spoke over the phone. He was a student in Ghazni, but his father and mother were still living in K. (he confirmed the name), the village where Mullah Omar had been in hiding. He said he didn't know that Mullah Omar was hiding there, and he didn't know Omari. 'That man didn't show himself.' He did know Ostaz personally. He said that not only did Ostaz live there, but also his family (including eight brothers), spread across perhaps seven to eight houses in the village. Having Ostaz's large family there must have given them a sense of security, because there were hardly any strangers around.

In the week I published the story, the Taliban also released a picture of the house in K. It was exactly how I thought it would look like. The guy who had contacted me through Twitter had already told me that the house was quite modern, with a proper door (and not a curtain in the doorway, which is common). In the photo, I saw the door, and a high wall. The situation in the house itself was also exactly how Omari had described it to me, with a simple bed, on which Mullah Omar sat for hours on end. In the picture you could see marks where Mullah Omar had leaned against the wall. The photo also showed the stove and the radio Omari had talked about.

Maybe a year after I saw Omari, he showed up on Facebook (he had left the safe house), standing in front of Mullah Omar's hiding place. It seems he had visited the region for a wedding. He filmed the hide-out with a group of men, and he related the same story he had told me.[13]

Omari's account of the twelve years that Mullah Omar spent in absolute secrecy in Zabul indicates that the Taliban leader was becoming more and more withdrawn from the world around him. He barely ventured outdoors as that was too risky. But even within the house, he kept very much to himself. When Omari asked Mullah Omar whether he missed his family, he would shake his head. Omari offered to bring his son Yaqub to see him, but he said that was not necessary. 'Look at us,' Omari said at one point to Mullah Omar. 'Here we sit, unable to go anywhere.' Mullah Omar barely responded. 'It is a blessing from Allah that we can be here,' was all he said. Omari's task was essentially to cook three meals a day for the mullah, but they never ate together. Once Mullah Omar had finished eating, Omari collected the dishes and washed them in the little kitchen next door.

Omari told me during our conversations that the Taliban leader no longer gave any sign of having unfulfilled wishes or ambitions. One of the few things Mullah Omar did want was a supply of henna, which he used regularly to dye his graying beard. He also liked to have some *naswar* to hand, the local chewing tobacco, which he would place under his lip. This was actually against his own rules. It reminded me of my conversations with Mullah Omar's dentist, who was also from Zabul. I texted him, after a gap of years, and asked him if he had seen the news about Mullah Omar hiding in his neighborhood. The dentist had told me lots of stories about his client Omar before 9/11, including the fact that Mullah Omar had bad teeth because of the un-Islamic tobacco he chewed. Once he sat back in the chair, and the dentist had trouble chasing out all Mullah Omar's Uruzgani companions who were staring around the dentist's room as if they had seen a ghost. 'I don't think any of them had ever visited a dentist before,' he smiled. The dentist had not approved of Mullah Omar's decision at one point to go to the hospital in Quetta when in serious trouble; he should have invested in Afghan health care instead. Now the dentist was surprised by the revelations. He had had no idea that Omar was ever in Zabul, he said.

Mullah Omar rarely talked about current affairs, although he did often listen to B.B.C. Pashto in the evenings, while Omari listened to the Voice of America in the room next door. On very rare occasions, Mullah Omar would comment on the news he had heard. He said nothing when he learned that his successor Obaidullah had died. Omari recalled that when the mullah heard the name Osama bin Laden dozens of times a day on the radio, he asked what was going on. Omari told him Bin Laden had been murdered by the Americans, but on this occasion too Omar barely said a word in response. The only thing he got worked up about occasionally was reports of civilian victims of attacks, and whether they had suffered at the hands of the Taliban or of foreign soldiers.

According to Omari, Mullah Omar spent most of his time buried in the Quran or some other religious text. He would spend hours seated in the same position with his eyes closed, deep in thought. Sometimes he would record Quran verses on his phone, a simple device without a SIM card, since that would have let the enemy trace his whereabouts. He recited the verses using the Classical Arabic in which the Quran was originally written, a language that is no longer spoken in daily life but that Mullah Omar was increasingly using.

Although Mullah Omar had never really learned to read and write properly, he now developed a script of his own that looked similar to Classical Arabic. Omari told me that the mullah filled four thick notebooks in this script that no one else could read. Omari was increasingly likely to find the leader in a kind of trance, in which he did not wish to be disturbed. Once Omari had nudged Mullah Omar because he thought the mullah had fallen asleep. Mullah Omar had snapped back at him furiously: Omari had interrupted him in his reflections on God's creation, the sky, the sun, and mankind and the overwhelming power of Allah, who let people breathe, or be angry if He so wished. Omari used the term *'wali'* to describe Mullah Omar and the state he had attained in this period. In Sufism, a *wali* is a messenger who receives *wahy* (revelations).

According to Omari, Mullah Omar was barely involved in the operational management of the Taliban after 2001; at most, he served as the movement's spiritual leader. Mullah Omar took the transfer of power in 2001 very seriously. He meant every word he had said in that meeting in the basement when he had delegated authority to Mullah Obaidullah. Any decisions Obaidullah made were by definition good decisions. 'You know the Taliban believe strongly in their *andiwal*,' said Omari, 'lifelong friends who trust blindly in one another.' Omar trusted in his *andiwal* in Quetta.

If Mullah Omar discussed politics and current affairs at all, such as the behavior of Al Qaeda or ISIS, it was usually from a religious perspective. He would analyze the different interpretations of Islam on which these movements were based. The way the Wahhabi Arabs and Al Qaeda believed they could know where God lived ran counter to Mullah Omar's

Sufi beliefs. 'If you know where God lives, you are making Him a human being and He is not that,' Omari explained to me.

A messenger would visit Mullah Omar about once every three months. Omari categorically refused to say his name, but I am fairly sure the messenger was Mullah Azizullah. In the early days, he came to pick up cassette tapes with recorded instructions from Mullah Omar for his successor Mullah Obaidullah. But the communication via cassette tapes soon stopped. Later on, the messenger visited Mullah Omar a couple of times a year. Omari said this was usually when his replacement in Quetta was facing some dilemma, and rarely at Mullah Omar's initiative. Unfortunately, Omari was never present during these meetings, although the messenger did sometimes speak to him afterwards. This was how Omari found out, for example, that the messenger and Mullah Omar had agreed that a Taliban office should be opened in Doha in Qatar, as a base for starting peace negotiations with the Americans. Regarding the Eid messages, Omari was able to tell me that Mullah Omar did not write them himself.

Mullah Omar died on April 23, 2013, Omari told me. There was a severe hailstorm that day in Kandahar, destroying many car windows. Mullah Omar had been coughing and vomiting for three months by then. He could no longer keep his food down, not even when Omari made him his favorite soup, *shorwa*. Omari had urged him to let a doctor see him, but Mullah Omar rebuffed his offer. Nor would he take any medication. He eventually agreed to be injected with a serum from the local bazaar, but by then it was too late.

'I still feel sick,' Mullah Omar said in Arabic right at the end. Shortly before he died, Omari found him unconscious, in a seated position and unbelievably pale. 'Oh Mullah sir, Mullah sir!' cried Omari, but his leader did not respond. When Omari gave him a gentle nudge, he toppled over. He regained consciousness one last time that night. The next day, Mullah Omar died.

The following night, Omari and two other helpers secretly buried Mullah Omar in an unmarked grave without a coffin. Then Omari fetched Mullah Omar's son Yaqub and his half-brother Abdul Manan from Quetta in Pakistan. Both opened the grave when they arrived to check that it really was Mullah Omar lying there. Omari had filmed the burial and given the recording to Yaqub, but Mullah Omar's oldest son wanted to see the body with his own eyes. Seventeen days later, the grave was reopened and Mullah Omar's corpse placed in a wooden coffin.

A little while later, Omari travelled to Pakistan to discuss the news with the Taliban leadership. They decided to keep Mullah Omar's death a secret for the time being. Like Atta Jan, Omari told me that the Taliban expected to be able to defeat the Americans in short order: a withdrawal had been announced. The idea was not to disrupt these developments with the tragic news of Mullah Omar's death. Not all the Taliban agreed with this decision; some said they should be honest and open about his death. Despite this, the movement's leaders were able to keep the death of their former mullah quiet for two years.

Mullah Omar died without leaving a will or any further instructions, whether in writing or on tape. Omari, Mullah Omar's son Yaqub, and his half-brother Manan searched his belongings in the hope of finding some kind of message for them, but they found nothing.

Epilogue

I FIRST wrote this book in Dutch and it was published in March 2019. I also published the last chapter of the book – about the hideout of Mullah Omar being in Afghanistan (and not Pakistan, as was widely believed) – in English in the same week. Journalists Emma Graham-Harrison of *The Guardian* and Jessica Donati of *The Wall Street Journal* knew me from our time together in Kabul and knew how I worked, so they trusted my research. Even though my account contradicted many of the standard narratives, their publications carried their reports on this news on their front pages.

I wonder if this would have happened without these connections. I say this mainly because of the response to my investigation. My reportage was confrontational for sure. For many, the news that the most wanted Taliban man was hiding near a U.S. base inside Afghanistan was a bolt from the blue. I myself still remember the moment in my research when it dawned on me: was Mullah Omar really in Afghanistan? I remember an almost physical sense of surprise, as if I could literally feel this paradigm shift in my mind, leaving me slightly dizzy.

We have lived in a very dominant narrative. Both the Afghan and the U.S. governments had consistently told the world that Mullah Omar was hiding in neighboring Pakistan, which fitted their account that the Taliban was the creation of Pakistan.

In the first interviews I did, I heard amazement in the interviewers' questions: How come a Dutch woman journalist was able to discover something in dangerous Afghanistan that thousands of C.I.A. agents had never found? My answer was: Why didn't more journalists investigate this story about the 'most wanted insurgent' that seemed to be almost public knowledge in Kandahar?

But the attitude of the interviewers soon changed after the officials in Afghanistan responded to my publication. In a press release, the Afghan president himself said that my research was a fabrication and that I was 'delusional'. The president claimed to have enough evidence and said he had never lied to the Afghan people about Mullah Omar.

Now that the Afghan palace was involved, the media questions turned more critical: 'So, Bette, what is your evidence? Because the palace says you are wrong.'

I saw the same patterns I had seen during my research: a heavy reliance on official sources who embrace the War on Terror. In this case it meant that the media accorded more weight to a press statement produced by Afghan officials with one quote, and without any supporting evidence, than a transparent twenty-page report full of footnotes, with hardly any anonymous sources and based on five years of research. I could feel my story ending up in the category of what is known in academia as the lower-caste voice, or the world of the underreported.

To me it also felt that the Afghan government had achieved what it had aimed for: silence. After the media storm died down, my research was not referenced. It also did not lead to discussions about the role of the Afghan government in the War on Terror, or the role of the C.I.A. for that matter. Of course Mullah Omar was not Osama bin Laden, but still there was no follow-up story, something that is almost a global script when it comes to breaking news (other media produce stories that are related).

In that same week I also noticed how powerful the official Western narratives are in the book publishing world. After my friends from *The Wall Street Journal* and *The Guardian* put me on the front page, one of the biggest book fairs of the year took place in London. I hoped that my Dutch book would sell to an American publisher. My agent was present and ready to take on this exciting job. *The Guardian* lay everywhere in the bookstands, and my name was on the front page. But one publisher after another turned the book down. According to them, there was no audience for this type of book. Some said, 'Afghanistan is no longer in the news.' Others said, 'The book has already had some attention, and we don't expect much more to come.'

It's true that there are not many books like mine out there, let alone specifically about the Taliban. Those that do get published, like *An Enemy We Created* by Alex Strick Linschoten and Felix Kuehn, are from niche publishers and sell in small numbers. Then there is *No Good Men Among the Living* by Anand Gopal, which received more attraction and was published by a mainstream publisher. We sent our pitch to several such publishers, but they replied that my narrative had already been published and that there was no appetite for more books on this subject.

This is a self-fulfilling prophecy: the Western publishing world generally decides that the American or European narrative is what interests readers and they therefore publish stories by Western soldiers, Western journalists, or of a Western rescue in Afghanistan. We checked, for example, the publications of one of the biggest publishers in the U.S. Of the around ninety books on Afghanistan (since 2001) that came up on their website, the vast majority were about the Western narrative, written by predominantly American authors; only four authors were Afghans (mostly living in the U.S.). As a consequence of this imbalance, readers are deprived of the Afghan perspective, let alone books by an Afghan author. Moreover, while the titles of books focused on the Western narrative mostly dwell on danger, terrorism, and military solutions – and while the books tend to paint the Afghans as the 'other' – the reality is that the Afghan story is sometimes about wars (often instigated by foreigners) but it is also peppered with examples of negotiations, access, hospitality, interest in the West, and peace initiatives.

It was my colleague Priyanka Shankar who told me not to wait for the unwilling Western world for an international publication. She is from India and, before I realized it, she had contacted HarperCollins India, which publishes books for India and the wider territory. They were eager to publish my book and said that Afghanistan is still an important topic for the region. We discussed publication online and via the usual platforms, concluding that we would be able to reach an international audience.

Thanks to the research for my Omar book, I am convinced we don't need to write about Afghanistan through a Western lens, or for a Western audience. Much more than many Western gatekeepers realize, we can learn to understand Afghans on their terms.

Bibliography

Archives

I made extensive use of Afghan newspaper archives, including archives of the Afghanistan Islamic Press (in English) and the archives of the Taliban newspaper *Shariat* (in Pashto and Farsi), parts of which were translated by my research team. Other local newspapers can be found through the Taliban Sources Project (Thesigers, Michael Innes, talibansourcesproject. com), which has an archive at the Norwegian Ministry of Defense's research institute (Forsvarets forskningsinstitutt, Oslo). Another key archive is that of *The Gazette*, which contains the Taliban's rules (http:// talibanbook.com).

Books

Bearden, Milton. *The Main Enemy: The Inside Story of the CIA's Final Showdown with the KGB*. New York: Random House, 2003.

Bergen, Peter. *The Osama bin Laden I Know*. New York: Free Press, 2006.

Benjamin, Daniel and Steve Simon. *The Age of Sacred Terror: Radical Islam's War Against America*. New York: Random House Trade, 2003.

Braithwaite, Rodric. *Afgantsy: The Russians in Afghanistan*, 1979-89. *London:* Profile Books, 2011.

Bruce, Riedel. *What We Won: America's Secret War in Afghanistan*. Washington D.C.: Brookings Institution Press, 2014.

Brynjar, Lia. *Architects of the Global Jihad: The Life of Al-Qaida Strategists Abu Mus'ab Al-Suri*. Oxford: Oxford University Press, 2009.

Burke, Jason. *Al-Qaeda: The True Story of Radical Islam*. New York: I.B. Tauris, 2004.

Coll, Steve. *Ghost Wars: The Secret History of the CIA, Afghanistan, and bin Laden, from the Soviet Invasion to September 10, 2001*. London: Penguin, 2004.

Coll, Steve. *Directorate S: The C.I.A. and America's Secret Wars in Afghanistan and Pakistan*. London: Penguin Press, 2018.

Dam, Bette. *A Man and A Motorcycle: How Hamid Karzai Came to Power*. Utrecht: Ipso Facto, 2014.

Farral, Leah and Mustafa Hamid. *The Arabs at War in Afghanistan*. London: Hurst, 2015.

Gall, Carlotta. *The Wrong Enemy: America in Afghanistan 2001-2014*. Boston M.A.: Mariner Books, 2014.

Grenier, Robert. *88 Days to Kandahar, a CIA Diary*. New York: Simon & Schuster, 2015.

Gopal, Anand. *No Good Men Among the Living: America, The Taliban, and the War Through Afghan Eyes*. London: Picador, 2015.

Giustozzi, Antonio. *Empires of Mud: Wars and Warlords in Afghanistan*. Oxford: Oxford University Press, 2012.

Griffin, Michael. *Reaping the Whirlwind: The Taliban Movement in Afghanistan*. London: Pluto Press, 2000.

Gutman, Roy. *How We Missed the Story: Osama bin Laden, the Taliban, and the Hijacking of Afghanistan*. Lincoln N.E.: Potomac Books, 2007.

Haq, Samiul. *Afghan Taliban War of Ideology: Struggle for Peace.* Islamabad: Emel Publications, 2017.

Howarth James, Bruce Lawrence and Osama bin Laden. *Messages to the World: The Statements of Osama bin Laden.* London: Verso, 2005.

Kean, Thomas and Lee H Hamilton. *The 9/11 Report: The National Commission on Terrorist Attacks Upon the United States.* New York: St. Martin's, 2004.

Maley, William. *Fundamentalism Reborn? Afghanistan under the Taliban.* New York: N.Y.U. Press, 1998.

Malkasian, Carter. *War Comes to Garmser: Thirty Years of Conflict on the Afghan Frontier.* Oxford: Oxford University Press, 2013.

Martin, Mike. *An Intimate War: An Oral History of the Helmand Conflict, 1978-2012.* Oxford: Oxford University Press, 2014.

Marsden, Peter. *The Taliban: War and Religion in Afghanistan.* London: Zed Books, 2002.

Matinuddin, Kamal. *The Taliban Phenomenon: Afghanistan 1994-1997.* Oxford: Oxford University Press, 2000.

Murshed, Iftikhar. *Afghanistan: The Taliban Years.* London: Bennett & Bloom, 2006.

Musharraf, Pervez. *In the Line of Fire: A Memoir.* New York: Free Press, 2006.

Mutmaeen, Abdul Hai. *Mullah Mohammad Omar, Taliban & Afghanistan, A documentary Collection of Taliban 23 Years History.* Afghanpublishers. com, 2017 (in Pashto).

Peters, Gretchen. *Seeds of Terror: How Drugs, Thugs and Crime are Reshaping the Afghan War.* London: Picador, 2010.

Rashid, Ahmed. *Taliban: Militant Islam, Oil and Fundamentalism in Central Asia.* New Haven: Yale University Press, 2000.

Reeve, Simon. *The New Jackals: Ramzi Youssef, Osama bin Laden, and the Future of Terrorism.* Boston: Northeastern University Press, 1999.

Riedel, Bruce. *The Search for Al Qaeda: Its Leadership, Ideology, and Future.* Washington D.C.: Brookings Institution Press, 2010.

Roy, Oliver. *Islam and Resistance in Afghanistan*. Cambridge U.K.: Cambridge University Press, 1990.

Smith, Graeme. *The Dogs are Eating them Now: Our War in Afghanistan*. Toronto: Knopf Canada, 2013.

Strick van Linschoten, Alex, and Felix Kuehn. *An Enemy We Created: The Myth of the Taliban–Al Qaeda Merger in Afghanistan*. Oxford: Oxford University Press, 2014.

Stenersen, Anne. *Al-Qaida in Afghanistan*. Cambridge: Cambridge University Press, 2017.

Stenersen, Anne. 'Brothers in Jihad: Explaining the Relationship between al-Qaida and the Taliban, 1996–2001.' PhD thesis, University of Oslo, 2012. https://www.nb.no/nbsok/nb/ b8bd987afec26cb85725a6cbe03591e8?lang=no , 2011.

Strick van Linschoten, Alex and Felix Kuehn. *Poetry of the Taliban*. London: Hurst, 2012.

Tenet, George. *At the Center of the Storm: The CIA during America's Time of Crisis*. New York: Harper Collins, 2009.

Woodward, Bob. *Bush At War*. New York: Simon & Schuster, 2002.

Wright, Lawrence. *The Looming Tower, Al-Qaeda and the Road to 09/11*. New York: Vintage, 2007.

Yousaf, Muhammad and *Mark* Adken. *The Bear Trap: Afghanistan's Untold Story*. Barnsley: Leo Cooper, 1992.

Zaeef, Abdul Salaam. *My Life with the Taliban*. London: Hurst, 2011.

Unpublished mahnuscripts

Hamid, Mustapha. 'The Night Kandahar Fell: The Last Arab Resistance! (1979-2001).' In a private collection.

Mohabbat, M. Kabir and L.R. McInnis. 'Delivering Osama. At Covert Meetings in October 2000 the Taliban gave the U.S. Three Ways to Take out Bin Laden: Trial, Assassination or Missile. So What Happened?' In a private collection.

Mutawakil, Wakil Ahmad. 'Afghanistan and Taliban, *Barialay Pohanyoon, Year: 1384.*' English translation in a private collection.

Muzhdah, Waheed. 'Afghanistan Under Five Years of Sovereignty.' In a private collection.

BIBLIOGRAPHY

Notes

Prologue

1.   I.E.D. means Improvised Explosive Device, I.D.F. Indirect Fire, and T.I.C. Troops in Contact.

2.   For a list of quotes about this restriction, which the journalists imposed on themselves, see *'Missie Waarheidsvinding'* [Establishing the Truth], an undergraduate thesis by Erik Beckers at Utrecht University, Holland. https://dspace.library.uu.nl/handle/1874/31111.

3.   While the Dutch mainstream media at that time, which dominated the daily news in Holland, tended to be embedded with the Dutch army, there were some exceptions. Among them was Minka Nijhuis, who reported on an unembedded basis from Uruzgan in 2006 for publications such as the Dutch newspaper *Trouw*. Deedee Derksen, who worked for *De Volkskrant* newspaper, came to Afghanistan later; although based in Kabul, she also visited Uruzgan unembedded. The Dutch journalist Arnold Karskens accompanied the militias of the local governor Jan Mohammed Khan rather than reporting from Camp Holland.

4.   Bette Dam, *A Man and a Motorcycle: How Hamid Karzai Came to Power* (Utrecht: Ipso Facto, 2014).

5.   This is a reference to Bart Nijpels' report for *Reporter*, a Dutch TV documentary program: http://www.human.nl/speel.KRO_1233076. html.

6.   The term 'global script' was coined in an academic paper on the reporting of terrorist attacks in four major mainstream media outlets; see: 'International Terrorism, Domestic Coverage? How Terrorist Attacks are Presented in the News of CNN, Al Jazeera, the BBC, and ARD,' *The International Communication Gazette* (2014). http://www.polsoz.fu-berlin.de/soziologie/arbeitsbereiche/makrosoziologie/mitarbeiter/lehrstuhlinhaber/dateien/Gerhards-_-Schaefer-2014-International-Terrorism—-International-Communication-Gazette.pdf.

7.   I wrote about this incident for the renowned think tank Afghanistan Analysts Network. See: Bette Dam, 'Beheaded by the Taleban? No, This Time it was about Sex.' https://www.afghanistan-analysts.org/beheaded-by-the-taleban-no-this-time-it-was-about-sex/.

8.   Idem.

9.   'Obama criticized for visiting Afghan intelligence official at US hospital,' *The Washington Post*, January 8, 2013. https://www.washingtonpost.com/politics/obama-criticized-for-visiting-afghan-intelligence-official-at-us-hospital/2013/01/08/0df70f92-59da-11e2-88d0-c4cf65c3ad15_story.html.

10.   'Roadside Bomb Kills Five in UN Vehicle,' A.B.C., April 17, 2007. http://www.abc.net.au/news/2007-04-17/roadside-bomb-kills-fivein-un-vehicle/2244430; *The New York Times*: http://www.nytimes.com/2007/04/17/world/asia/17ihtafghan.1.5316936.html.

11.   'Afghan Governor's Rights Abuses Known in '07,' C.B.C. News, April 12, 2010. http://www.cbc.ca/news/politics/afghan-governor-s-rightsabuses-known-in-07-1.906659.

12.   Idem.

13.   Bette Dam, C.N.N., transcript, June 29, 2011. http://edition.cnn.com/TRANSCRIPTS/1106/29/ita.01.html.

14.   Bette Dam, 'Kabul Hotel Attack is Down to Political Gameplay,' *The Guardian*, June 29, 2011. https://www.theguardian.com/commentisfree/2011/jun/29/kabul-hotel-attack-political-gameplay.

15.   A good example is the work of the journalist Matthieu Aikins about Abdul Razeq. See: 'Our Man in Kandahar,' *The Atlantic*, November 2011. https://www.theatlantic.com/magazine/archive/2011/11/our-man-in-kandahar/308653/. Among Anand Gopal's extensive publications is a book on the same topic. See: Anand Gopal, *No Good Men Among the*

Living: America, the Taliban and the War through Afghan Eyes (New York: Metropolitan Books, 2014).

CHAPTER 1

1. 'U.S. Might Send Ground Troops To Assist In The Search For Omar,' *The New York Times*, January 1, 2002.
2. 'Mullah Omar Calls for a Taliban Surge,' *The New York Times*, March 6, 2009.
3. Authoritative books by such authors as Bob Woodward repeatedly claim that Osama bin Laden was bankrolling Mullah Omar. See, for example: Bob Woodward, *Bush At War* (Simon & Schuster, 2002), p. 31.
4. This information can be found, for example, on the B.B.C. website: 'Profile: Mullah Mohammed Omar,' July 29, 2015. It is also claimed in Lawrence Wright, *The Looming Tower: Al Qaeda and the Road to 9/11* (Knopf Doubleday Publishing Group, 2007), p. 326, that Mullah Omar and Osama bin Laden were friends (and went fishing together), especially after Bin Laden had sworn an oath to the mullah. In a long article that appeared in the Dutch newspaper *De Volkskrant* shortly after 9/11, the attacks in Saudi Arabia were also ascribed to Bin Laden, who was described as a major terrorist in the 1990s and a close friend of Mullah Omar's family. According to the journalist, Mullah Omar was married to Osama bin Laden's daughter. Rob Vreeken, '*Osama bin Ladens missie: vergelding met gepaste munt*,' [Osama bin Laden's mission: revenge in kind]. https://www.volkskrant.nl/nieuws-achtergrond/osama-bin-ladens-missie-vergelding-met-gepaste-munt~bedc9395/.
5. Ahmed Rashid, *Taliban: The Story of the Afghan Warlords* (Pan MacMillan, 2001), p. 139.
6. Idem.
7. Alex Strick van Linschoten writes about this in his article 'The Myth of Talqaeda,' January 10, 2011.
8. Dan Lamothe, '"Probably the largest" al-Qaeda training camp ever destroyed in Afghanistan,' *The Washington Post*, October 30, 2015, https://www.washingtonpost.com/news/checkpoint/wp/2015/10/30/probably-the-largest-al-qaeda-training-camp-ever-destroyed-in-afghanistan/.
9. For example, this article: Rivera Gall, 'Rebutting Afghan Spy Agency, Taliban Say their Leader isn't Dead,' *The New York Times*, May 23, 2011.
10. Interview with Ahmed Rashid, via Skype.

11. After Mullah Omar's death had been confirmed in 2015, the Wanted notice remained on the website.

12. Interview with Najibullah from Uruzgan, who had seen the flyers when they were being burned in this city. Also, an interview with the B.B.C. Pashto journalist Rahimullah Yousafzai, who received a phone call from the man in one of the photos, hoping that Yousafzai would be able to help him put the Americans right.

13. National Security Archive. https://nsarchive2.gwu.edu//NSAEBB/ NSAEBB97/poster.htm.

14. 'Searching For Mullah Omar,' *Vanity Fair*, March 2003.

15. See, for example, my deconstruction of the story behind one of the killings in *The Sydney Morning Herald*: Bette Dam, 'The Cycle of Revenge,' https:// www.smh.com.au/national/the-cycle-of-revenge-20110521-1exzc.html

16. 'Drone Strike Statistics Answer Few Questions, and Raise Many,' *The New York Times*, July 3, 2016. I quote this article from *The New York Times*. At the same time I don't see a further incorporation of this lack of precision (90 per cent miss their target and there is the problem of biased intelligence) in the follow-up coverage. An example is here: Eric Schmitt and Matthew Rosenberg, 'C.I.A. Wants Authority to Conduct Drone Strikes in Afghanistan for the First Time,' *The New York Times*, September 15, 2017, https://www.nytimes.com/2017/09/15/us/politics/cia-drone-strike-authority-afghanistan.html?searchResultPosition=6; or this article: Eric Schmitt, 'Pentagon Tests Lasers and Nets to Combat a Vexing Foe, *The New York Times*, September 23, 2017, https://www.nytimes.com/2017/09/23/world/middleeast/isis-drones-pentagon-experiments.html?searchResultPosition=11.

17. One year after we met, Mir Hamza was shot dead by a marksman on a scooter who managed to attack him at the door to his house. According to Najibullah, a rival was behind the murder.

18. Text of the State of the Union Address, *The Washington Post*, January 29, 2012.

19. 'In U.S. Report, Brutal Details of 2 Afghan Inmates' Deaths,' *The New York Times*, May 20, 2005.

20. Interview with the wife of one of the Afghan men I interviewed, whose family often spent time together with Mullah Omar's family. The Afghan man I interviewed asked me not to reveal his identity or report that I'd interviewed his wife. He said that it was forbidden by local traditions for his wife to be interviewed by a stranger.

21. Rodric Braithwaite, *Afgantsy: The Russians in Afghanistan 1979–89* (Profile Books, 2012), p. 16.

22. 'When Duke Ellington Played in Kabul,' B.B.C., September 20, 2013.

23. 'In Small Things Remembered, The Early Years of Afghan-U.S. Relations,' http://www.meridian.org/insmallthingsremembered/local-afghans-and-ica-rural-development-workers-share-a-relaxing-moment.

24. Interview with Mutawakil, Kabul; interview with Mutasim, Kabul; interview with Abdul Rahman Hotaki, Kabul.

25. Interview during a visit to the cemetery in Kandahar with the man in charge of tending to the cemetery.

26. Interview with Mutasim Agha Jan, Ankara, Turkey; interview with Mullah Omar's half-brother, Mullah Manan. For the formal biography, see: https://hansdevreij.com/2015/04/05/official-biography-of-taliban-leader-mullah-omar/.

27. Interview with Abdul Ahad, Deh Rawod and Kabul.

28. Interview with Mullah Mutawakil, Kabul.

29. Interview with Ghulam Haider, Deh Rawod and Kabul; interview with Abdul Ghaffour, governor of Deh Rawod in 2013, who knew Mullah Omar as a child. In the course of my investigations, I discovered that Mullah Omar did not have a good relationship with his stepfather. I also heard from Latif that Mullah Omar did not want much to do with his stepfather during his period in power either.

30. Afghanistan Analysts Network (A.A.N.) published a report in June 2017 that includes my sources and Latif's on the *hujras*. The report can be found at: https://www.afghanistan-analysts.org/publication/aan-papers/ideology-in-the-afghan-taliban-a-new-aan-report/.

31. The book has not yet been published.

32. For example, in an article by the well-known author William Dalrymple: http://www.newstatesman.com/politics/international-politics/2014/04/inside-islams-terror-schools. In his authoritative book *The Looming Tower*, Lawrence Wright claims that Mullah Omar already spoke Arabic back then and took classes in the Pakistani city of Peshawar. This is based on an interview with the Egyptian journalist Faraj Ismael, who worked a lot for the newspaper *Al Muslimoon* in Peshawar at the time. See also: *The Looming Tower*, p. 256-257.

33. 'Many of [the Taliban] had been born in Pakistani refugee camps, educated in Pakistani madrassas and had learnt their fighting skills from Mujaheddin parties based in Pakistan. As such the younger Taliban barely knew their own country or history, but from their madrassas they learnt about the ideal Islamic society created by the Prophet Mohammed 1400 years ago and this is what they wanted to emulate.'

34. B.B.C., 'Where the Taliban's Warriors are Born,' *The Independent*.

35. Reuters, 'I Knew Bin Laden,' Al Jazeera, December 27, 2011. http://www.aljazeera.com/programmes/general/2011/05/201151014338715787.html.

36. Samiul Haq, *Afghan Taliban: War of Ideology, Struggle for Peace* (Emel Publications, 2015).

37. Anand Gopal and Alex Strick van Linschoten, 'Ideology in the Afghan Taliban,' Afghanistan Analysts Network.

38. Its Wikipedia entry, for example, gives Mullah Omar as one of the 'notable alumni'. See: https://en.wikipedia.org/wiki/Jamia_Uloom-ul-Islamia. The American publishing company McClatchy makes the same claim. See: https://www.mcclatchydc.com/news/nation-world/world/article29940219.html.

39. Interview with Saleemudeen, the son of Nizamudeen Shamzai, Karachi, Pakistan. When asked, Omar said that he could not remember having visited the madrassa.

40. Interview with B.B.C. journalist Rahimullah Yousafzai, Peshawar, Pakistan. Yousafzai told me about this quote by Mullah Omar. He had interviewed Mullah Omar on several occasions.

CHAPTER 2

1. See more on this in: Mike Martin, *An Intimate War: An Oral History of the Helmand Conflict* (Hurst Publishers, 2017).

2. These murders, which some experts have called 'crimes against humanity,' have been remarkably neglected in accounts of Afghanistan's history. To read more about them, go to the Afghanistan Analysts Network website: http://www.afghanistan-analysts.org/death-list-published-families-of-disappeared-end-a-30-year-wait-for-news/. On the events prior to the Russian attack on Kabul, see: Rodric Braithwaite, *Afgantsy*.

3. Bruce Riedel, *What We Won, America's Secret War in Afghanistan: America's Secret War in Afghanistan, 1979–89* (Brookings Institution Press, 2014), p. 105.

4. There is still uncertainty surrounding the statistics on ISIS militants in Syria and Iraq. The U.S. government claims there have been at least 40,000 combatants but other sources, including Russian ones, speak of 25,000.

5. Jason Burke, *Al-Qaeda*.

6. For more on this, see: Leah Farrall and Mustafa Hamid, *The Arabs at War in Afghanistan* (Hurst Publishers, 2015), https://www.hurstpublishers.com/book/the-arabs-at-war-in-afghanistan/.

7. For a detailed account of the Arab Afghans – as they were known – see: *The Arabs at War in Afghanistan*.

8. Martine van Bijlert describes in detail how Deh Rawod District fell rapidly to the Russians. See her paper 'Unruly Commanders,' July 6, 2009.

9. There were some exceptions, such as Graeme Smith, who regularly visited Kandahar, reporting for the Canadian media, between 2005 and 2011.

10. My good friend and colleague Borhan Osman has written a lovely article about these legendary trucks. See: Afghanistan Analysts Network, 'Poetry in Motion: Love, War and Politics on Trucks,' August 17, 2013.

11. The photo is from the book by Mullah Zaeef, *My Life with the Taliban* (Columbia University Press, 2010).

12. Interview with Wakil Mutawakil, Kabul.

13. Interview with Haji Ghausedin, Kandahar. Ghausedin, who must have been at least sixty by then, was a prominent tribal leader who had lived next to Mullah Omar's command post in Haji Ibrahim. His house was destroyed in the fighting that broke out in Haji Ibrahim after 9/11. I spoke to him in Kandahar City.

14. Mullah Zaeef, for example, claims in his book *My Life With the Taliban* that he witnessed the incident but I have found no evidence of that. His presence has not been confirmed by residents of Haji Ibrahim or Mullah Omar's fellow combatants there. Neither do my sources, such as the doctor who attended to Omar, remember Zaeef being there. In the bestseller *The Looming Tower*, Lawrence Wright claims that Omar lost his eye in Jalalabad, a city in eastern Afghanistan. But he never went there during the jihad, according to my sources, so he could not have lost his eye there.

15. Interview in Kandahar with Mullah Ezatullah, who came from Haji Ibrahim and fought in the jihad. He is now a truck driver and lives in Kandahar.

16. For more information, see the article in *Vanity Fair*, although it should be noted that the two other photos that the magazine published in the article are not actually photographs of Mullah Omar. Edward Grazda, 'Searching for Mullah Omar,' *Vanity Fair*, March 7, 2007, https://www.vanityfair.com/news/2003/02/mullah200302. See the film *The Caliphate* (Arte 2014) on how we tracked down the man in these fake photos of Mullah Omar. He explains how he was tricked by the photographer Hadi, who photographed him in profile and then sold this in America as a picture of Mullah Omar.

CHAPTER 3

1. Milton Bearden and James Risen say this in their book *The Main Enemy.
    The Inside Story of the C.I.A.'s Final Showdown with the K.G.B.* (Random
    House, 2003). In 2002, when Hekmatyar was still a prominent leader
    in Afghanistan, the Americans tried to kill him using a Predator UAV
    (unmanned aerial vehicle), but the attack failed. See: http://news.bbc.
    co.uk/2/hi/south_asia/1978619.stm. Hekmatyar is now a member of
    the current Afghan Government headed by President Asraf Ghani.
2. See, for example: Jason Burke, *Al-Qaeda: The True Story of Radical Islam*
    (I.B. Tauris, 2004), p. 142. See also: Peter Bergen, *The Osama bin Laden I
    Know* (2006), p. 104. He had left Peshawar in 1989 and lived for a while
    in Jeddah, Saudi Arabia. He was back in Peshawar in 1991 and 1992, after
    which he moved to Sudan.
3. For more examples of extreme measures under President Rabbani,
    see: Jonathan Steele, '10 Myths About Afghanistan,' *The Guardian*,
    September 27, 2011.
4. The British U.N. official Joylon Leslie kept the decree by the Islamic State
    of Afghanistan and its Supreme Court setting out the restrictions that
    apply to women. He sent it to me in an email.
5. For more details, see the book by Peter Tomsen, *The Wars of Afghanistan:
    Messianic Terrorism, Tribal Conflicts, and the failures of Great Powers* (Public
    Affairs, 2011).
6. I never found out the real names of Mullah Omar's four wives. His family
    refuses to tell me. It's against their conservative views to share the names of
    the women. This is not only a Taliban custom: in large parts of Afghanistan
    it is not only seen as disrespectful for the female relatives but also risky for
    the family and the tribe. According to thse patriarchical ideas, the women
    should be living in seclusion so as not to threaten their family. I saw women
    themselves embracing this notion in the south. For more on this topic, see
    this article: https://www.afghanistan-analysts.org/en/reports/rights-
    freedom/whats-in-a-womans-name-no-name-no-public-persona/.
7. Two of them were allegedly killed in an attack on Omar in 1998.
8. The uncle I spoke to hardly had any contact with his brother (whose
    daughter married Mullah Omar) because they were *turburs* – family
    rivals. He still lived in Haji Ibrahim and his brother had moved to Quetta,
    Pakistan.
9. Source: Mutasim.
10. Interviews with Mohammed Issa.

CHAPTER 4

1.   See, for example: Bob Woodward, *Bush at War*, p. 31. I reconstructed
      the rise of Mullah Omar as leader of the Taliban using the accounts of
      eyewitnesses, including Issa, Haji Ghausedin, Haji Bashar's deputy and
      Dr. Baluch. I also interviewed Abdullah Khan, a Taliban leader now and a
      young student back then who assisted Mullah Omar in Dand, Kandahar.
2.   For more insight into U.S. perspectives on the role of Pakistan, see:
      The National Security Archive, 'Pakistan: "The Taliban's Godfather"?,
      Documents Detail Years of Pakistani Support for Taliban, Extremists.' It
      is also important to note the sources the U.S. uses in these documents,
      and how often statements are corroborated by more than one source. See:
      https://nsarchive2.gwu.edu/NSAEBB/NSAEBB227/index.htm.
3.   Transcripts of the court case on Haji Bashar, September 2008, New York.
4.   Gretchen Peters, *Seeds of Terror*, loc. 1211 of 6579 (Kindle).
5.   Gretchen Peters, 'How Opium Profits the Taliban,' D.E.A. documents,
      2009.
6.   Court records of the trial of Haji Bashar in the U.S.
7.   Such as the notorious Haji Lalek, one of the principal Afghan traders in
      that city and a major donor to the Taliban.
8.   William Maley, ed., *Fundamentalism Reborn? Afghanistan and the Taliban*
      (NYU Press: 1998), p. 77.
9.   From an interview with Haji Bashar's deputy, who was at the meeting.
10.   Interview with Haji Bashar's deputy.
11.   Interview with Haji Ghausedin, Kandahar.
12.   At a meeting at the U.S. embassy in Islamabad, a man who was possibly
      Mullah Ghaus told the Americans about the origins of the movement, and
      connected this to Haji Bashar and his madrassa. See: NSA cable: https://
      nsarchive2.gwu.edu/NSAEBB/NSAEBB97/tal7.pdf. In *Seeds of Terror*
      (Kindle edition, loc. 1205), the author Gretchen Peters describes why she
      thinks this Taliban member must have been Mullah Ghaus. Hamid Karzai
      too, who according to my sources was also talking to the U.S. embassy
      in 1995, connected Haji Bashar to 'us' – the Taliban, and Mullah Omar.
      See the N.S.A. document here: https://nsarchive2.gwu.edu/NSAEBB/
      NSAEBB97/tal8.pdf.
13.   Gretchen also describes this scene in her book *Seeds of Terror*.
14.   Interview with Esmat (from Haji Ibrahim and a member of Mullah
      Omar's jihad group), Kabul; interview with Issa and interview with Haji
      Ghausdin (both Kandahar). Interview with Sharafat, member of the

N.G.O. commission, Dubai, in Pakistan. He is writing a Taliban biography of Mullah Omar in Pashto. It is not clear when this book will be published. According to Sharafat, Mullah Omar immediately fired Abdul Samad, one of the leaders of the nascent movement and the man who had given permission for the honor killing.

15. A good profile of Naquibullah, including about his switch to the American side after 9/11, can be found in Sarah Chayes' book *The Punishment of Virtue: Inside Afghanistan After the Taliban* (Penguin Press: 2006).

16. Michael Griffin, *Reaping the Whirlwind: The Taliban Movement in Afghanistan* (Pluto Press, 2000).

17. Interview with one of Amir Lalai's commanders, Ahmad Akhundzada, who was there when Mullah Omar came along. Interview with Daru Khan, who manned one of the commando posts on the Highway. 'We didn't fight with them and they didn't fight with us.'

18. Interview with one of Amir Lalai's commanders who was there when Mullah Omar came along.

19. Abdul Salaam Zaeef, *My Life With the Taliban*, p. 69.

20. Interview in Kabul with Esmat, Mullah Omar's friend from Sangisar.

21. Idem.

22. Read more about Hamid Karzai's past in: Bette Dam, *A Man and A Motorcycle*.

23. Antonio Giustozzi, *Empires of Mud: Wars and Warlords in Afghanistan* (Hurst Publishers), p. 74.

24. Interview with Agha Jan Mutasim, Ankara, Turkey.

25. Interview with Farouck Azam, Kabul; interview with Ostad Abdul Halim, Kandahar; both were supporters of President Rabbani.

26. Latif also remembered Ahmad Shah Massoud and President Rabbani giving their support. The phrase 'angels of peace' was often used at that time, he said.

27. Interview with Abdul the pilot, Kabul.

28. Interview with Mutawakil, Kabul. These Rabban services are also mentioned in *Fundamentalism Reborn?* by William Maley and in a leaked diplomatic letter from the U.S. embassy in Islamabad. They call the Taliban an 'unknown group' that is well armed and consists largely of young religious students who have had enough of the status quo in Kandahar. 'The group's immediate objective seems to be to reopen the Chamman-Kandahar Highway, where there has been a great deal of fighting recently, which has made many people believe that the Taliban is supported by Pakistan. Another objective is the commercial interests in reopening the trade route between Pakistan and central Asia.'

29. *Frontier Post*, September 25, 1994, see A.C.K.U. clipping. http://www. afghandata.org:8080/xmlui/handle/azu/6574. *Frontier Post*, December 11, 1994. 'For Nasrullah Babar's consideration!' William Maley, *Fundamentalism Reborn?*, p. 80.

30. Interview in Kandahar with Akhundzada, Amir Lalai's deputy. Amir Lalai died from natural causes in 2008.

31. See, for example, the diplomatic communications from the U.S. embassy in Islamabad, which state that opening the highway was a priority for Pakistan, which had engaged Western diplomats in the issue by getting them to pay a visit to Herat. Furthermore, large sums of money were invested in a new highway in southern Afghanistan. See: N.S.A. Archive, 'Weekly South Asia Report,' November 4, 1994, and 'New Fighting and New Forces in Kandahar,' November 3, 1994. See also: https:// nsarchive2.gwu.edu/NSAEBB/NSAEBB97/tal1.pdf.

32. Carlotta Gall, *The Wrong Enemy: America in Afghanistan 2001–2014* (Houghton Mifflin Harcourt: 2014), p. 36.

33. N.S.A. Archive, 'New Fighting and New Forces in Kandahar.'

34. Source: https://nsarchive2.gwu.edu/NSAEBB/NSAEBB97/tal1.pdf. Here the convoy is described as having been planned independently of the Taliban, and the Taliban are said to act like 'surrogates' of the Rabbani government.

35. Idem.

36. 'Taliban Vow to Establish Islamic Rule in Afghanistan,' *The News*, January 27, 1995.

37. Not to be confused with Abdul Rahman, the Sufi tutor who taught Mullah Omar in Haji Ibrahim.

38. In this N.S.A. document Hamid Karzai speaks to the U.S. embassy about these councils. His name is not mentioned, but I know from my sources that this is Hamid Karzai: https://nsarchive2.gwu.edu/NSAEBB/ NSAEBB97/tal8.pdf.

39. 'Kandahar Falls to the Taliban,' *Afghanistan Islamic Press*, November 8, 1994. The B.B.C. correspondent William Read, whom I interviewed in Kabul, also saw this council meet in Kandahar when he visited the city in 1994.

40. Diplomatic cable from the U.S. embassy in Islamabad, January 20, 1995.

41. Article from an as yet unpublished archive of the Taliban Sources Project at F.F.I. in Oslo; translations by Alex Strick van Linschoten and team. Source: *Tolo Afghan* (local newspaper). The date of publication in the Afghan calendar: 1373 (1994), Qaws (September) 30. Translated by Alex Strick van Linschoten and his Afghan team. The newspapers will be published by the Norwegian think tank F.F.I.

42. 'The Taliban, What We Have Heard,' National Security Archive, information released by the U.S. embassy in Islamabad, January 20, 1995.

43. U.S. cable; see also: Anand Gopal and Alex Strick van Linschoten, 'Taliban Ideology,' Afghanistan Analysts Network.

44. Interview with Latif, who was one of Mullah Omar's secretaries at the time and later worked in a Taliban embassy abroad.

45. In the fall of 1994, William Read traveled to Kandahar and requested an interview with Mullah Omar. His request was refused. Interview with William Read, Kabul.

46. Source: 'Pakistan Ex-I.S.I. Officer Claims To Have Trained Taliban, Mullah Omar, Met Usama, Karachi Umat,' July 8, 2005, translated from Urdu.

47. Interview in Kandahar with Sheik Hotak, the brother of one of Mullah Omar's wives.

48. I discovered in my conversations with Abdul Rahman Hotaki and Mutawakil that they were also present at this interview.

49. For a detailed account of the Taliban's capture of Helmand, see: Mike Martin, *An Intimate War*, p. 98 onwards.

50. Michael Griffin, *Reaping the Whirlwind*, p. xiv.

51. Mullah Muhammad was a member of the movement from the very start, when they seized control of the Highway at Sangisar. Interview in Dubai with Abdullah Khan, head of the Taliban's Civilian Casualties Commission. Abdullah Khan said that he met Mullah Omar for the first time in that battle for the Highway.

52. Interview with Abdul the pilot. Mullah Omar had told him that he would go to Gereshk now that Mullah Muhammad was dead.

53. *Tolo Afghan*, 13737, Dalwa 12, 1995.

54. William Maley, *Fundamentalism Reborn?*, p. 77.

55. Mike Martin, *An Intimate War*, p. 98; a U.S. cable states the same: https://nsarchive2.gwu.edu/NSAEBB/NSAEBB227/3.pdf.

56. See Mike Martin, *An Intimate War*, p. 98.

57. N.S. Archive, October 1995, https://nsarchive2.gwu.edu/NSAEBB/NSAEBB227/4.pdf.

58. 'Who Should Be the Caliph and What Should He Do?' *Tolo Afghan*, June 7, 1995 (author's archive).

59. Interview with Mullah Akhundzada of the Muj Mubarak mosque, who was at this meeting in the school. Leading mullahs such as Mullah Deobandi wanted Mullah Omar to stay.

60. Amnesty International, 'Afghanistan: Grave Abuses in the Name of Religion,' November 18, 1996.

61. He forgot the name Omar here. Mullah Omar's full name is Mullah Muhammad Omar. Akhund means 'son of the mullah'.
62. Interview with the gatekeeper of the cloak, Mr. Akhundzada, Kandahar.
63. Interview with the gatekeeper of the cloak, Mr. Akhundzada; see also Norimitsu Onishi, 'A Tale of the Mullah and Muhammad's Amazing Cloak,' December 19, 2001, *The New York Times*, http://www.faughnan.com/scans/011219_MuhammedCloak.pdf.
64. Claire Billet, Leslie Knott, and I interviewed the cameraman for our film *The Last Caliphate*, Arte.com. You can see parts of the BBC footage here: https://vimeo.com/506846132PW: Uruzgan.
65. Radio Afghanistan, Kabul, in Pashto, 15:30 G.M.T., April 16, 1996.

CHAPTER 5

1. Interviews with Mutasim Agha Jan.
2. Eckhart Schieweck, an employee in the U.N. Al Qaeda Taliban Monitoring Team. Schieweck was involved in organizing Mutasim's hospital visit.
3. In 2017, the German researcher Annika Schmeding started an interesting study of Sufism in Afghanistan. I helped her and drew her attention to the importance of dreams for the Taliban. After I introduced her to Mutasim, he gave her more details, telling her how important dreams were and how the fighters used to meet up regularly to discuss their dreams. Annika Schmeding shared her recording of the interview with Mutasim with me. Her doctoral thesis was completed at Boston University and is called 'Sufis in Afghanistan - Religious Authority and Succession in an Insecure Age,' 2020.
4. Osama bin Laden also believed in dreams. He apparently told his underlings that they should make sure they did not dream of specific attacks on America as that information would then be leaked to Mullah Omar, who might see the attacks in his own dreams.
5. See also my blog on these two men, at Afghanistan Analysts Network: https://www.afghanistan-analysts.org/death-of-a-sahebzada-a-story-of-different-strands-of-thought-in-the-taleban-movement/.
6. See, for example, the book *The Interpretation of Dreams* by Ibn Sirin, available via: https://www.amazon.com/Interpretation-Dreams-Ibn-Seerin/dp/187058208X/ref=sr_1_4?dchild=1&keywords=ibn-seerin&qid=1594207025&s=books&sr=1-4.
7. Interview with Mutasim, Ankara, Turkey.
8. *Shariat Weekly*, July 15, 1996.

9. See also: Afghanistan Analysts Network, 'Flash to the Past: When the Taliban wanted un-Monitored Elections,' (2013).

10. See my blog on Afghanistan Analysts Network: https://www.afghanistan-analysts.org/death-of-a-sahebzada-a-story-of-different-strands-of-thought-in-the-taleban-movement/ (2014). Annika Aneko was also told by envoys of the Sufi leader Baba that he had advocated peace negotiations but this advice had been rejected by Mullah Omar.

11. 'Guerrillas take Afghan Capital as Troops Flee,' *The New York Times*, September 28, 1996.

12. 'Kabul Falls to Taliban,' Peshawar (A.I.P.), September 26, 1996.

13. 'Guerrillas take Afghan Capital as Troops Flee,' *The New York Times*, September 28, 1996.

14. Interview in Kabul with B.B.C. Pashto journalist Daud Junbish, who met Bor Jan and Mullah Omar in 1996.

15. Interview with Mutawakil, Kabul.

16. See also: Kamal Matinuddin, *The Taliban Phenomenon: Afghanistan 1994–1997* (Oxford University Press, 1999), p. 88. See also: 'Obituary of Mohammad Rabbani,' *The Independent*, April 18, 2001. *The Independent* – in the person of Kate Clark – speaks of the rivalry between Rabbani and Najibullah, even though Rabbani denies this in the article.

17. See the diplomatic letter in the National Security Archive: https://nsarchive2.gwu.edu/NSAEBB/NSAEBB227/17.pdf.

18. 'Masood Confident of Taking Kabul,' *Dawn*, August 1, 1997.

19. Interviews with Mutasim Agha Jan and Abdul Rahman Hotak. See, for example, also the book by Mullah Zaeef.

20. Interview with a member of Mullah Obaidullah's staff who wishes to remain anonymous, Kabul. Interview with Saad, secretary to Yaqub, Mullah Omar's son, Dubai, United Arab Emirates.

21. Interview with Dr. Wardak, Kabul.

22. These traders have remained important and powerful donors to the Taliban down to this very day.

23. *Shariat Weekly*, January 31, 1997.

24. *Shariat Weekly*, February 5, 1997.

25. Omar made preparations for Kabul: 'Kabul Falls to Taliban,' Peshawar (A.I.P.), September 26, 1996.

26. Michael Griffin, *Reaping the Whirlwind*, p. 157.

27. Interview via Skype with Alan Eastham, the American deputy ambassador in Islamabad, who visited Afghanistan five times between 1998 and 2001.

28. Interview with a poet who won one of the prizes in Kandahar.

29. Source: Mullah Abdul Rahman, Mutasim Agha Jan, and Mullah Mutawakil.

30. Anna M. Pont, *Blind Chickens and Social Animals, Creating Spaces for Afghan Women's Narratives under the Taliban*, Mercy Corps International, 2000.

31. Extreme ideas circulating among the Taliban, such as banning passports (because God rules the world and does not recognize borders between countries), were rejected by Mullah Omar. He said that what he wanted was an Islamic state in Afghanistan – he did not have any international ambitions.

32. See: J.L. Anderson and Thomas Dworzak, *Taliban* (Trolley, 2003).

33. See: *Blind Chickens and Social Animals*, Merci Corps, April 2000, http://www.afghandata.org:8080/xmlui/bitstream/handle/azu/3278/azu_acku_pamphlet_ds371_3_p668_2000_w.pdf?sequence=1&isAllowed=y

34. 'Scenesetter for your Visit to Islamabad, Afghan Angle,' a background document produced by the American embassy in Islamabad in preparation for the visit by Ambassador Robin Raphel, January 16, 1997. https://www.hsdl.org/?abstract&did=477828.

35. *Faces of Change – Afghan Women*, film essay, N.S.F., A.U.F.S., Nancy Dupree and Louis Dupree, 1976, A.C.K.U. library, Kabul.

36. U.S.I.P., 2021, Ibraheem Thurial and Borhan Osman.

37. Interview with former minister Arsala Rahmani, Kabul.

38. Interview with former minister Arsala Rahmani, Kabul; interview with Mutawakil, Kabul.

39. For more background information, see: Amir Mohammed Mansory, 'Mathematics Achievements among Afghan Primary School Children,' Masters' thesis in International and Comparative Education, 2000, p. 10.

40. 'Mullah Mohammad Omar with Shariat Weekly: University is Intellectual Center of Afghanistan's Development,' April 30, 1997. The *Shariat Weekly* wrote: 'Islam states that the highest priority should be given to education and it has always said that both boys and girls must receive an education.'

41. See Taliban newspapers. Also an interview with Robert Kluijver and Martine van Bijlert, Den Bosch, Holland. Van Bijlert was working in Kabul at the time.

42. Interview with Mutawakil, Kabul.

43. See also: 'Survey on S.C.A. Supported Girls Education,' August 27, 1997, p. 6.

44. People in Kabul disagreed on the quality of the home schooling. The B.B.C. reported on November 16, 1997 that the Taliban were allowing home schooling, a move that the British broadcaster said was welcomed by Afghan families. However, Western aid organizations were not happy as they said the standard was too low. The in-house education scheme could not be responding adequately to the needs of Afghan students in the era of contemporary education schemes, claimed the NGOs.

45. 'Scenesetter for your Visit to Islamabad, Afghan Angle,' a background document produced by the American embassy in Islamabad in preparation for the visit by Ambassador Robin Raphel, January 16, 1997. https://www.hsdl.org/?abstract&did=477828.

46. 'The Taliban's War on Women: A Health and Human Rights Crisis in Afghanistan,' Physicians for Human Rights, August 1998.

47. 'Scenesetter for your Visit to Islamabad, Afghan Angle,' a background document produced at the American embassy in Islamabad in preparation for the visit by Ambassador Robin Raphel, January 16, 1997. https://www.hsdl.org/?abstract&did=477828. 'In the past few weeks, Mullah Omar has tried to create a kinder, gentler Taliban occupation, warning his soldiers that they would be beaten if they beat up citizens for not conforming to Taliban mores.'

48. For example, one stated that any woman who went out with a 'bared face' ought to be reprimanded. But in such cases it was her husband rather than the woman herself who should be punished. The same applied to women 'who sang too loudly or danced too much at weddings'. In those cases too, the husband had to be tracked down and sent to prison. Only if a woman were to order clothes from a male tailor without a chaperon should she be punished in person, according to the *Gazette*. This was because the Taliban assumed her measurements must have been taken by a male stranger.

49. 'The Little White Book,' *Gazette*, translation by Bette Dam.

50. See also: Hamid Khan, *Islamic Law, Customary Law, and Afghan Informal Justice*, U.S.I.P., March 6, 2005.

51. This is often claimed in Western media reports. I had also assumed that there were executions or stonings every Friday, for example in the Ghanzi stadium in Kabul. See, for example: *The New Republic*, October 3, 1996, A.C.K.U. library, or read the Reuters article 'Taliban Executions still Haunt Afghan Soccer Field.'

52. 'Taliban Public Punishments, 1996-2001, A Different Place,' blog entry. https://www.alexstrick.com/talibanexecutions.

53. Interview with Wakil Mutawakil, Kabul.

54. I heard the rumor that Mullah Omar was supposed to have a tail from my Afghan friend Rafiq in Mazaar-e-Sharif. These rumors were spread by General Ahmad Rashid Dostum's soldiers.
55. Interview with Taliban leader Suhail Shaheen, Doha, Qatar.
56. Michael Griffin, *Reaping the Whirlwind*, p. 53.
57. 'Taliban Declare Beard in Force, Veil for Women Compulsory,' A.I.P., September 24, 1996.

CHAPTER 6

1. 'By the fall of Kabul administration, the hand of outsiders has been cut off from our country,' *Shariat Weekly*, September 29, 1996, edition 39.
2. See a cable from 1996: https://nsarchive2.gwu.edu/NSAEBB/NSAEBB227/12.pdf.
3. See a cable from 1996: https://nsarchive2.gwu.edu/NSAEBB/NSAEBB227/9.pdf.
4. See a cable from 1996: https://nsarchive2.gwu.edu/NSAEBB/NSAEBB227/15.pdf.
5. Source: 'Pakistani Ex-I.S.I. Officer Claims to Have Trained Taliban, Mullah Omar, Met Usama, Karachi Ummat,' July 8, 2005, translated from Urdu.
6. U.S. cable, 1996, https://nsarchive2.gwu.edu/NSAEBB/NSAEBB227/9.pdf.
7. Steve Coll, *Ghost Wars: The Secret History of the CIA, Afghanistan and Bin Laden* (Penguin Putnam: 2005), p. 293. In this chapter about the conversation with Benazir Bhutto, Steve Coll also explains that Pakistan was not behind the creation of the Taliban in 1994. At that time, the I.S.I. was still dependent on Hekmatyar, whose training camps were used as a source for Pakistani jihad fighters. They were then sent to Kashmir to fight the eternal enemy, India. Only later did the I.S.I. let it be known that it saw the Taliban as an interesting option for a partner. Coll also writes that the recently appointed I.S.I. leader, an admirer of the British Raj, was not keen on Islamic fundamentalism. When a Taliban delegation paid a visit, he was quite shocked: the men wore slippers and some had only one leg.
8. Interview with Iftikhar Murshed, Islamabad; see also his book: *Afghanistan: The Taliban Years* (Bennett & Bloom, 2006), p. 62.
9. Interview with Dr. Baluch, Kandahar; interview with Mutasim Agha Jan, Ankara, Turkey.
10. 'The Godfather of the Taliban: Hamid Gul and his Legacy,' Deutsche Welle, August 16, 2015.

11. 'HuM Vows Fight against India, the Northern Alliance,' Kashmir News, December 17, 2001.

12. For a detailed description of their activities, see: http://www.atimes. com/c-asia/CJ26Ag01.html, 'But charity and relief work are its main goals – not jihadis against 'infidels'. Al-Rashid says that its activities include providing financial and legal support to jailed Muslim militants around the world, and that all of its actions are purely humanitarian.'

13. The Al Rashid employee claims to have advised Mullah Omar not to blow up the Buddhas in 2001, but Omar would not listen.

14. For the description of Al Rashid on the U.N. sanctions list, see: https:// www.un.org/sc/suborg/en/sanctions/1267/aq_sanctions_list/ summaries/entity/al-rashid-trust.

15. 'Banned Organisation Seeks Unfreezing of Accounts,' Dawn, April 27, 2016, https://www.dawn.com/news/1254662.

16. 'Flash to the Past when the Taliban Wanted U.N. Monitored Elections,' Afghanistan Analysts Network. In 1998, Mullah Omar decided to move into one of the abandoned workers' houses next to the old factory so that he could live as cheaply as possible. He no longer felt safe in Haji Ibrahim; he was afraid of being attacked on his journeys between the village and Kandahar City. The workers' houses were closer to the city, although it was still a ten-minute drive. They had a Western layout with a low wall around the garden (that you could look over) and a kitchens with a sink and gas stove, which was still quite unusual in Kandahar at that time. People often cooked on the floor. Although it was a small, abandoned house, it must still have seemed a big improvement for Mullah Omar's family compared with what they had in Haji Ibrahim, even if the women in the family may have felt nostalgic pangs for their familiar old mudbrick hut. When I visited the place in 2013, Amir Lalai's son and his family were living there; I found they were still cooking with burners on the floor and were not using the kitchen with its gas stove at all.

17. A 'Taliban insider' talked with the American embassy in Islamabad in September 1995. He claimed that the Taliban were not interested in fomenting ethnic divisions; on the contrary, they wanted to protect the rights of minority groups. For the report of this conversation, see the National Security Archive, February 1995. A good description of the Americans' attitude to the Taliban can be found in the diplomatic letter 'Dealing with the Taliban in Kabul,' September 28, 1996. See also: William Maley, Fundamentalism Reborn?, p. 91. When the Taliban decided to make the Sikhs – a minority in Afghanistan – wear a yellow star, this caused a huge

stir in America and Europe, with comparisons soon being drawn with the Second World War. The Taliban's motivation was rather different, though: letting them wear a yellow star in public would make it easier for the religious police to exempt them from the rules. The police would know they did not have to force these Sikhs to pray five times a day as Sikhs are not Muslims.

18. The then U.S. ambassador Robin Raphel confirmed this in an interview with me in Washington D.C. She said that many Taliban thanked the Americans for their assistance during the jihad and thought they were helping the U.S. now too.

19. This is from the book *How We Missed the Story: Osama bin Laden, the Taliban and the Hijacking of Afghanistan* (Potomac Books, 2007), p. 77, by Roy Gutman.

20. The Americans' attitude to the Taliban is described in the diplomatic letter 'Dealing with the Taliban in Kabul,' September 28, 1996.

21. Idem.

22. Statement by Robin Raphel, head of the American delegation, U.N. Meeting on Afghanistan, November 18, 1996. The conversation was conducted in private, according to Ahmed Rashid; see: *Taliban*, pp. 178, 261.

23. In a cable in early 1995, Hamid Karzai told the Americans that the Taliban wanted to be an inclusive movement and would not interfere with the Shia; see: https://nsarchive2.gwu.edu/NSAEBB/NSAEBB97/tal8.pdf.

24. The book with Sufi poems by Abdul Ghafar Baryalay, Mutawakil's father, is still very popular in Kandahar. It was no longer available in the bookshops at the time when the Taliban came to power, so Mullah Omar had it reprinted. Mutawakil knew which poems Omar particularly liked, for example, 'Your Splendor' (about love). Some of the poems focus on the comforting effect of alcohol, a subject also dealt with by the famous Persian poet Rumi.

25. Hamid Karzai also told the Americans in early 1995 that recognition by the U.N. was important for the Taliban. See: https://nsarchive2.gwu.edu/NSAEBB/NSAEBB97/tal8.pdf.

26. Member of the U.N. delegation in Kabul. Interview via email.

27. Interview by email with Norbert Holl. For a report of his press conference, see: https://www.un.org/press/en/1996/19961119.afghn.18n.html.

28. Interview with Latif, Kabul. The Taliban ambassador at the time, Abdul Hakim Mujahed, also told me in an interview that the Taliban did not want Karzai as a U.N. representative, but he would not say why. However, Karzai does seem to have been an ambassador for the Taliban in December 1996

(and he had contact with the American ambassador Robin Raphel); see: 'U.S. Engagement with the Taliban on Usama bin Laden,' July 16, 2001.

29. Interview with Latif; interview with Dr. Baluch.

30. Francesc Vendrell, who became the U.N. representative responsible for both Afghanistan and Pakistan in 2000, says that the choices made by the credentials committee in this 'technical part' were not actually as technical as they seemed; the real criteria driving the decision were informal as this was a 'political' decision. 'It reflects the member states' political judgment of some governments,' says Vendrell. If the criteria were to be applied strictly, other countries would have to be excluded too. That is the case for Saudi Arabia, for example, a country that discriminates against women and requires them to wear clothes that cover the entire body. What is more, stoning is permitted as a punishment for men and women in Saudi Arabia.

31. See John F. Burns, 'New Rulers Won't Ease Restrictions, Afghan Says,' The New York Times, October 9, 1996, http://www.nytimes.com/1996/10/09/world/new-rulers-won-t-ease-restrictions-afghan-says.html.

32. Interview with Norbert Holl, by email.

33. 'Russians are Back in Afghanistan, Aiding Rebels,' The New York Times, July 27, 1998.

34. Abdul Rahman Hotaki was present at this meeting.

35. On the friendship between Bout and Massoud, see: Nicholas Scmidle, 'Disarming Viktor Bout', New Yorker, August 27, 2014, http://www.newyorker.com/magazine/2012/03/05/disarming-viktor-bout.

36. In the documentary The Notorious Mr. Bout, he relates how Mullah Omar showed him the door because he had supplied Omar's enemy with weapons. So according to Bout himself, he did indeed meet Mullah Omar.

37. The American senator Hank Brown also visited Mullah Omar, and the mullah asked him too for an 'exchange of prisoners,' whereby Omar would hand over the Russian pilots he was holding prisoner in return for the Afghans who had disappeared. See: 'Daredevil Airmen Receive Warm Homecoming,' A.P., August 19, 1996.

38. Interview with Abdul Rahman Hotaki, who received the delegation together with Mullah Mutawakil. Friends who were living in Kabul at the time can also clearly remember announcements by the Taliban on the radio calling on people to report missing persons.

39. Interview with Latif, Kabul; interview with Mutawakil, Kabul. See also: 'The Taliban Enacted a Radio Statement on 29 August 1997' via Radio Voice of Shari'ah, Kabul, in Pashto (translated by the B.B.C.): 'We have a well-known proverb about having 'one roof with two kinds of weather''

[double standards]. (...) Those who make a loud noise about human rights and shed tears about prisoners, making accusations against our Islamic State, are not making a noise because of human rights but because they want to protect criminals and cruel people. If this is incorrect and they are really defending human rights, then why are you [the Western media], the defenders of human rights, not yet able to visit the poor, persecuted and trapped Taliban prisoners in Mazar-e-Sharif?' Excerpt from 'Taliban Radio Rejects Claims of Abuse of Human Rights, B.B.C. Reports,' B.B.C. Asia-Pacific Monitoring Service, September 1, 1997.

40.   'Russian hostages describe escape,' Reuters, August 19, 1996, http://nl.newsbank.com/nl-search/we/Archives?p_product=WT&p_theme=wt&p_action=search&p_maxdocs=200&p_topdoc=1&p_text_direct-0=0EB0F20B7AD3A37E&p_field_direct-0=document_id&p_perpage=10&p_sort=YMD_date:D&s_trackval=GooglePM.

41.   I have carried out a media survey in the archives of the French university Sciences Po together with my student, Elodie Le Fur. Elodie has written a paper about this that can be found on my website, www.bettedam.com.

42.   'Afghan Opposition Makes Huge Gains, 3,000 Taliban Killed or Held: Envoy,' A.F.P., May 30, 1997.

43.   Interview with Patricia Grossman, who was monitoring Afghanistan at the time for Human Rights Watch. An exception was the International Committee of the Red Cross, which repeatedly raised the subject, both locally and internationally, throughout the summer of 1997.

44.   Research Paper, Sciences Po, Elodie Le Fur.

45.   'Taliban Foreign Ministry Protests over U.S. Secretary of State's Remarks on Women,' Radio Voice of Shari'ah, Kabul, in Pashto, 15:00 G.M.T., November 20, 1997. 'In Afghan Refugee Camp, Albright Hammers Taliban,' The New York Times, November 19, 1997.

46.   Interview with Jolyon Leslie, Kabul, U.N. diplomat in Afghanistan during the Taliban period.

47.   'Bonino Calls for Solidarietà Day with Afghan Women,' La Repubblica, via B.B.C. Summary of World Broadcasts, October 2, 1997.

48.   S. Iftikhar Murshed, Afghanistan: The Taliban's Years, p. 289.

49.   'Taliban Seek Recognition from 55 Muslim States,' U.P.I.

50.   'Afghanistan: The Massacre in Mazar I Sharif,' Human Rights Watch, November 1998.

51.   Brahimi said they were mainly drivers and other staff working at the Iranian consulate, not actual diplomats. Interview with Brahimi, Paris, France, 2016.

CHAPTER 7

1.   A great deal has been written about this flight. My information comes from Osama bin Laden's son Omar bin Laden. Omar was on the flight that took the family from Sudan to Afghanistan, stopping over in Iran.
2.   Interview with Omar bin Laden, Doha, Qatar.
3.   'Anti-Soviet Warrior puts his Army on the Road to Peace,' *The Independent*, December 6, 1993.
4.   For a journalistic analysis of Osama's life, see: Jason Burke, *Al-Qaeda*.
5.   Jason Burke, *Al-Qaeda*, p. 103.
6.   Two young men involved in the attacks on the two American embassies in Africa (in 1998) came from the Khalden camp; see: Jason Burke, *Al-Qaeda*, p. 106.
7.   See the 9/11 Commission Report, from p. 57.
8.   Idem, p. 58. An example of an article that incorporates these assumptions is 'Born into Privilege, Bin Laden Became the Face of Global Terror,' *The New York Times*, May 3, 2011. It links Osama bin Laden to numerous terrorist attacks without giving any evidence.
9.   'U.S. was Foiled Multiple Times in Efforts to Capture Bin Laden or Have him Killed,' *The Washington Post*, October 3, 2001.
10. Page 101 of the book *An Enemy We Created* by Strick van Linschoten and Kuehn states the following: 'The plots and attacks that were carried out in the mid-1990's – the World Trade Center bombings of 1993, for example – reveal the nature of the early threat: unorganized and lacking unity but nevertheless able via some key individuals, to rely on support and draw together and backing from the wider community of jihadists and former Afghan Arabs.'
11. Read the introduction to Jason Burke, *Al-Qaeda*.
12. For a description of the attack, see the 9/11 Commission Report, which also assumes that Al Qaeda was behind the attack, p. 71. Moreover, Condoleezza Rice said – under oath – that this attack should be seen as an attack by Al Qaeda. For a report of her statements, see: http://test.www.wnd.com/2004/04/24091/. Jason Burke notes that the perpetrator Ramzi Yousef is often described as an 'Al-Qaeda agent' but he doubts whether that was actually the case. 'A close examination reveals broad associative links, mainly through mutual acquaintances, but little more' (p. 110). According to reports from the time, the C.I.A. knew that the connection with Osama bin Laden was always 'mysterious and confusing' but secret service agents invariably assumed those connections existed. In interviews given by the

C.I.A. about the '1993 attack', they state without giving evidence that they are convinced Osama was linked to that attack. For more on how the C.I.A. interprets evidence of a link with Osama, see: Simon Reeve, *The New Jackals. Ramzi Yousef, Osama bin Laden and the Future of Terrorism*, which was published in 1999. Other media adopted the C.I.A.'s line of reasoning. This is evident in an article about Ramzi Yousef in the leading Dutch newspaper *NRC Handelsblad*; it states that there is little evidence for what Ramzi is supposed to have done and his alleged connections, but the author still concludes that Yousef was very probably working with Osama bin Laden, or had received training 'in one of Bin Laden's camps.' 'Het Slechte Voorbeeld,' [The Bad Example], *NRC Handelsblad*, October 20, 2001.

13.   There is a lot that is unclear and unknown about this. The Pakistani journalist Hamid Mir is cited in the book *The New Jackals*. He says that he interviewed Osama in 1997, and claimed then that Osama was behind the attack in Somalia. I have not been able to find the original interview. Osama told C.N.N. in 1997 that he was not behind the attack; he said the perpetrators had collaborated with Arabs who had fought in the jihad in Afghanistan (*Al-Qaeda*, p. 148). In 1998 the lawsuit dealing with Osama bin Laden's involvement in the Somalia attack was dismissed because the American justice department could not find enough evidence. Even so, many news outlets still claim he was involved in the attacks in Somalia, as is evident for example in articles in *The New York Times*. See: https://archive.nytimes.com/query.nytimes.com/gst/fullpage-9906E3DB123 AF930A35756C0A9679D8B63.html. The Dutch media still makes this assumption too; see, for example, the Dutch daily *Trouw*, which states that 'Osama's right-hand man' carried out the attacks in 1993 and that Al Qaeda was involved: https://www.trouw.nl/home/bin-laden-helpt-somalie~add0ed82/.

14.   Burke, pp. 17, 148.

15.   Saudi Arabia convicted four Saudi men in April 1996. They were executed because they allegedly had links to Osama bin Laden. Yet it is important to realize that even today it is not clear who was behind this attack; these young men were convicted for an attack that has never been properly investigated. Much has been written about the attack. I quote one viewpoint: one U.S. source claims Iran was behind it, saying that the Saudi state already knew the attack was actually the work of foreign agents from Iran when it convicted the four men. This claim is made by Bruce Riedel, the C.I.A. agent who played a role in the Afghan jihad and who was Deputy Assistant Secretary of Defense for Near East and South Asian Affairs, a Pentagon department, in 1995. He was in charge of the reporting on this attack and

he says Saudi secret agents had told him Iran was behind the attack. See
Riedel, *The Search for Al Qaeda, Its Leadership, Ideology, and Future*, p. 51.

16. Burke, p. 154.

17. Think tanks and the media still regularly link Osama bin Laden to
this attack. For an analysis, see: the Combating Terrorism Center,
'Deconstructing the Myth about al-Qa`ida and Khobar.' https://ctc.
usma.edu/deconstructing-the-myth-about-al-qaida-and-khobar/.
While the Saudi authorities talking directly to American officials in the
Pentagon (such as Bruce Riedel) did not suspect Osama of the attack,
other Saudi sources were telling *The New York Times* that jihadists *were*
behind the bombing. https://www.nytimes.com/1996/08/15/world/
saudi-rebels-are-main-suspects-in-june-bombing-of-a-us-base.html.

18. Daniel Benjamin and Steve Simon, *The Age of Sacred Terror: Radical
Islam's War Against America* (Random House, 2003), p. 246. See also: *The
Looming Tower*. '"The F.B.I. did not believe we had enough evidence to
indict bin Laden at that time, and therefore opposed bringing him to the
United States," said Samuel R. "Sandy" Berger, who was deputy national
security adviser then.' Quote from 'U.S. was Foiled Multiple Times in
Efforts to Capture Bin Laden or Have him Killed', *The Washington Post*,
October 3, 2001. http://www.washingtonpost.com/wp-dyn/content/
article/2007/11/18/AR2007111800593.html. Three staff members
of the Clinton administration 'fantasized' about Saudi Arabia accepting
Osama bin Laden now that a court case was out of the question and
beheading him 'real quick', just like the four falsely accused young men
earlier that year. Others in the U.S. government were actually wondering
whether it was not focusing too much on counter-terrorism rather than
the peace negotiations between Israel and Palestine, given that for many
jihadists the Palestinian question was a key reason why they opposed the
West. See: *The Washington Post*: http://www.washingtonpost.com/wp-
dyn/content/article/2007/11/18/AR2007111800593.html.

19. 'U.S. was Foiled Multiple Times in Efforts to Capture Bin Laden
or Have him Killed,' *The Washington Post*, October 3, 2001. http://
www.washingtonpost.com/wp-dyn/content/article/2007/11/18/
AR2007111800593.html.

20. Ahmed Rashid, p. 134.

21. Interview with Omar bin Laden.

22. In 1997, a delegation from Mullah Omar discussed the subject of Osama
bin Laden with American diplomats. The delegation explained that he
had not been invited by the Taliban. See: National Security Archive,

December 1997. https://nsarchive2.gwu.edu/NSAEBB/NSAEBB97/ tal24.pdf. Osama bin Laden landed in territory that was not controlled by the Taliban at that time. Osama came at the invitation of local leaders in eastern Afghanistan. Interview with Omar bin Laden, who reproduced the timing of the plane landing with his father. See also Omar bin Laden's book, which says more about the relationship between Mullah Omar and Osama bin Laden.

23. The notion of Osama bin Laden as the rich donor bankrolling Afghanistan is enduring; although there are numerous signs that this was not the case, that is not the dominant narrative. His son Omar bin Laden writes at length about the poverty-stricken conditions in Bin Laden's home, where good food was a rarity because of the lack of money. Taliban leaders such as Mutasim Agha Jan who visited Osama confirm this as well.

24. I tried hard to arrange an interview with the Saudi ambassador while I was in Saudi Arabia, but without success. This visit by the ambassador is mentioned in the book by the Egyptian Mustafa Hamid, a former jihadist who was living with his family in Kandahar at the time. He was in contact with both Mullah Omar and Osama bin Laden, although he clearly sides with Mullah Omar in his manuscript. The manuscript is called 'The Night Kandahar Fell' and has not been published. I also talked with the Palestinian journalist Jamal Ismail about this visit. He still remembers the Saudi ambassador's visit and his intention to resolve the Osama bin Laden problem. According to Ismail, the ambassador said he would be able to arrange Osama bin Laden's extradition. 'I thought when he said that: I'm not so sure,' Ismail told me in his office in Islamabad, Pakistan.

25. See, for example: Kamal Matinuddin, *The Taliban Phenomenon*, pp. 85-86.

26. In her book *Al-Qaida in Afghanistan*, Anne Stenersen gives a detailed account of which camps were closed by the Taliban and which not.

27. See also a cable from the C.I.A. from that time. They have their own list of camps that were closed and that were not closed: https://nsarchive2.gwu. edu/NSAEBB/NSAEBB227/11.pdf.

28. Interview with Pakistan's Interior Minister at the time, Haider. This gives the gist of Haider's conversation with Mullah Omar. Another book that gives a precise account of what happened with the jihad camps is *Al-Qaida in Afghanistan* by Anne Stenersen. However, it is still not at all clear how many camps Afghanistan had (some say hundreds).

29. Al-Quds Al-Arabi, interview with Abdel Bari Atwan, November 1996. This is also reported in: Peter Bergen, *The Osama Bin Laden I Know*, p. 235.

30. Interview with Omar bin Laden, who was there. See also his book and see Mutawakil's autobiography, which claims that Mullah Omar wanted Osama bin Laden in Kandahar.

31. Mutawakil wrote a manuscript that has not been translated into English but for which I do have an informal English summary. On Osama's move to Kandahar, he writes the following (p. 10, sic): 'How Osama Ben Laden became supporter of Taliban? After participating in Afghan Jehad (holy war), Osama went to Saudi Arabia and then to Sudan. But he was brought back to Afghanistan and stationed in Nengarhar province. When the eastern provinces came under control of Taliban, he strengthened his relations with Taliban and proposed construction of highways, agricultural farms. Thus he attracted much attentions of the Taliban leadership. Since the government of Saudi wanted him and stressed that he must be controlled, he and his friends were asked to go to Kandahar. He did not do any work of reconstruction or other activities for progress of this country. He always put a cross-Islamic brotherhood sprit and anti-American dialogue. He also would stress on details of anti-American feelings in the Arab world.'

32. Al Hayat, October 5, 1996. Furthermore, Ahmed Rashid claims that Pakistan played a role in their relationship because it wanted to use the Khost camps for its own soldiers fighting in Kashmir (*Taliban*, pp. 138-139).

33. Ahmed Rashid, *Taliban*, p. 133.

34. Anne Stenersen, *Brothers in Jihad*, p. 308.

35. For example, Mullah Rabbani was educated at a school in Kandahar that was funded by Saudi Arabia; see: Steve Coll, *Ghost Wars*, p. 294.

36. For the text of this statement, see James Howarth and Bruce Howarth, *Messages to the World: The Statements of Osama bin Laden*, p. 23; 'Anti-Soviet Warrior Puts his Army on the Road to Peace,' *The Independent*, December 6, 1996.

37. For the whole interview, see James Howarth and Bruce Howarth, *Messages to the World: The Statements of Osama bin Laden* (Verso, 2005), p. 44.

38. This was in spring 1997.

39. The meeting between Osama and Omar is recounted in Mustafa Hamid's book. In his book, Mustafa Hamid describes this meeting between Mullah Omar and Osama bin Laden at great length. See also U.S. WikiLeaks Cable, 'Afghanistan: Taliban Official Confirms that Mullah Omar Asked Bin Laden to Refrain from Anti-Saudi Activities.'

40. In March 1997, Osama bin Laden met C.N.N.'s Peter Arnett. He had managed to get the interview via Osama's N.G.O., A.R.C. (Advise and

Reform Committee) in London, which regularly sent faxes that were extremely critical of the regime in Saudi Arabia. In this C.N.N. interview, Osama spent a long time talking about the 'occupation' of Saudi Arabia by the Americans and the anger this was causing among young Arabs. 'Every action has its reaction,' said Osama when he was asked if more attacks would follow in Saudi Arabia. On his own plans, Osama said, 'You will see them, and hear about them in the media, God willing.' A transcript of this interview can be found in: James Howarth and Bruce Howarth, *Messages to the World: The Statements of Osama bin Laden*, pp. 44-57.

41. Unpublished manuscript by Mutawakil, 'Afghanistan and the Taliban,' p. 10. See also Mullah Omar's colleague Mutawakil, who told the American embassy in Islamabad, 'Everyone says Osama is rich, but he comes across to us as someone who has just enough money to feed his family.' https://nsarchive2.gwu.edu/NSAEBB/NSAEBB134/Document%20 4%20-%20STATE%20220495.pdf. Mutasim says it was soon clear that Osama did not have much money. In conversations with him, Osama bin Laden suggested imposing an international tax so that he could get financial support from Muslims all over the world. 'He wanted to use this to get more money,' says Mutasim. According to Bin Laden's staff, these promises never amounted to much. 'The wind blew them away,' said one of them. See: Brynjar Lia, *Architect of Global Jihad: The Life of Al Qaeda Strategist Abu Mus'ab Al-Suri* (Columbia University Press, 2008), p. 287. See also the unpublished manuscript by Mutawakil, in which he says nothing came of Osama's promises to start construction projects.

42. https://nsarchive2.gwu.edu/NSAEBB/NSAEBB134/Document%20 4%20-%20STATE%20220495.pdf.

43. 'He is going to be trouble for us,' said an American diplomat to Alan Eastham, who was Deputy Chief of Mission in Pakistan at the time. Eastham says Bin Laden was seen by the U.S. as a real danger after he started issuing fatwas and giving interviews in 1997. (Interview via Skype.)

44. This long article in the reputable Dutch daily *De Volkskrant*, which appeared quite soon after 9/11, ascribed the attacks in Saudi Arabia to Osama bin Laden. In the article, he is portrayed as one of the top terrorists of the 1990s, and also close friends with Mullah Omar and his family. According to the journalist, Omar was even married to Osama bin Laden's daughter. https://www.volkskrant.nl/nieuws-achtergrond/osama-bin-ladens-missie-vergelding-met-gepaste-munt~bedc9395/.

45. It is also claimed in *The Looming Tower* (p. 326) that Mullah Omar and Osama bin Laden were friends (and went fishing together), especially after Bin Laden had sworn an oath to Mullah Omar. A Reuters article stated, after an interview with Omar bin Laden, that on the contrary there was no love lost between the two: https://www.reuters.com/article/us-security-afghanistan-binladen-intervi/bin-laden-son-no-love-between-qaeda-taliban-idUSTRE60P4A320100126.

46. Anne Stenersen, *Al-Qaida in Afghanistan*, p. 71.

47. Idem, p. 175.

48. For example, an employee of Osama's organization A.R.C. in London did not agree. He thought someone was having a bad influence on Osama. Ayman al-Zawahiri had joined Osama bin Laden in 1998, which had already caused a stir in his Egyptian jihad movement. See also: *The Osama bin Laden I Know*, pp. 194-195.

49. Jason Burke, *Al-Qaeda*, p. 175; see also the 9/11 Commission Report, which starts with this fatwa when describing how Bin Laden's war against the Americans began.

50. Anne Stenersen, *Al-Qaida in Afghanistan*, p. 71.

51. On the signatures, see: Peter Bergen, *The Osama bin Laden I Know*, p. 196.

52. This was also the conclusion drawn later by Anne Stenersen, who has done a great deal of research on Al Qaeda in Afghanistan. See her book *Al-Qaida in Afghanistan*.

53. https://nsarchive2.gwu.edu/NSAEBB/NSAEBB134/Document%20 4%20-%20STATE%20220495.pdf

54. Interview with Rahimullah Yousafzai, Peshawar, Pakistan.

55. Mustapha Hamid, 'The Night Kandahar Fell,' p. 105.

56. *The New York Times*; see also: *Al-Qaida in Afghanistan* by Anne Stenersen.

57. Muhammed Salah, *Al Hayat*, August 10, 1998 (manuscript by Anne Stenersen, 'Brothers in Jihad').

58. Muhammed Salah, *Al Hayat*, August 19, 1998 (manuscript by Anne Stenersen, 'Brothers in Jihad').

59. Lawrence Wright, *The Looming Tower*, p. 316. Incidentally, the author writes that the man in question was fighting 'against the Taliban' when he received training in Khalden. That does not seem likely to me as the Arabs in Afghanistan did not usually oppose the Taliban back in 1998.

60. Marc Lacey, 'Look at the Place! Sudan Says, "Say Sorry," but U.S. Won't,' October 20, 2005, *The New York Times*, https://www.nytimes.com/2005/10/20/international/africa/20khartoum.html.

61. Omar bin Laden, *Growing Up*, Kindle edition, loc. 5177-86.

62. Idem.
63. Interview with Daud Junbish, Kabul.
64. 'Bin Laden is Not Involved in Terrorist Activity Omar Says,' *Afghanistan Islamic Press*, August 19, 1998.
65. 'U.S.A. a Big Terrorist, Says Omar,' *Afghanistan Islamic Press*, August 21, 1998.
66. Idem.
67. Interview with Spozhmai Maiwandi, via Skype.
68. Interview with Michael Malinowski, via Skype.
69. 'Afghanistan: Taliban's Mullah Omar's 8/22 Contact with State Department,' The National Security Archive.
70. Interview with Michael Malinowski, via Skype.
71. 'Delivering Osama bin Laden' (p. 24), a fascinating unpublished manuscript by the Afghan businessman Kabir Mohabbat, who was asked informally by the U.S. State Department to persuade the Taliban to hand over Osama bin Laden. The manuscript can be obtained from me.
72. 'I thought this request for evidence was really a maneuver to distract us, and I didn't take it seriously.' Interview with R. Pickering, former Under Secretary for Political Affairs (19972000), Washington D.C.
73. This is confirmed by the Deputy Chief of Mission at the time, Alan Eastham. There was the public charge and a video, possibly showing Osama bin Laden's media appearances.
74. 'Osama bin Laden: Taliban Spokesman Seeks New Proposal for Resolving bin Laden Problem,' The National Security Archive, November 1998. https://nsarchive2.gwu.edu/NSAEBB/NSAEBB134/Document%20 4%20-%20STATE%20220495.pdf.
75. Lawrence Wright, *The Looming Tower*, p. 327.
76. The former Pakistani president Musharraf also says that Omar had hoped Turki had come to talk about Iran; see: Pervez Musharraf, *In the Line of Fire: A Memoir* (Free Press, 2006), p. 213.
77. Musharraf, p. 213.
78. U.S. cable, September 19, 1998, diplomatic intercourse in which an Arab journalist informed the American diplomats in Islamabad that the relationship between Saudi Arabia and the Taliban had deteriorated.
79. Lawrence Wright, *The Looming Tower*, p. 327, reports on an interview with Prince Turki about this incident.
80. In his manuscript with the working title 'Final Kandahar', Mustapha Hamid recounts an earlier meeting, after which Mullah Omar warned

Osama bin Laden and told him that he really needed to stop now as the pressure from Saudi Arabia was increasing.

81.   Latif, who was in Kandahar back then, did not know either whether Mullah Omar had indeed promised to hand Bin Laden over that first time. 'But it is perfectly possible that he changed his mind after the American rocket attack,' he said.

82.   *The Osama bin Laden I Know*, p. 226. Samiul Haq, the head of the Haqqania madrassa in Pakistan, also had this impression. 'America turned Bin Laden into someone with superpowers. If there was a terrorist attack, everyone immediately thought of him. Bin Laden became the symbol of resistance for the entire Islamic world,' concluded Haq.

83.   This is confirmed by Latif, who also knows about this incident. He says the Taliban had ordered Osama to withdraw his previous statements but he ignored that request.

84.   Anne Stenersen, *Al-Qaida*, p. 86; interview with Jamal Ismail, Islamabad, Pakistan.

85.   'U.S. Engagement with the Taliban on Usama bin Laden,' July 16, 2001. https://www.scribd.com/document/13279767/US-Government-Document-Summarising-Contacts-with-Taliban-as-of-July-2001.

86.   U.S. embassy (Islamabad) Cable, 'Usama bin Laden: Charge Underscores U.S. Concerns on Interviews; Taliban Envoys say bin Laden Hoodwinked them and it Will Not Happen Again,' National Security Archive, December 30, 1998.

87.   General Butt of the Pakistani secret service the I.S.I. (who did not agree to be interviewed by me) said in 2011 that Mullah Omar had told him during the Taliban period that Osama bin Laden was 'a bone in the throat that can neither be swallowed nor thrown out.' Breaking all links with Osama would have been difficult by then as he had become a hero for some Taliban members. Carlotta Gall, *The Wrong Enemy*, p. 51 (I quote from her book but I do not agree with her description of Mullah Omar on p. 51). According to Anand Gopal in his book *No Good Men Among the Living* (p. 13), Mullah Omar gave this quote himself, although it is not clear when and where.

88.   *Al Hayat*, February 20, 1999; cited in the book *Al-Qaida in Afghanistan* by Anne Stenersen (p. 88).

89.   'U.S. Engagement with the Taliban on Usama bin Laden,' July 16, 2001. https://www.scribd.com/document/13279767/US-Government-Document-Summarising-Contacts-with-Taliban-as-of-July-2001.

90. *Taliban* by Ahmed Rashid contains an interesting reconstruction of this potential oil deal.

91. 'How Afghanistan Went Unlisted as Terrorist Sponsor,' *The Washington Post*.

92. Idem.

93. For the resolution, see: http://unscr.com/en/resolutions/doc/1267.

94. http://articles.latimes.com/1999/oct/16/news/mn-22891.

95. The Islamic Emirate, no. 5/6 (November/December 2000), via Anne Stenersen.

96. *Al Hayat*, Ahmad Muwaffaq Zaydan, October 30, 1999. (Cited in Anne Stenersen's manuscript 'Brothers in Jihad.') According to Stenersen, this article states that Osama bin Laden offered to leave in 1999. Stenersen says that Mutawakil apparently also gave a press conference on that day in which he sought to give the impression that the Taliban were not trying to extradite Bin Laden but there would be no problem with 'him leaving of his own accord if he wished.'

97. 'Osama bin Laden: Taliban Spokesman Seeks New Proposal for Resolving bin Laden Problem,' The National Security Archive, November 1998.

98. 'Taliban once wanted Osama killed,' *The Times of India*, August 22, 2015.

99. Interview with the C.I.A. chief in Islamabad, Robert Grenier, via Skype.

100. Robert L. Grenier, *88 Days to Kandahar*, p. 44.

101. Lawrence Wright, *The Looming Tower*, p. 301.

102. Interview with Alan Eastham, Deputy Chief of Mission in Pakistan for the United States from 1997-1999, and subsequently Principal Deputy Assistant Secretary for South Asian Affairs.

103. Interview with Robert Grenier, via Skype. See also: 'Taliban Offered Bin Laden Trial Before 09/11,' Al Jazeera, September 11, 2011.

104. 'U.S. Engagement with the Taliban on Usama bin Laden,' July 16, 2001. https://www.scribd.com/document/13279767/US-Government-Document-Summarising-Contacts-with-Taliban-as-of-July-2001.

105. S. Iftikhar Murshed, *The Taliban Years*, p. 294.

106. B.B.C. Monitoring, Radio Shariat, July 30, 2000. In 1996 too, Mullah Omar called on people to pray for rain in his newspaper *Shariat Weekly* (December 16, 1996).

107. Interview with Lakhdar Brahimi, Paris, France.

108. 'Mullah Omar Asks the U.N. to Help Eradicating Drugs,' B.B.C., January 7, 2000.

109. 'Funding Shortfall to Halt U.N. Drugs Control Program in Afghanistan – Iran,' Voice of the Islamic Republic of Iran, Mashhad, in Persian, December 17, 2000.

110. *Afghanistan Islamic Press*, October 14, 1998.

111. http://www.nytimes.com/2000/03/03/world/ghani-khel-journal-distress-in-the-opium-bazaar-can-t-make-a-profit.html.

112. This story in *The Observer* is from the Taliban period and gives a good account of what exactly happened with the poppy cultivation ban. 'World's Opium Source Destroyed,' April 1, 2001.

113. 'Where have all the Flowers Gone,' *International Journal of Drug Policy*, March 2005.

114. 'Learning Lessons from the Taliban Opium Ban,' The Transnational Institute (T.N.I.), March 1, 2005.

115. Idem.

116. U.N. Security Council, report dated July 21, 2001. https://www.globalpolicy.org/images/pdfs/0713sgreport.pdf.

117. Relations had also soured with B.B.C. Radio, the station that Mullah Omar had once listened to so enthusiastically. Interview with Kate Clark, B.B.C.

118. Pakistan's ambassador in Kabul at that time, Aziz Khan, says that many people around him were unconvinced at the time. 'A court case would have not stood a chance.' Interview in Islamabad, Pakistan.

119. Read more about this in these articles, written at the time: https://www.nytimes.com/2001/03/19/world/taliban-explains-buddha-demolition.html; https://www.theguardian.com/books/2001/mar/03/books.guardianreview2.

120. 'Omar Vows to Go Ahead with Statues Demolition,' *Afghanistan Islamic Press*, February 27, 2001.

121. This is also mentioned in this article: https://www.theguardian.com/books/2001/mar/03/books.guardianreview2.

122. Charles Masson, *Narrative of Various Journeys in Balochistan, Afghanistan, and the Panjab*, Vol. II (London: Richard Bently, 1842), pp. 392-93.

123. SPACH 2000: 17.

124. 'Why the Buddhas of Bamian were destroyed,' Afghanistan Analyst Network, March 2011, https://www.afghanistan-analysts.org/en/reports/context-culture/guest-blog-why-the-buddhas-of-bamian-were-destroyed/.

125. Idem.

126. 'Why the Buddha's of Bamian were destroyed,' Afghanistan Analyst Network, March 2011, https://www.afghanistan-analysts.org/en/

reports/context-culture/guest-blog-why-the-buddhas-of-bamian-were-destroyed/

127. Human Rights Watch, 'IV Massacre in Yakaolang,' January 2001, https://www.hrw.org/reports/2001/afghanistan/afghan101-03.htm

128. B.B.C., 'Taliban bar press from "massacre site",' January 28, 2001, http://news.bbc.co.uk/2/hi/south_asia/1140942.stm.

129. B.B.C., 'Taliban accuse rebels of massacre,' February 21, 2001, http://news.bbc.co.uk/2/hi/south_asia/1182586.stm.

130. Interview with Francesc Vendrell, London, U.K.

131. Interview with Latif, Kabul. A journalist working for the *Observer* was in Afghanistan in April and wrote that the destruction of the Buddhas was partly motivated by the lack of international support for the poppy cultivation ban.

132. Interview with Daoud Junbish; interview with Mutawakil.

133. Interview with the pilot Abdul, Kabul.

134. Kate Clark, 'Revealed: The Taliban minister, the US envoy and the warning of 11 September that was ignored,' *Independent*, September 6, 2002.

135. 'Osama bin Laden: Taliban Spokesman Seeks New Proposal for Resolving Bin Laden Problem,' The National Security Archive.

136. On Colin Powell's 'request for action,' see the leaked American diplomatic letter: https://wikileaks.org/plusd/cables/01STATE61624_a.html; see also: Al Jazeera, April 8, 2000.

CHAPTER 8

1. Interview with Mutawakil; see also: *An Enemy We Created*, p. 217.

2. Interview with Mullah Zaeef, Dubai, United Arab Emirates. See also his book: *My Life With the Taliban*, p. 143.

3. Interview with Robert Grenier, via Skype. See also his book: *88 Days to Kandahar*, pp. 119-122, for the complete dialogue as Grenier interpreted it.

4. Idem.

5. The statements made at the *ulema* gathering can be found here: https://www.theguardian.com/world/2001/sep/21/afghanistan.september115.

6. Interview with Spozhmai Maiwandi, via Skype; see also: http://edition.cnn.com/2001/US/09/24/gen.voa.taliban/.

7. Interview with delegation member Mufti Hazarwy, Islamabad, Pakistan. For a recording of this interview, see: https://www.youtube.com/watch?v=4RdkPkmA6IU.

8.   Interview with delegation member Mufti Hazarwy, Islamabad, Pakistan.
        'Mullah Omar remained hospitable, even though he was having to
        welcome his enemy,' he recalled. It became evident during this meeting
        that the delegation from Pakistan was hopelessly divided. For a start, it
        was not clear what the agenda was, said Mufti Hazarwy. The government's
        vague instructions were 'that we were to go there to nurture fraternal
        relations between our country and the Muslim country of Afghanistan.'
        The delegation included Mufti Nizamudeen, who many Pakistanis –
        Hazarwy among them – thought was someone with influence among the
        Taliban. He was the leader of the Binori madrassa in Karachi, Pakistan.
        Nizamudeen went frequently to Kandahar and often visited Mullah
        Omar. Omar respected the mufti but he did not obediently follow all the
        Pakistani's advice. For example, in February 1999 Nizamudeen apparently
        demanded that the *ulema* should resolve the conflict between Mullah
        Omar and Osama bin Laden, but Omar ignored this. According to Mufti
        Hazarwy, it became clear when they arrived in Kandahar that they would
        be requesting Osama bin Laden's extradition. But then it transpired that
        delegation members had differing views on this too. The I.S.I. general
        Mahmoud and Mufti Nizamudeen were sitting right next to Mullah Omar,
        according to Mufti Hazarwy. Mahmoud asked for Osama bin Laden to
        be handed over but Mufti Nizamudeen, who also spoke, did not keep to
        the line laid down by the government in Islamabad. Mufti Hazarwy could
        not hear everything, but he heard Nizamudeen say he agreed with Mullah
        Omar that he should not have to hand over Bin Laden, as the U.S. would
        still invade even if he did. When they returned to Islamabad, General
        Mahmoud was fired by the Pakistani dictator Pervez Musharraf because
        the delegation had failed to give Mullah Omar a clear message. Musharraf
        and General Mahmoud were under a lot of pressure from Washington. The
        fact that the delegation visiting Mullah Omar had had no effect whatsoever
        made the Americans suspicious, so Musharraf decided to fire Mahmoud.

9.   Grenier, *80 Days to Kandahar*.

10.   Bob Woodward, *Bush at War*, p. 33.

11.   Idem.

12.   George Tenet, *At the Center of the Storm*, p. 178.

13.   To find out more about what led up to this declaration, listen to this
        interesting podcast by Radiolab: https://www.wnycstudios.org/
        story/60-words/.

14.   See note 12.

CHAPTER 9

1. The attack on Mullah Omar is described in detail in *The Atlantic*. https://www.theatlantic.com/international/archive/2015/05/america-first-drone-strike-afghanistan/394463/. See also: http://edition.cnn.com/2001/US/10/07/ret.attack.bush/

2. *The New York Times*, 'A Nation Challenged: The President; President Rejects Offer By Taliban For Negotiations,' October 15, 2001.

3. Seymour Hersh, 'The Getaway,' *The New Yorker*, January 20, 2002, https://www.newyorker.com/magazine/2002/01/28/the-getaway-2.

4. Idem.

5. Al Watan.

6. Interview with Hamid Karzai, Kabul, 2009. See also: Bette Dam, *A Man and A Motorcycle*, about Karzai's plans for peace with the Taliban in 2001. See further: 'De vrede die Amerika niet wilde,' [The Peace the America Did Not Want] *Vrij Nederland*.

7. Interview with Abdul Salaam Rocketi.

8. See: Bette Dam, *A Man and A Motorcycle*; see also: Anand Gopal, *No Good Men Among The Living*.

9. For the full story of his advance, see: Sarah Chayes, *The Punishment of Virtue*.

10. In addition to Abdul Salam, I also interviewed Rais Bagram, who was present at this meeting too; he confirmed Salam's account.

CHAPTER 10

1. For more on this, see *A Man and A Motor Cycle*, which is based on interviews with Hamid Karzai, Mullah Naquibullah's son, Aziz Agha, Ibrahim Akhundzada, and Jason Amerine.

2. Interview with Jason Amerine; see also: Anand Gopal, *No Good Men Among the Living*.

3. Interview with Ibrahim Akhundzada, a confidant of Hamid Karzai.

4. Interview with Karzai. Ahmad Issa also remembers these broadcasts.

5. For the first reports of this unknown surrender, see: Bette Dam, *Expeditie Uruzgan* [Expedition Uruzgan]. See also: *Vrij Nederland*, https://www.vn.nl/hoe-de-amerikanen-in-2001-de-vredesdeal-met-de-taliban-onder-het-vloerkleed-veegden/. This surrender was only picked up by

the mainstream media in 2017 after the well-known author Steve Coll described it in detail in his book *Directorate S.*

6. For example, I spoke to the prominent U.S. diplomat Barney Rubin, who worked on Afghanistan from 2001 onwards. He told me that he only heard about this surrender in 2008 when I sent him an email about it. Leading advisers such as Carter Malkasian also knew nothing about this surrender by the Taliban.

7. For a report of the press conference that Rumsfeld gave on December 6, 2001, see: http://archive.defense.gov/Transcripts/Transcript. aspx?TranscriptID=2604.

8. See also Mullah Zaeef's account of how he ended up in Guantanamo Bay.

9. Rory Stewart, 'Time to End the War in Afghanistan,' https://www.ted. com/talks/rory_stewart_time_to_end_the_war_in_afghanistan, TED Talk, July 2011.

10. https://eu.usatoday.com/story/news/world/2015/07/29/taliban-leader-mullah-omar/30819359/.

11. B.B.C. Radio 5 Live, July 29, 2015. See also: Samiha Shafy, 'Journalist Bette Dam on the Death of Taliban Leader Mullah Omar,' *Der Spiegel*, July 30, 2015.

12. That this offer was indeed made was confirmed by the head of the N.D.S., Massoum Stanekzai; interview in Kabul.

13. When I checked in February 2021 the film was no longer on Facebook. I have the film in my archive, and can send it if someone is interested.

Epilogue

1. For my TED Talk, see: https://www.ted.com/talks/bette_dam_why_western_media_promotes_war.

2. An initial pool of potential articles was identified by performing an advanced Google keyword search for each media outlet, using terms like 'training camp' or 'terrorist camp' but also including various terrorist-organization or country names to broaden the results. Ten articles were then chosen from that pool for each of the selected media outlets on the basis of whether the article discussed the existence of a specific terrorist training camp. No other limitations were imposed (such as geographical location or attributed terrorist group).

Index

in Dar es Salaam, bombing, 204;
embassy in Kabul, 176, 207;
feminists, 211; and Iran hostage
crisis, 74; military, 5, 16, 235, 251,
256; and Pakistan relation, 73;
representative of Omer to, 206;
troops in Afghanistan, 27, 267;
and Vietnam War, 72; weapons in
Afghanistan, 73
U.N. Office on Drugs and Crime
(U.N.O.D.C.), 216
uprising, 113–114, 116, 123, 129
Uruzgan, 4, 6–8, 13–17, 32, 36, 53,
79, 83, 116–117, 154, 242–243;
groups, 83, 98, 101, 106–107;
'in the middle of the day' 2;
surrendering of, 117

Vanity Fair, photo of Omar in, 30
Vendrell, Francesc, 223
Vietnamese Communists, 72
Vietnam War, 72
Voice of Shariat, 166–167, 215, 236
The Voice of the Mujahideen. *See*
Radio Kabul

Wahabis, 27, 77; Arabs as, 271
Wardak, 152, 158; meeting Omar,
152
warlords (*see also under separate
entries*), 24, 74, 77, 92, 94, 96,
114, 116, 120–121, 127, 131, 136,
166, 170, 217, 236–238, 243,
250–253
'War on Terror,' 4, 40, 46, 48,
232–233

Western: allies, 29, 42; military
forces, 20–21, 24, 37; narratives,
221, *see also* media, Western
Westerners, 8, 23, 37, 67, 220
white Toyotas, 16, 36, 41, 80, 265
widows, 56, 79; remarriage and,
164
women, 12–13, 34–36, 47, 49, 52,
54–56, 65, 69–70, 72, 94–97, 153,
155–162, 177, 185, 213–214; ban
on working, 158; and bride-price,
157; clothing and, 34, (*see also*
punishment); freedom of, 95; in
Haji Ibrahim, 158; inheritance
of, 157; mujahideen and, 94;
rights of, 177–178, 185, 212;
segregation of men from, 159;
sufferings of, 96
Woodward, Bob, 105, 231
World Trade Center, attack on 9/11,
3–4, 7, 23, 25, 190–191, 194,
197, 199–200, 228, 230–232,
250–252, 255, 257, 261

Xinhau, Chinese press agency, 22

Yousafzai, Rahimullah, 128–130,
203, 210, 215
Yousafzai, Sami, 67

Zabul, 53, 244, 259–263, 265,
268–269, 274; as tribe's area of
Omar, 262
Zaeef, Abdul Salam, 133, 227, 243
Zaibiullah Mujahed, 253
al-Zawahiri, Ayman, 202
Zia-ul-Haq, military coup of, 73

Acknowledgements

WHENEVER I fly over Afghanistan, I have mixed feelings. I am incredibly grateful for all the wonderful things the country has given me, as a person, in my work, and in everything it has taught me. At the same time, I find it very distressing that every time I take that flight, the country I am flying over is in a worse state, suffering more pain and more trauma.

I often feel powerless, wishing I could do more but not knowing how, or what channels I should use. At any rate, now I have this book. Perhaps it will help people understand the conflict better.

This book is at least one small contribution. And I want to thank the people of Afghanistan above all for that. Najibullah Sahibzada, Ahmad Issa, Patmal Abdul Hadi, Safi Khairullah, and Fazl Rahman Muzhary helped me hugely in finding people who had known Mullah Omar and could tell me about his life. I would like to thank Mohammad Afzal Zarghoni for turning the entire Afghanistan Research and Evaluation Unit (A.R.E.U.) library upside down to uncover various old Taliban newspapers for me. It was terrible when the Taliban abducted Najibullah and held him captive for about eighteen months, but fortunately he escaped and is free again. We fear he would not have survived otherwise.

I am grateful to all the Afghans who were interlocutors for me. Tahir Khan, thank you for arranging my contact with Mutasim. Mohammed (you know who you are): it's great that you introduced me to so many Taliban in the Emirates. D. knows how crucial he was, as does H., especially about the Taliban in the first few years after 9/11. Thank you to R. in Norway. I am also eternally grateful to all the Afghans who gave me a place to stay during my investigations. The man in Khoshal Khan whose name I cannot reveal but who always had a bed for me, everyone at *The Wall Street Journal* in Kabul, and my home in Kandahar: Ahmad Issa, Patmal, and my dear friends R. and A. and their daughter whom I often stayed with when I visited the province, where I saw how devastated R. was when her father was murdered in the city.

This book would never have come to fruition without the help of Toof Brader. Turning the material into an accessible text turned out to be more difficult than I had expected. I am infinitely grateful to him for his help.

I would also like to thank the Dutch publisher De Bezige Bij for their faith in my story in its original Dutch incarnation, of course, and now also HarperCollins India for their belief in the English translation. Siddhesh Inamdar has been an amazing editor who agreed almost immediately to publish the book.

As regards the content, I got my information from my Afghan contacts and crosschecked it with independent experts. I would like to thank Martine van Bijlert for reading the draft texts. Few people have such a nuanced, informed view of Afghanistan as she does. I would also like to thank the Afghanistan Analyst Network team: Thomas Ruttig, Kate Clark, and Fabricio Foscini. Alex Strick van Linschoten has been another constant source of information about the Taliban for me. Robert Kluijver came up with some good suggestions from his time living in Afghanistan in the days of the Taliban regime. Anne Stenersen, thank you for your friendship and your knowledge of Al Qaeda in Afghanistan. I found like-minded journalists in Anand Gopal and Matthieu Aikin, journalists who have tried to steer their own course and have produced work that did not bow to the master narrative. I have invariably found them to be ideal intellectual sparring partners and just what I needed for this book.

My most recent trips to Afghanistan would not have been possible without D. and H. I was able to stay with H., and D. helped me with my request to get closer to the crucial eyewitness Omari.

I'd like to thank Leslie Knott for being a good friend and supporting me wherever I went. My friends at *The Wall Street Journal*, Nathan Hodge, Margherita Stancati, Jessica Donati, and Yaroslav Tromifov, should not go unmentioned. Elsbeth Koning, Misha Galustov, and Matthieu Aikins, who were my housemates in a wonderful pink bungalow in Kabul, made my time in Afghanistan so much nicer.

In the Netherlands, I wish to thank Tjitkse Holtrop and Julien McHardy and their daughters Nanne and Sol (my godchild). Harm Botje has always been a great support: for years, we published stories together that Harm believed in even though they ran counter to the mainstream.

My friends Fanny Verwoerdt, Jan Willem Petersen, Jain Holsheimer, Matthijs Brouwer, Arezo Malakooti, and Jos Winters made coming home and writing this book so much easier. They had all travelled in Afghanistan and knew exactly how I could feel at times. Anne Marieke Samson, thank you for reading drafts and for your comments. Saskia de Jong, thank you for your friendship.

This English edition took shape in Brussels, Belgium, where I now live.

Priyanka Shankar was crucial for the contact with HarperCollins India: Thank you! And Inbar Preis for assisting us when the sales process started.

And of course my family, my brother Douwe, my dear sisters Jacoba and Mettje, and my mother and father. It's not easy to be the home front when your daughter chooses such an insecure life. It's not easy to stay behind and accept that your daughter feels she has a story that needs to be told and is prepared to run a lot of risks to do so. Yet my parents have managed that and I'm incredibly grateful to them for it.

List of people interviewed

This list of the people interviewed is not complete: some interviewees have been left anonymous for their own safety, while some names have been changed for the same reason.

Abdul, head of Kandahar Airport during the time of the Taliban; Kabul.

Abdul Ahad, a relative of Mullah Omar's third wife; Deh Rawod, Kabul.

Khateb Akhundzada, mullah in Muj Mubarak mosque; Kandahar.

Farouk Azam, Minister for the Repatriation of Refugees from 1991 to 1993, Kabul.

Dr. Baluch and his wife Sharifa Baluch; Kandahar.

Haji Barwari, Deh Rawod resident at the time when Mullah Omar was living there; Assen (Holland), Kabul.

Martine van Bijlert, worked in Kabul during the Taliban time as a diplomat for the E.U., former director of Afghanistan Analysts Network; Amsterdam (Holland), Kabul.

Lakhdar Brahimi, the U.N. Special Representative for Afghanistan; Paris (France).

Kate Clark, former B.B.C. journalist; Kabul.

Dalili, businessman in Kabul and real estate developer in Doha (Qatar); Kabul.

Mawlawi Shahabuddin Delawar, former ambassador for the Taliban regime in Pakistan and Saudi Arabia, judge in Kabul until 2001, currently a member of the Taliban's political committee in Doha; Doha (Qatar).

Alan Eastham, from 1997 to 1999 deputy chief of mission for the U.S. in Pakistan, subsequently Principal Deputy Assistant Secretary for South Asian Affairs in Washington D.C.; Skype.

Haji Esmat, member of Mullah Omar's jihad group in Haji Ibrahim; Kabul.

Mullah Ezattullah, a former resident of Haji Ibrahim who fought there in the jihad; Kandahar.

Moheeb Spin Gar, journalist in Kandahar at the time of the Taliban; Kabul.

Haji Ghausedin, tribal leader from Haji Ibrahim; Kandahar.

Abdel Halim Ghazaly, journalist who interviewed Mullah Omar for Al Jazeera; Doha (Qatar).

Ostad Abdul Halim, prominent jihad commander, supporter of President Rabbani in Kandahar; Kandahar.

Haji Gilani, Haji Ibrahim resident who fought in the jihad there; Kandahar.

Anand Gopal, author of *No Good Men Among the Living*; Kabul, New York.

Robert Grenier, head of the C.I.A. in Islamabad; email and Skype.

Daud Gulzar, Hotak leader from Zabul, former head of the Provincial Council of Zabul, friend of Samad Ostad; Kandahar.

Moinuddin Haider, former Minister for the Interior in Pakistan; Karachi (Pakistan), phone.

Mir Hamza, tribal leader in Deh Rawod; Deh Rawod.

Atmal Al Hamrie, employee of the Organization of Islamic Cooperation; Jeddah (Saudi Arabia).

Mufti Hazarwy, religious leader in Pakistan, visited Mullah Omar after September 11, 2001; Islamabad (Pakistan).

Norbert Holl, the U.N. Special Representative for Afghanistan; email.

Sheikh Hotak, relative of Mullah Omar's second wife; Hotak was murdered in 2017; Kandahar.

Abdul Rahman Hotaki, former employee working personally for Mullah Omar, now a member of the Afghan Human Rights Commission; Kabul.

Jamal Ismail, journalist in Islamabad; Islamabad (Pakistan).

Mohammed Issa, owner of Mullah Omar's mosque in Haji Ibrahim, his son Ahmad, and his wife Bibi; Kandahar.

Aziz Agha Pir Jan and his son Najibullah; Tarin Kowt, Deh Rawod.

Daud Junbish, B.B.C. Pashto journalist who interviewed Mullah Omar several times; Kabul.

Hamid Karzai, former president of Afghanistan; Kabul.

Abdullah Khan, chairman of the Taliban Commission for Civilian Victims; Dubai (United Arab Emirates).

Robert Kluijver, who worked during the Taliban period in Kabul for the Society for the Preservation of Afghan Cultural Heritage, and subsequently worked for the U.N. in Kabul; Paris (France).

Abdul Koudouz, school friend of Mullah Omar; Deh Rawod.

Omar bin Laden, son of Osama bin Laden; Doha (Qatar).

Haji Agha Lalai, former head of the Provincial Council of Kandahar; Kandahar.

Latif, former employee and diplomat working for Mullah Omar, now an author; Oslo (Norway), Kabul.

Jolyon Leslie, U.N. diplomat during the Taliban period; Kabul.

David Loyn, former B.B.C. journalist in Kabul; London (U.K.).

Mullah Malang, prominent jihad commander, taught Mullah Omar during the jihad; Kabul.

Michael Malinowski, American diplomat, formerly employed in the Bureau of South Asian Affairs of the Department of State; Skype.

Carter Malkasian, author of *War Comes to Garmser*, and Pentagon employee; Kabul.

Mullah Muhammad, pupil in the madrassa next to Mullah Omar's office in Kandahar, friend of one of Mullah Omar's uncles; Kandahar.

Sibghatullah Mojaddedi, one of the leaders of the Peshawar Seven, former interim president of Afghanistan; Kabul.

Abdul Manaan, half-brother of Mullah Omar; Zoom.

Abdul Hakim Mujahed, Taliban representative at the U.N.; Kabul.

Iftikhar Murshed, Pakistan's ambassador to Afghanistan in the Taliban period; Islamabad (Pakistan).

Agha Jan Mutasim, former Taliban Minister of Finance; Ankara (Turkey), Kabul.

Wakil Akmad Mutawakil, former Minister of Foreign Affairs for the Taliban; Kabul.

Waheed Muzhda, former employee in the Ministry of Foreign Affairs during the Taliban period; Kabul.

Mullah Nizami, former radio presenter at the Voice of Shariat; Kabul.

Jabbar Omari, governor during the Taliban period, Mullah Omar's protector after September 11, 2001; Kabul.

Thomas R. Pickering, former Under Secretary of State for Political Affairs (1997–2000); Washington D.C.

Mullah Qalamudeen, former deputy Minister for the Promotion of Virtue and Prevention of Vice; Kabul.

Qari, worked as a pilot during the Taliban era; Kandahar.

Burhanuddin Rabbani, former president of Afghanistan; Kabul.

Doctor Rahila, midwife who assisted at the birth of Mullah Omar's children; Kandahar.

Arsala Rahmani, former minister under President Rabbani, subsequently a deputy minister in the Taliban regime; Kabul.

Robin Raphel, Assistant Secretary of State for South and Central Asian Affairs from 1993 to 1997; Washington D.C.

Ahmed Rashid, author of *Taliban*; Skype.

William Reeve, former B.B.C. journalist; Kabul.

Abdul Salam Rocketi, former Taliban commander, became a member of Parliament after September 11, 2001; Kabul.

Barney Rubin, American diplomat; New York.

Thomas Ruttig, former U.N. employee, now co-director of the Afghanistan Analysts Network; Marienburg (Germany).

Saad, secretary to Mullah Omar's son Yaqub; Dubai (United Arab Emirates).

Khalilullah Safi, former employee at Pugwash, the organization that acted as an intermediary between the Taliban and the Afghan government in peace talks; Doha (Qatar), Dubai (United Arab Emirates), Kabul.

Said, who lives in Mullah Omar's old house in Deh Rawod; Deh Rawod.

Eckart Schiewek, security officer working for the U.N. during the Taliban era, now a security expert on Al Qaeda and the Taliban at the U.N.; Kabul, New York.

General Shafi, with the Afghan secret service, guarded Jabbar Omari; Kabul.

Suhail Shaheen, represented the Taliban at the U.N. until 2001, now a member of the Taliban's political commission; Doha (Qatar).

Sharafat, member of the Taliban's N.G.O. commission in Pakistan, author of the Taliban biography of Mullah Omar; Dubai (United Arab Emirates).

Massoum Stanekzai, head of the Afghan secret service; Kabul.

Francesc Vendrell, the U.N. Special Representative for Afghanistan and Pakistan; London (U.K.).

Moheeb Woleswal, tribal Hotak leader in Zabul; Kandahar.

Rahimullah Yousafzai, journalist for B.B.C. Pashto; Peshawar (Pakistan).

Mullah Abdul Salam Zaeef, Taliban ambassador in Islamabad; Dubai (United Arab Emirates), Kabul.

Wakil Zergey, tribal Hotak leader in Zabul; Kabul and Kandahar.

About the Author

BETTE DAM is a Dutch investigative journalist who made a career working in Afghanistan, Syria and Iraq. She is currently a lecturer at the prestigious Sciences Po university in Paris. She is also the author of *A Man and a Motorcycle: How Hamid Karzai Came to Power.*